François Truffaut

MANCHESTER
UNIVERSITY PRESS

DIANA HOLMES and ROBERT INGRAM *series editors*
DUDLEY ANDREWS *series consultant*

Jean-Jacques Beineix   PHIL POWRIE

Luc Besson   SUSAN HAYWARD

Bertrand Blier   SUE HARRIS

Robert Bresson   KEITH READER

Claude Chabrol   GUY AUSTIN

Diane Kurys   CARRIE TARR

Marguerite Duras   RENATE GÜNTHER

Georges Méliès   ELIZABETH EZRA

Jean Renoir   MARTIN O'SHAUGHNESSY

Coline Serreau   BRIGITTE ROLLET

François Truffaut   DIANA HOLMES AND ROBERT INGRAM

Agnès Varda   ALISON SMITH

FRENCH FILM DIRECTORS

Francois Truffaut

DIANA HOLMES
AND ROBERT INGRAM

Manchester University Press
MANCHESTER AND NEW YORK

distributed exclusively in the USA by Palgrave

Published by Manchester University Press
Oxford Road, Manchester M13 9NR, UK
and Room 400, 175 Fifth Avenue, New York, NY 10010, USA
www.manchesteruniversitypress.co.uk

Distributed exclusively in the USA by
Palgrave, 175 Fifth Avenue, New York,
NY 10010, USA

Distributed exclusively in Canada by
UBC Press, University of British Columbia, 2029 West Mall,
Vancouver, BC, Canada v6s 1z2

British Library Cataloguing-in-Publication Data
A catalogue record is available from the British Library

Library of Congress Cataloging-in-Publication Data applied for

ISBN 0 7190 4553 3 *hardback*
    0 7190 4554 1 *paperback*

First published 1998

08 07 06 05 04 03 02 01   10 9 8 7 6 5 4 3 2

Typeset in Scala with Meta display
by Koinonia, Manchester
Printed in Great Britain
by Biddles Limited, Guildford and King's Lynn

Contents

List of plates

All stills courtesy of BFI Stills, Posters and Designs

Series editors' foreword

To an anglophone audience, the combination of the words 'French' and 'cinema' evokes a particular kind of film: elegant and wordy, sexy but serious – an image as dependent upon national stereotypes as is that of the crudely commercial Hollywood blockbuster, which is not to say that either image is without foundation. Over the past two decades, this generalised sense of a significant relationship between French identity and film has been explored in scholarly books and articles, and has entered the curriculum at university level and, in Britain, at high-school level. The study of film as art-form and (to a lesser extent) as industry, has become a popular and widespread element of French Studies, and French cinema has acquired an important place within Film Studies. Meanwhile, the growth in multi-screen and 'art-house' cinemas, together with the development of the video industry, has led to the greater availability of foreign-language films to an English-speaking audience. Responding to these developments, this series is designed for students and teachers seeking information and accessible but rigorous critical study of French cinema, and for the enthusiastic filmgoer who wants to know more.

The adoption of a director-based approach raises questions about *auteurism*. A series that categorises films not according to period or to genre (for example), but to the person who directed them, runs the risk of espousing a romantic view of film as the product of solitary inspiration. On this model, the critic's role might seem to be that of discovering continuities, revealing a necessarily coherent set of themes and motifs which correspond to the particular genius of the individual. This is not our aim: the *auteur* perspective of film, itself most clearly articulated in France in the early 1950s, will be interrogated in certain volumes of the series, and throughout, the director will be treated as one highly significant element in a complex process of film production and reception which includes socio-economic and political determinants, the work of a large and highly skilled team of artists and technicians, the mechanisms of production and distribution, and the complex and multiply determined responses of spectators.

The work of some of the directors in the series is already well known outside France, that of others is less so – the aim is both to provide informative and original English-language studies of established figures, and to extend the range of French directors known to anglophone students of cinema. We intend the series to contribute to the promotion of the formal and informal study of French films, and to the pleasure of those who watch them.

DIANA HOLMES

ROBERT INGRAM

Acknowledgements

The idea for this book emerged from the collaborative work that went into teaching Truffaut's cinema at the universities of Wolverhampton and Keele and into the annual short courses or 'Truffaut study days', run between 1988 and 1996. Our thanks therefore go to the third member of the teaching team, our close friend and colleague Yves Milhavy, and to all the teachers and students of French cinema who have worked with us over these years and contributed their ideas and enthusiasm.

We would also like to thank Madame Madeleine Morgenstern for her help over copyright and for kindly according the permission of the Films du Carrosse to reproduce stills and photos from the films.

This book is dedicated, with love, to Gretchen, Richard and Allen, and to Nick, Thomas and Martha.

1 <u>Nouvelle vague</u>
Freshness
low budget
unknown actors

Les Mistons: an introduction

A summer's day in the Midi, a young woman, carefree and graceful, skirt billowing to reveal long, lithe legs, cycles along the tree-lined streets of a provincial town, passing through sunlight and shadows to the accompaniment of a musical score that defines her mood of freedom and happiness. Lying in wait at the river is a group of five young boys. They spy on her bathing, creep up to her bicycle, propped against a tree, sniff its saddle and, as she returns from her swim, rush off into the undergrowth.

This incident sets the scene for a series of encounters between the boys and the couple: Bernadette and her boyfriend Gérard. From underneath the arches of the arena, from the other side of the wire netting at the tennis court, from the back rows of the local cinema, from behind a wall outside her house, the spying on the beautiful Bernadette continues, unrelenting, developing on occasion into a rowdy tormenting of the couple by the boys. Their jeering and hooting express the frustration of conflicting emotions: on the one hand Bernadette's beauty and what they perceive as her total otherness exert a magnetic sexual and emotional attraction, on the other they produce a sense of angry and puzzled resentment. Their activities gradually escalate into a campaign waged remorselessly against the couple and culminating in Gérard cuffing one of the kids. Gérard leaves to do his military service, suggesting to Bernadette that he will return to marry her. However, as the summer wanes, news filters through of his tragic death in a mountain accident. The boys, now subdued and somewhat chastened, see Bernadette again, dressed for the first time in dark clothes, as she walks alone beneath the autumnal trees of the town. As the musical score, now melancholic in tone, rises to a crescendo, the camera tilts upwards above her head to end the film with a shot of the trees against the sky which conveys an impression of inconclusiveness and indefinable melancholy.

When challenged by Anne Gillain to explain his motives in making *Les Mistons* (1957) Truffaut was somewhat vague and unhelpful, deflecting the critic's attention to the short story on which the film is based: 'C'est assez proche de la nouvelle de Maurice Pons, mais je n'ai jamais considéré que c'était proche de moi'[1] (Gillain 1988: 84). No amount of authorial (im)modesty can, however, disguise the presence of what were to become recurrent themes and formal devices. Much of the subject matter of the films is sketched out in this twenty-three-minute long film: childhood, male fascination with women, construction of masculinity, the obsession with death, the fumbling towards an understanding of love, the relationship of the individual with order and authority, the links between fiction and reality. At the same time, this first major encounter with the mechanics of film-making brings early decisions in the areas of adaptation, narration and vital questions of *mise en scène*. The focus on the *auteur* approach to film-making, together with its inherent contradictions, is reflected in the opening credits. They identify the preponderant role of the director in the creation of this film but at the same time his evident dependence on a team comprising producer, assistant directors, cameraman, editor, composer, etc.

Running, falling, laughing, plotting, spying, shouting, the eponymous kids occupy virtually every frame of the film. Their continuous presence is an affirmation of the central theme of childhood in this and later films and is evidence of an awareness of their vulnerability. On another level, in their innocence and unfulfilled potential, their exuberant presence is a vibrant manifestation of life and dispels thoughts of mortality. The energy and resilience of children act as vital counters to a morbid preoccupation

1 'It follows Maurice Pons's short story pretty closely. I've never believed it had much to do with me.'

with death, visible here in the fatal ending to the couple's romantic idyll.

Another interesting aspect of *Les Mistons* is that of gender representation. Bernadette is the only female character in the film. She is throughout unequivocally the subject of the male gaze, the voyeuristic nature of which is confirmed in repeated shots in which the camera spies on Bernadette from behind trees, walls, balustrades, wrought-iron gates. The famous tennis sequence is a classic of its kind, presenting Bernadette's fragmented body in a series of single shots – breasts, thighs, legs – which fetishise and dehumanise the young woman. The spectator is not invited to share directly her thoughts and feelings and she is shown as submissive, somewhat petulant (at the station as Gérard leaves) and compliant in following his agenda, for example the destination of their walk and bike ride. Significantly, although we are told Gérard is a gym teacher and although we frequently see his young, athletic body, at no point in the film does the camera concentrate its gaze upon it, and certainly not on fragmented parts of it. The construction of masculinity is nevertheless a feature of *Les Mistons* and is articulated mainly in terms of the contrast between Gérard and the five kids. The former is fit, strong and self-confident, a model of accomplished masculinity. The kids, on the other hand, are awkward and ungainly, ignorant and aggressive, mere brats with everything to learn. If only in embryo, the character of Antoine Doinel, hero of Truffaut's famous *Bildungsroman* cycle, is here in the making.

By choosing as subject for his film an exploration of the young male's sexual awakening, by situating it in a French provincial town and by adopting the realist mode, Truffaut was making an important statement: one of the first shots to be fired in the campaign to launch a new way of making films, the campaign that was to become the Nouvelle Vague (the New Wave). What *Les Mistons* is as a film is less significant than what it is not: it cannot be easily ascribed to a particular genre. If its simple story line at first suggests a romance, the presence of the boys as focalisers, the objectivisation of the couple, and the tragic outcome all militate against such a reading. It is, rather, an attempt to capture a moment in the formation of the male psyche: the nuanced observation of the boys' attitudes and behaviour and the sympathetic, deftly ironic manner in which they are evoked, constitute first steps in the elaboration of a style, in the construction of the *auteur*. On another, perhaps for Truffaut more important, level the film is an attempt to define what a new French cinema should be. Put simply, it should be French; it should hark back to French sources, it should present a contemporary France, it should broach themes of interest to French audiences. Though displaying awareness of and respect for the achievements of North American cinema, it should not seek to emulate Hollywood.

Another theme of this and other films and one which will be explored in more detail in a later chapter is that of the act of creation itself. From the beginning, Truffaut's cinema displays a fascination with virtually anything connected to the process of artistic creation, including even its most mechanical aspects, witness the sequence from *Antoine et Colette* (1962) in which the camera lingers on Antoine as he presses and trims a vinyl record or the shots of the printing press in *L'Homme qui aimait les femmes* (1977). The creative act is introduced into *Les Mistons* through the quotation of another film, that of a fellow film-maker and colleague of the Nouvelle Vague, Jacques Rivette. It is his film, *Le Coup du berger*, that Gérard and Bernadette, dogged by the brats, go to see at the *cinoche* (local cinema). The connection with the creative act is only indirect. Nonetheless, it is present and reflects a recurrent theme: the relationship of life to art. Does the latter imitate the former or vice versa? In this particular instance it would appear that life is imitating art as Gérard and Bernadette re-enact in the cinema stalls the actions and words of the lovers on the screen. Indeed, for a moment, it is difficult to separate the two couples as the darkness of the cinema conspires to mask the source of the sound and the words could be attributable to either couple.

On another level, Truffaut took a keen aesthetic interest in other forms, most significantly writing. Evidence of this theme is not a major feature of *Les Mistons* but it is not a coincidence that the boys do write, even if the form of writing they adopt is crude, limited to street graffiti and postcards. Writing is, however, present in *Les Mistons* in another, less visible, way. Although the film and its themes are undeniably shaped by the director, they are closely based on a short story by Maurice Pons (from the volume *Les Virginales*), and retain a degree of fidelity to the original text. The anonymous narrator's voice-over reproduces passages from it, past historics included, thus imparting to *Les Mistons* a literary feel.

Alongside such literary allusions there are other allusions, for example to filmic texts. The quotation from Jean Vigo's *Zéro de conduite* (1933) (the boys walking in single file along the wall of the arena) is echoed by the brief sequence which constitutes a 'remake' of a brief classic of early French cinema, the Lumière brothers' *L'Arroseur arrosé*. These 'homages' were no doubt on one level intended as jokey acknowledgements, friendly winks from one *auteur* to another, but often passing unrecognised by an untutored public. They can, however, be seen to have other, perhaps more serious, meanings. Truffaut was, in later films, to persist with such allusions, allusions to his own films as well as to the films of others, thus developing a wide range of inter-connected references. Borrowings of this type have more recently been identified as a form of postmodern play: quotation for pleasure, quotation in imitation (pastiche) and ironic quotation (parody) are features more readily associated with the 'Nouvelle Nouvelle Vague' of 1980s French cinema, but already visible here. Such quotations serve to briefly destabilise the fictional illusion, to produce a pleasurable moment of detachment and recognition, to draw attention to the history and the language of film itself.

A final important thread running through the films of Truffaut is the tension that exists when the individual is confronted with figures of authority. The phrase *en situation irrégulière* would be a most fitting epitaph for Truffaut: from childhood through to early adulthood, and possibly beyond, he tended to project the image of the outsider. Whether as childhood delinquent or adolescent organiser of a film club with debts, as truculent soldier or angry young film critic, he seemed at odds with those in authority and at times constrained beyond the point of tolerance by the fetters of an authoritarian and unsympathetic society. The films reflect this maverick behaviour and signs of it emerge in the behaviour of the brats whose taunting of the couple goes well beyond the socially acceptable: they deface walls, rip down posters and harass, not to say stalk, a woman. They exist in a kind of social vacuum with none of the usual reference points, such as family or elders, and appear free to roam unaccompanied and unchecked in the streets and woods of the locality.

In terms of narrative structure, the films tend to avoid closure, to shy away from conclusions and definitive statements. Many are open-ended, fittingly so in the case of stories which are often no more than pegs on which to hang investigation of themes and ideas. *Les Mistons* provides evidence for this approach. As in many of the later films, there is, on the surface, a plot which holds the film together. Very simply, *Les Mistons* recounts the tormenting, over one summer, of a couple by kids whose incomprehension and sense of exclusion lead them to launch increasingly aggressive 'attacks' on a young couple. On examination, however, this plot is quite flimsy and the film is composed of a series of sequences tied only loosely together, in temporal and spatial terms, by the passing of summer in a southern town. The real interest of the film, for its maker, lay less in the unravelling of a story and a dramatic denouement and more in the series of short tableaux each of which sketched out an aspect of the relationship between the boys and the couple and each of which painted in a further nuance in the evocation of the young male psyche.

While Truffaut was neither inclined nor motivated to revolutionise *mise en scène* in the manner of a Godard, the comparisons drawn between the two film-makers have tended to obscure the creativity and skill of Truffaut's *mise en scène* and the imaginative ways in which he exploited well-established and common conventions the better to make a point or underline a theme.

Frame composition makes a significant contribution to *Les Mistons*, reinforcing one of the main features of the film: the age gap separating the couple from the boys. On one side of this divide are Gérard and Bernadette, with their knowledge of love, on the other are the boys, driven by instinct, knowing that the couple has possession of something magical, powerful, wonderful but unable to either share in or understand it. Hence their sense of inferiority and exclusion which is skilfully confirmed in visual terms by one instance of frame composition which situates the boys at the bottom of the frame, sitting huddled together under one of the arches of the arena, in the dark, while at the top of the frame embracing, in bright sunlight, stands the couple. Conforming to one of the basic conventions of film language, that of structuring a film using patterns of repetition and variation, this frame composition is repeated at the point at which Gérard collects Bernadette from her home to take her for a walk. Again, the boys are at the bottom of the frame with the couple above them. Again there is a barrier, this time in the form of a stone wall, separating the couple from the kids.

A second important element of the *mise en scène* of *Les Mistons* is lighting. Given that this was a low-cost production of a kind which inevitably sought the less expensive option of exterior shooting with natural lighting and direct sound, this may at first seem surprising. From the very first frames, however, the importance of lighting is evident. As Bernadette, captured in a series of tracking shots taken from a moving vehicle, makes her graceful way to the river, cycling along the tree-lined streets of Nîmes, she moves from light to dark, dark to light. The 'lighting' is, of course, natural, but, significantly, the director has done nothing to attenuate the effects of Bernadette moving frequently through patches of comparative darkness. Reinforced by the music which also has two tones, joyful and melancholic, this chiaroscuro lighting underlines the vicissitudes of life. From one moment to the next Bernadette is plunged from happiness at the prospect of a shared life with Gérard, to despair at his sudden and unpredicted death. The end of the film, with the panning shot upwards to leaves and sky mentioned earlier, suggests that the 'widowed' but youthful Bernadette will move 'back into the light' again and refind happiness.

Further, the medium of lighting is another way in which the film adheres to the convention of repetition and variation. That Bernadette is in some way associated with Gérard is signalled to the spectator before the two are first seen together through a repetition of the chiaroscuro effect that accompanied Bernadette's first appearance. Gérard is introduced walking through the streets of Nîmes towards the arena and a rendezvous with Bernadette. The pattern of light and dark, created by shadows and sunlight on the walls of the buildings behind him, echoes that seen in the opening sequence with Bernadette and thus immediately suggests a connection between them. Significantly, Gérard does not move from sunlight to shadow, but remains all the time in shadow and where Bernadette moved fluently on her bicycle, he is on foot. Thus, not only does a gap open up between couple and kids, but also between Gérard and Bernadette, between male and female.

The twenty-three fleeting minutes of *Les Mistons* are, then, pointers not only to themes and filmic practices which will nourish and sustain the later work, they are also a key to the Nouvelle Vague, to its approach to cinema and its desire to create a cinema that is French. A pattern of meaning emerges from this apparently slight and nostalgic film. *Les Mistons* may be narrated as an adult's wistful memories of childhood, but it is never mawkishly sentimental, it does not linger long enough on any moment of emotion to become that. Though a first film, it is never amateurish in its execution; Truffaut already at this early point in his career had too professional a grasp of the possibilities of *mise en scène* for that. Above all, *Les Mistons*, despite its brevity, is rich and diverse, open, like the later films, to readings other than those intended by its author.

This study sets out to follow the avenues opened up by this brief introduction. Chapters 1 and 2 are intended as contextualisation, the first seeking to situate Truffaut both historically and culturally and the second aiming to give a broad overview of his films and their critical reception. Chapter 3 provides a closer analysis of one film, *Jules et Jim* (1961), both as a means to discuss more precisely Truffaut's style of film-making, and to provide an example of how a film may be 'read'. On these foundations rests the wide-ranging analysis of the four remaining chapters. A chronological, if easily referenced, account of the films has been rejected in favour of a thematic approach organised around issues that are central to the

whole of Truffaut's work: the '*auteur*–genre' tension, the representation of gender, the relationship between paternity and authorship
and, finally, the conflict at the heart of the films between the
'absolute' and the 'provisional'.

References

Gillain, Anne (1988), *Le Cinéma selon François Truffaut*, Paris, Flammarion.

1

The context: cinema saved my life

The films as autobiography

Truffaut's work invites biographical readings. His first full-length film, *Les 400 Coups* (1959), told a story of growing up in Paris so close to the facts of his own childhood that the fictional Antoine Doinel became confused in the popular imagination with the real François Truffaut. The subsequent appearance of four sequels, charting Doinel's development from delinquent teenager to thirty-something divorcee, confirmed the generalised belief that Truffaut's work could be read as a form of autobiography, a belief supported by the uncanny physical resemblance between the director and Jean-Pierre Léaud, the actor who played Doinel, once Léaud reached maturity. *La Nuit américaine* (1973), in which Truffaut played the part of a film-director and represented on-screen many of his own film-making practices, further blurred the distinction between life and fiction, and Truffaut's willingness to acknowledge, in interviews and letters, the relationship between his own experience and the stories he told has contributed to the elaboration of a mythical Truffaut, an amalgamation of the historical individual and certain of the characters he created. 'Tribute' books[1] tend to juxtapose stills from the films with photos of the director in poses befitting his public persona: in conversation with female stars ('the man who loved women'), intent on the

[1] For example see Annette Insdorf: *François Truffaut: Les Films de sa vie*, Paris, Gallimard, 1996.

process of filming ('the man who loved film', as a BBC documentary entitled him).

To read the films as direct transpositions of Truffaut's life is neither accurate nor rewarding. The relevance of biography lies not in tracing all those names, places, situations and dialogues that Truffaut 'borrowed' from life, but rather in recognising the relationship between his films and the social context of both creation and reception. If we begin here with a brief account of François Truffaut's early life in occupied and post-war France, it is in order to situate his highly personal vision within the society and culture that shaped his imagination and made his success possible. First, certain aspects of Truffaut's, on the whole, unhappy childhood and adolescence enter his films not at the level of narrative detail, but at that of underlying structures and themes, the significance of which goes well beyond the personal. Second, Truffaut's personal development rapidly became inextricably interwoven with the history of a specific era of French society and of French cinema. In the words of Truffaut's mentor, the film critic and theorist André Bazin, a successful artist brings together 'unquestionably personal talents, a gift from the fairies, and a moment in history' (Hillier 1985: 252).

Discovering cinema: the Occupation years

François Truffaut was born in 1932 as the result of an unwanted and illegitimate pregnancy; his mother, Janine de Montferrand, was – as the particle 'de' in her name suggests – of an aristocratic family, and her marriage to an undistinguished architect's assistant, Roland Truffaut, some twenty-one months after the birth of her son, seems more likely to have been the result of social pressure than of romance. The identity of François's biological father remained a mystery throughout his childhood and early youth.[2]

2 The 1996 biography by Antoine de Baecque and Serge Toubiana (*François Truffaut*, Paris, Gallimard) reveals that Truffaut did eventually trace his father, in 1968, and that his father was Jewish. Truffaut seems to have been unsurprised by the discovery of his Jewish blood: it corresponded to that sense of being an outsider he had known since childhood.

The child spent his early years being passed around between grandmothers and other surrogate carers, though his maternal grandmother, with whom he spent the most time, provided him both with his only experience of being 'mothered', and with an introduction to what was to be a lifelong passion for books. After her death in 1942, François finally took up residence in his parents' cramped flat, where from his own account his mother scarcely tolerated him and his father was kind but weak and preoccupied. The intense desire for a lost or withheld maternal love, the quest for an absent father who could facilitate entry into the social world – these emotional drives structure many of Truffaut's fictions and resonate with spectators also formed by the Oedipal triangle of the Western nuclear family.

Emotionally deprived, granted little support in his entry into the social world, the young Truffaut not surprisingly failed to become a model pupil and began a pattern of systematic minor delinquency that was to lead from non-attendance at school and serial expulsion to petty crime, through a period in a detention centre and on to desertion from the army. Though Truffaut's films are, as we shall see, almost devoid of explicitly political content or reference, they are nonetheless informed by a consistent suspicion of authority and a sympathy for the delinquent, the rebel and the outlaw – not an unusual ideological stance for a film-maker, but one which contributes to the films' capacity to please and engage certain audiences.

What saved the disaffected young Truffaut from a life of petty crime was the cinema: in his own words 'J'aurais peine l'impression d'exagérer en disant que le cinéma m'a sauvé la vie.'[3] (Gillain 1988: 19). Here the historical context of his early life becomes paramount: Truffaut was only eight when France was invaded by Hitler's army, and he spent the years from eight to twelve in occupied Paris, in a city of material shortages and scarcely concealed brutalities. Living close to Montmartre in the ninth *arrondissement*, however, he was also surrounded by refuges from bleak everyday reality, for the Boulevard Clichy alone had twenty-

3 'I feel it would hardly be an exaggeration to say that cinema saved my life'.

five cinemas, and although the war meant that France was deprived of imported American films, the Occupation was paradoxically a rich period for indigenous French film production. Though his practice of planning the week around cinema programmes (rather than school) and that of watching the same film up to twenty times were no doubt exceptional, Truffaut's identification of the cinema with physical and emotional warmth and with the pleasure of escapism ('le cinéma devint un refuge pour tous, et pas seulement au sens figuré'[4] (Bazin 1975a: 17)) was shared with much of the urban population of occupied France. Jacques Siclier, born five years before Truffaut and later to become an eminent film critic, also recalls the emotional importance of cinema in those years. Cinema was 'un spectacle auquel nous demandions la distraction, l'oubli passager des difficultés et des épreuves quotidiennes, un plaisir et une forme de liberté'[5] (Siclier 1981: 17). In *Le Dernier Métro* (1980), Truffaut transposes this function to theatre, but retains the image of the shared pleasure of illusion in the darkened auditorium, the suspension of anxiety emphasised by the shot of a young Jewish girl so absorbed in the stage as to forget the damning yellow star she wears. Throughout his films, cinema itself would become a central element of meaning, both as the site of key narrative events, and as the provider of profound emotional and aesthetic pleasure.

Emotional deprivation, and a consequent need both for a refuge and for some help in making sense of the world, led the child François Truffaut to the cinema. These are matters of personal biography – though perhaps of a not uncommon kind – but the availability of cinemas and of particular films connect the individual to social and cultural history. What Truffaut absorbed during these years was a particular cinematic heritage, shaped both by the history of the first forty-five years of French cinema and by the particular circumstances of the Occupation, and this in turn would help to mould his own work as a film-maker.

4 'the cinema became a refuge for all, and not only in the figurative sense'.

5 'a spectacle from which we demanded entertainment, the chance briefly to forget our problems and the hardships of everyday life, pleasure and a sort of freedom'.

The birth of cinema can be traced to that day in Paris in December 1895 when the Lumière brothers first presented their films – shot and projected with the *Cinématographe* they had invented – before a paying audience. It can equally well be traced to the other side of the Atlantic where, in April 1894, Edison opened his Kinetoscope Parlor on Broadway and demonstrated the potential of his new machine by showing the motion pictures *Horse-shoeing* and *The Barber Shop*. Even in the story of its origins, rivalry with the USA is inscribed in the history of French cinema, and the (often creative) tension between the two would play its part in Truffaut's work. Early French dominance of the film market was lost to the USA after World War I, but indigenous film production continued throughout the 1920s, and the 1930s can be seen in many senses as one of the great eras of French cinema. Competition from the USA, and financial problems caused by the Depression, made the decade a troubled one: once effective dubbing mechanisms had been introduced, the language problem posed by the introduction of 'talkies' ceased to be an advantage for national European cinemas, and the cheaper dubbed American films attracted distributors struggling to make a profit in a harsh economic climate (Hayward 1993: 24). The two major French film companies, Pathé and Gaumont, both collapsed in the 1930s, and the economic crisis also led the American company Paramount to close down its operation in Paris. However, the closure of the big firms allowed some smaller independent film producers to thrive, and at the same time the social inequalities exacerbated by the Depression produced a vibrant Left-wing critique of society. The combination of these two factors determined the nature of many of the films now canon-ised as the French classics of the 1930s.

Despite the political upheavals of a decade which saw the rise of Fascism and Nazism, the Spanish Civil War and, within the borders of the hexagon, the election of the Popular Front coalition of the Left (1936), most French studios in the 1930s continued to turn out well-crafted melodramas, comedies and stage adaptations which made little allusion to contemporary events but met the audience's demand for entertainment. Towards the end of the decade, however, there also appeared what are now thought of as the great films of the period, notably those made by the directors Jean Renoir and Marcel Carné (with his scriptwriter, the poet Jacques Prévert), representing an original and peculiarly French cinematic vision which would influence later generations of film-makers, including the directors of the Nouvelle Vague. Renoir and Carné directed films which were realist, depicting contemporary society through the stories of representative individuals, and which transcended realism through the poetic use of cinematic language. In sympathy with the values of the Popular Front, they depicted the exploitation of the working class through techniques which encouraged spectator identification with the underdog, the proletarian, the working-class hero, played both in Renoir's seminal *La Grande Illusion* (1937) and in Carné's *Le Jour se lève* (1939) by the actor Jean Gabin.

The French cinema was never nationalised, but governments of Right and Left recognised a need to support what was both an important industry and an artistic medium that represented, abroad, the qualities of French civilisation. The beneficent influence of French culture on the rest of the world is one of the founding credos of French Republicanism, and cinema has benefited from this both by being taken more seriously as an art-form in France than elsewhere, and by receiving a reasonably consistent degree of State support. In 1936, in response to the threat posed by competition from the American film industry, the French government imposed an import quota on dubbed films. In the same year, an archive to guard the legacy of French cinema was founded, though the *Cinémathèque française* would only be fully recognised as a national institution after World War II, when it would become both meeting place and source of inspiration for the future directors of the New Wave, amongst them Truffaut. In 1938 five National Film Prizes were instituted by the Ministry of Education, and the project for an annual national film festival at Cannes was launched, though its realisation was to be delayed until 1946 by the outbreak of war in September 1939.

When the German armies entered Paris in June 1940, every cinema in the city was closed (Chirat 1983: 8). The occupying powers were keen to re-open them, both to provide rest and relaxation for the German soldiers, and to keep the French population entertained and out of trouble: Goebbels's 1941 instructions to Alfred Greven, director of the German-run Parisian film company *Continental*, specified that films made for the French public should be 'légers, superficiels, divertissants mais nuls'[6] (Chirat 1983: 30). The government of Marshall Pétain, nominally in power in the 'Free Zone' of France until late 1942, was equally anxious to resume film production and distribution, if only to inaugurate a truly *French* era of film-making in the spirit of Pétain's traditionalist National Revolution. With all American competition banished by the war, production companies were set up and those French directors and stars who had not fled across the Atlantic were re-employed. The films produced ranged from melodramas that at least superficially subscribed to the Vichyite virtues of *Travail, Famille, Patrie* (Work, Family, Nation), to complex masterpieces such as Carné's *Les Enfants du paradis*, but the fact that the ideological significance of these films is in many cases still disputed suggests that neither Goebbels nor Pétain were able to gain full control of cinematic meanings. Parisians, Truffaut amongst them, flocked to the cinema to enjoy a range of films that continued the pre-war mainstream tendency to sidestep contemporary issues, though this now had the added advantage of providing a much-needed escapism and avoiding the danger of censorship. There were literary adaptations, many of them costume dramas (e.g. Baroncelli's *La Duchesse de Langeais*, 1941), tear-jerking melodramas (e.g. Jean Stelli's *Le Voile bleu*, 1942), American-style wise-cracking comedies (e.g. Marcel L'Herbier's *L'Honorable Catherine*, 1942, with Edwige Feuillère attempting a Katherine Hepburn role), murder stories (Clouzot's *L'Assassin habite au 21*, 1942), colonial dramas (Delannoy's *Pontcarral, colonel d'empire*, 1942) – and for Truffaut the most memorable of all, Carné's magical and enigmatic *Les Visiteurs du soir* (1942) and Clouzot's skilful and ambiguous story of small town intrigue *Le Corbeau* (1943). Traces of all of these genres and sub-genres can be found in Truffaut's own eclectic production, as can the avoidance

6 'light, superficial, entertaining but devoid of content'.

of any direct engagement with contemporary political reality. As Truffaut comments in his introduction to André Bazin's *Le Cinéma de l'Occupation et de la Résistance*, the emphasis on entertainment and escape from the present meant that 'le cinéma de l'Occupation a réussi à quatre-vingt-dix-huit pourcent à ne pas être pétainiste'[7] (Bazin 1975a: 29).

The particular circumstances under which Truffaut discovered cinema intensified the experience of spectatorship. It has become almost a commonplace of film theory that the cinema positions the spectator as *voyeur*, watching from the darkness a scene that ignores the spectator's presence. The *voyeur* sees both what he or she wants to see, and also perhaps what he or she fears to see: Freud's association of voyeurism with the child's horrified fascination at witnessing his or her parents engaged in the sexual act underpins the theory of cinematic voyeurism. Thus the pleasure of watching film would have its roots in pre-conscious experience and would mobilise some of our deepest emotions, blending desire and guilt. For the boy illicitly absent from school, or secretly leaving the family flat at night while his parents were out, and, more often than not, having entered the cinema without paying, the darkened auditorium was 'lié à ... une idée de clandestinité'[8] (Gillain 1988: 16–17) in a particularly acute way: the cinema was both a warm, womb-like refuge and the site of transgression, the flickering images were both the medium that could make narrative sense of a chaotic world, and the medium through which he encountered, as a pre-adolescent, sex, love and death. In his films, cinema frequently fulfils both of these functions, serving in *L'Argent de poche* (1976) for example both as illicit refuge for Julien, the abused and unloved child, and as the site of tentative sexual experiments for Patrick and his friends, who learn what is expected of them from male behaviour on the screen.

The historical situation added yet another layer to the intensity of the experience, for in a city occupied by a hostile foreign power, the cinema, with its largely French-produced stories, represented

---

7 'the French cinema of the Occupation succeeded in remaining 98 per cent free of Petainist propaganda'.

8 'associated with ... the idea of clandestinity'.

a haven not only of relative warmth and comfort but also of French identity. The frequently hostile reaction of French audiences to the screening of German news bulletins confirms this: local police forces were warned that misplaced applause or laughter should be dealt with severely, and by 1944 cinemas were obliged to screen the news with the lights half-on so that offenders could be identified, which often meant that the ticketless Truffaut, let in through the back door by a more fortunate friend, had to hide in the lavatories until the news was over and the lights went down (Gillain 1988: 18; Siclier 1981: 45–55; Chirat 1983: 12). Thus the cinema, with its sense of collective pleasure secured against the world outside, took on some connotations of resistance: Elsa Triolet's Resistance story *The Lovers of Avignon*, published by the underground press, has its heroine retreat into the cinema at a point of crisis, and regain her will to fight in part through the release offered by French images and music. Truffaut's intense identification with the characters on-screen 'chaque fois que quelqu'un était emmerdé ..., chaque fois que quelqu'un était en situation irrégulière'[9] (Gillain 1988: 19), arose in part from his own sense of being 'out of order' (*en situation irrégulière*), but may well have coincided with the identifications of many of his French fellow spectators, aware that they were in constant danger of finding themselves *en situation irrégulière* in the eyes of the occupying forces. Truffaut's film *Le Dernier Métro*, 1980, set in the Occupation years, evokes this sense of passive resistance through culture in the story of a small Parisian theatre surviving censorship, anti-Semitism and material shortages to emerge triumphant at the war's end.

Entering the cinema world: from the Liberation to the early 1950s

At the time of the Liberation in 1944 Truffaut was twelve-years old, a precociously literate and knowledgeable filmgoer, intellectually and emotionally committed to cinema, thus far primarily French

9 'whenever anyone was being given a hard time ..., whenever anyone was out of order'.

cinema. The end of the Occupation left the French film industry – like most sectors of French life – divided, disorganised and lacking in resources. Now competition from Hollywood, suspended since 1940, returned dramatically with the influx of all the films of the war years: 70 per cent of the films screened in France in 1946–47 were American (Hayward 1993: 26). Though French governments recognised the importance of cinema in polishing up France's rather tarnished international image, the conditions agreed for much-needed American economic aid reduced the possibility of protectionism, and the pre-war import quota on American films was replaced by the Blum–Byrnes agreement which provided only for a screening quota: French cinemas must show French-produced films for four weeks out of thirteen (increased in 1948 to five). Lobbying by the cinema industry convinced the government that more positive support strategies were needed: as part of the Fourth Republic's First Plan (1947–50), designed to kick-start the reconstruction of the country, taxes on cinema were reduced, a programme of cinema renovation and rebuilding was established, the *Centre National de la Cinématographie* (CNC) was set up to encourage national production, and the *loi d'aide* established the principle that a proportion of cinema's profits should be ploughed back into film production through the CNC. Financial support was first offered to film producers who had already proved themselves, through the system of *aide automatique* which made investment in a new film project dependent on the previous film's profits. In 1953 the system of *aide sélective* was added, offering investment based not on commercial success but on the quality of the project proposed, or the capacity of the film to 'serve the cause of French cinema' (Prédal 1991: 70). Finally in 1959 the *avances sur recettes* scheme granted interest-free loans to film-makers with a promising project, the loans being repayable from profits made. The latter scheme in particular was to encourage the wave of new film-makers whose careers began at the turn of the decade, and of whom Truffaut was to be one.

Fuelled by the huge numbers of good and bad Hollywood movies that crossed the Atlantic, and in France by state encouragement, the post-war decade was one of the great periods of cinema-going in Europe. Pierre Sorlin states that in 1955 more than three thousand million cinema tickets were sold in Europe, which, he calculates, is the equivalent of every European, including the newborn, attending the cinema at least sixteen times in the year (Sorlin 1991:81). In France a thousand new cinemas opened during the 1950s. François Truffaut alone contributed considerably to Sorlin's statistics, continuing to visit the cinema several times per week and sometimes per day; by his own reckoning, he saw three thousand films between 1946 and 1956 (Winston Dixon 1993: 73). Not surprisingly, given the obsessive attraction it held for him, it was the cinema that finally got Truffaut into serious trouble with the law: an attempt to start up one of the film clubs that proliferated in Paris in the 1940s and 1950s led to disaster when the film failed to turn up and the customers demanded their (already spent) money back. Truffaut's father, in a move that was to be built into the narrative of *Les 400 Coups*, handed his son over to the police and thence to a detention centre. His exit from the detention centre was equally tied up with his enthusiasm for film: through the various film clubs of which he had been a member Truffaut had met the film critic and theorist André Bazin. Bazin offered Truffaut (now in his mid-teens) a home and a job as a projectionist with the organisation *Travail et Culture*, set up to take cinema (and discussion of cinema) to the workers, through screenings in factories and other worksites. Through Bazin, Truffaut found himself in a milieu that shared his passion, and from then on – apart from a brief and mistaken foray into military life, from which Bazin also rescued him – Truffaut's life and his career as a film journalist, critic and director were one and the same.

André Bazin was only fourteen years Truffaut's senior, but by the time they worked together he was already established as a writer on film and as one of the organisers of *Travail et culture*. Bazin shared his protégé's passion for cinema and encouraged him to see the medium in a historical perspective, as an art-form that was still evolving and that could be supported and shaped by well-informed criticism. Bazin's aesthetic was a humanist one, based on an optimistic faith that through a realism that showed people and events in all their complexity, and that involved the spectator actively in the production of meaning, film could contribute to the construction of a better world. The Italian neo-realist films of the late 1940s corresponded to his ideal: an article written in 1948 asks the reader/spectator 'mais dites-moi si, en sortant de voir un film italien, vous ne vous sentez pas meilleur, si vous n'avez pas envie de changer l'ordre des choses, mais de préférence en persuadant les hommes...'[10] (Bazin 1975b: 264). Admiring also in neo-realism the generous treatment of characters, the fact that 'Aucun n'est réduit à l'état de chose ou de symbole, ce qui permettrait de les haïr confortablement sans avoir à dépasser au préalable l'équivoque de leur humanité'[11] (Bazin 1975b: 264). Bazin brought a similar generosity to his personal life, from which Truffaut greatly benefited and which he recalled with gratitude: 'je crois qu'il avait une morale civique, sociale, humaine, extraordinaire, telle qu'on pense que si beaucoup de gens étaient comme ça, la vie serait meilleure, je crois'[12] (Desjardins 1993: 29).

The *Cahiers du cinéma*

In April 1951 Bazin, Jacques Doniol-Valcroze and Lo Duca founded the film journal *Cahiers du cinéma*. *Cahiers* was by no means the first scholarly review to deal with film in a country which had always taken the medium seriously: *Revue du Cinéma* for one had been published from 1929–31, and again from 1946–9, and had employed many of the same writers and adopted a broadly similar approach to that of the new *Cahiers*. But *Cahiers* was to bring together a group of young men – Truffaut amongst them – equipped with an extensive familiarity with film history and

10 'just tell me, when you come out of an Italian film, if you don't feel a better person, if you don't feel you want to change the way things are, preferably by persuasion ...'.
11 'no one is reduced to the condition of an object or a symbol that would allow one to hate them in comfort without having first to leap the hurdle of their humanity'.
12 'I believe he had an extraordinary sense of morality, civic, social, human ... if more people were like that I think the world would be a better place.'

contemporary cinema, gained in part at the *Cinémathèque* where they often met, and fuelled by a righteous Oedipal anger at what they saw as the inadequacies of the *cinéma de papa*, or the French mainstream cinema of the 1950s. Their sense of themselves as young men with a mission of renewal was in tune with the age: the 1950s was a period in which youth and modernity began to appear as national ideals in France, as governments of the Fourth Republic (1946–58) pursued pro-nationalist, modernising policies designed to make France a successful consumer economy. After 1958, with the arrival in power of de Gaulle at the head of a new Republic, the emphasis on renewal became still more marked: some of the *Cahiers* team (Claude Chabrol, Jean-Luc Godard, Jacques Rivette, Eric Rohmer – and Truffaut) would be helped in their transition from film critic to film director by the willingness of the press to christen them the New Wave of French cinema and thus foster the curiosity of the public.

Truffaut began to write for *Cahiers* in 1953, having already gained some experience as a film journalist, writing for (amongst others) *Elle* magazine. The *Cahiers* team were united in their Bazinian respect for a particular kind of realism, their enthusiasm for Hollywood genre films, and their dislike of the kind of cinema that was dominant in France. Within this broad consensus, Truffaut (twenty-one in 1953) tended to adopt a more virulent and uncompromising tone than the rest: self-educated where most of his colleagues had followed more conventional routes through school and (in some cases) university, he wrote lively, tendentious and hard-hitting film reviews, some of which he later regretted and omitted from his collected articles. Contempt for the *tradition de qualité* or mainstream French cinema of the day, extended to the conservatism of more established film critics who, according to Truffaut, were indiscriminate supporters of the status quo and unable to recognise new or experimental modes of cinema. In an appreciative review of Vadim's *Et Dieu créa la femme* (1956), he sets his own pleasure in the 'daring photography' and the 'anti-theatrical laconicism' of the dialogue against the animosity of 'the mealy-faced critic', who 'arrives in the movie theatre his eyes glazed over, his view obstructed by foolish prejudices', all too willing to 'blame the film for not being consistent with what he expected' (Wheeler Dixon 1993: 72–4).

The attacks on the *cinéma de papa* and its defenders undoubtedly carried an element of the ritual rejection of the father with which young male intellectuals tend to begin their careers – the entire *Cahiers* team was male, as were all the older film-makers whom they criticised. Demonisation of what went before is also a standard rhetorical ploy for new movements in the arts, and the definition of what was wrong with the *tradition de qualité* equally served the more constructive purpose of formulating a vision of what would constitute 'good' cinema. In his article *A Certain Tendency of French Cinema* (1954), Truffaut grouped together the commercially successful and celebrated French directors of the day (Yves Allégret, Claude Autant-Lara, René Clément, Jean Delannoy, Marcel Pagliero) as practitioners of 'psychological realism', which he compared negatively to the poetic realism of the 1930s. He objected primarily to the central role played by script-writers in the making of their films: the team of Jean Aurenche and Pierre Bost had been responsible, over the preceding decade, for the adaptation of many literary works into film scenarios, and Truffaut found their apparent versatility to be no more than an ability to reduce widely differing works to the same old formula.

> Les coucheries s'effectuent selon une symétrie bien concertée, des personnages disparaissent, d'autres sont inventés, le script s'éloigne peu à peu de l'original pour devenir un tout, informe mais brillant, un film nouveau, pas à pas, fait son entrée solennelle dans *La Tradition de la Qualité*[13] (Truffaut 1987: 219).

It was not merely the specific failings of the most respected script-writers of the day that displeased him, but the fact that they were considered central to the quality of the film, that these were 'script-

13 People hop in and out of bed with each other in neat, rhythmical patterns, characters disappear, others are invented, the script deviates little by little from the original and becomes a whole, formless but brilliant: a new film, step by step makes its solemn entrance into the *tradition de qualité*. (Nicholls 1976: 229. In Nicholls 1976 the first words of the quotation are mistranslated as 'The sun rises and sets like clockwork.').

writers' films' in which the director was merely 'le monsieur qui met les cadrages là-dessus'[14] (Truffaut 1987: 224). For Truffaut as for the rest of the *Cahiers* team, this was heresy, for if film was to be an art-form in its own right, then the artist was surely the one who 'wrote' in film-language, that is the director.

The primary role accorded to the script-writers betrayed a failure to conceive of film as a medium with its own specific codes of meaning. In *A Certain Tendency...* Truffaut acknowledged that many 'quality' films aspired to social relevance and to expressing a broadly 'anti-bourgeois' ideology, either through the adaptation of literary texts dealing with problematic social issues (Autant-Lara's *Le Diable au corps* (1947) and *Le Blé en herbe* (1954) were both adapted by Aurenche and Bost from novels whose frank treatment of adolescent sexuality had provoked scandals at the time of publication[15]), or through scenarios that made their proletarian protagonists 'heroic' (Truffaut cites for example Allégret's *Manèges* (1950), Pagliero's *Les Amants du Brasmort* (1951) and *Un Homme marche dans la ville* (1950)). Truffaut applauds the principle of 'audacity' in film but insists that regardless of the script, the 'cadrages savants, éclairages compliqués, photo "léchée"'[16] (Truffaut 1987: 220) of the *tradition de qualité* determine conservatism of meaning; the 'realism' of left-wing directors such as Autant-Lara he reduces to 'donne[r] au public sa dose habituelle de noirceur, de non-conformisme, de facile audace'[17] (Truffaut 1987: 221). The true 'audacities' of post-war cinema are performed by those 'men of the cinema' who experiment with the medium: Truffaut mentions Jacques Tati's Hulot films, Abel Gance's 'studies in Polyvision', and Renoir's *Le Carrosse d'Or*.

Out of the critique of the *qualité* cinema then, there developed the subsequently famous *politique des auteurs*, the assertion of the

14 'the gentleman who adds the pictures to (the scenario)' (Nicholls 1976: 233).

15 See Keith Reader: '"Tous les garçons et les filles de leur âge": representations of youth and adolescence in pre-new-wave French cinema', *French Cultural Studies*, 7: Part 3: 21, 259–70.

16 'scholarly framing, complicated lighting effects, "polished" photography' (Nicholls 1976: 230).

17 'giv[ing] the public its customary dose of seaminess, non-conformity and facile audacity' (Nicholls 1976: 230).

primary role of the film director in the creation of a cinematic text, and of a continuity of artistic inspiration throughout a director's work. The *Cahiers* team argued that despite the complex process of film production, and the inevitable involvement in the creative process of large numbers of actors and skilled technicians of various kinds, the controlling creative force in any film worthy of respect was the director. A good (or *Cahiers*-approved) director was the *auteur* (author) of a corpus of work in which every film would display a recognisable style expressive of a consistent personal vision, a mere *metteur-en-scène* was judged intrinsically incapable of creating a good film.

This image of the film director derives from a view of the artist as source and guarantor of meaning and artistic value, a view already becoming outdated in the early 1950s. Its similarity to Romantic images of the writer, painter or musician are not accidental: the *Cahiers* team was engaged in a continuation of the struggle to have cinema viewed as equal in status to earlier art-forms, and since the nineteenth century art had been defined as a product emanating from the inspiration of the exceptional individual. The application of such a model to a medium based on complex technologies was in some senses inappropriate, as Bazin himself pointed out in a sympathetic but carefully critical article 'On the *politique des auteurs*': '...the cinema is an art which is both popular and industrial' and thus any analysis of, for example, the excellence of Hollywood cinema must go beyond 'the quality of certain directors' to include 'a sociological approach to its production' (Bazin 1957, (ed. Hillier 1985): 251). In its minimising of the socio-historical determinants of a film's meaning, and of the contribution of a large, skilled team of workers, the *politique* could be read as reactionary and misleading.

However, in other respects the re-evaluation of the director's role was progressive. The *politique* provided a useful corrective to dominant critical and film-making practices in its emphasis on the specifically visual and aural language of film as the key to a film's meaning and its quality: the insistence that the medium was itself the message, aligned 'New Wave' theory with modernist thinking on literature and painting. Moreover, true to their initial enthusiasms, the *Cahiers* team did not subscribe to an elitist or hierarchical view of cinema, finding their 'true *auteurs*' as often amongst the makers of Hollywood B-movies as amongst the less commercial French directors such as Jean Cocteau or Robert Bresson. An authentic *auteur*, they seemed to feel, could impose his [*sic*] personal vision even on the production-line methods of the Hollywood studio system. Cinema as entertainment industry, and cinema as art, were not mutually exclusive categories. Working within and against the *genre* codes of the popular cinema was seen not as a constraint but as a further creative possibility.

The positive value accorded to genre was an important counter-balance to the individualist emphasis of the *auteur* argument. In recognising that the recurring structures and motifs of Westerns, gangster films or musicals represented not a failure of creativity, but an acceptance of cinema's mythic function, the *Cahiers* critics related the *auteur*'s achievements to the ability to tap into the collective imagination. Bazin articulated their shared admiration for American cinema's ability to do precisely this: 'La beauté du western proc[ède] notamment de la spontanéité et de la parfaite inconscience de la mythologie dissoute en lui, comme le sel dans la mer'[18] (Bazin 1975a: 243), and conversely a regret that French cinema should lack 'good basic genres that thrive, the way they do in America' (Bazin 1957 (ed. Hillier 1985): 33). Whilst the more extreme versions of the *auteur* position seemed to evaluate films according to the director's ability to express an individual vision on the screen, and thus to ignore the box-office as a criterion of success, this willingness to take genre seriously, implied a recognition that film is an important *social* medium, and that the popularity of certain types of film arises from their ability to address shared emotions, anxieties or desires. In his own film-making, Truffaut was both to experiment with the use of genre codes, and to take box-office success as an important criterion of quality.

The work done by *Cahiers du cinéma* in the 1950s was central to the development of film theory and criticism not only in France

18 'The beauty of the Western proceed[s] notably from its spontaneity and from its perfect unconsciousness of the mythology dissolved in it, like salt in the sea' (Bazin 1957 (ed. Hillier 1985): 170).

but also in the USA, Britain and the rest of Europe. Truffaut's polemical attacks on the *tradition de qualité* and his championing of the work of Hollywood directors such as Alfred Hitchcock and Nicholas Ray (director of *Johnny Guitar* and *Rebel Without a Cause*) were not always rigorously fair or accurate, but they contributed to the development of a text-based film criticism that took popular cinema as seriously as 'art' films. As in the case of his colleagues Chabrol, Godard, Rivette and Rohmer, the period spent as a critic constantly engaged in the analysis and evaluation of films allowed Truffaut to formulate a view of what film should be which he was subsequently able to put into practice.

From critic to director

Whilst writing for *Cahiers* Truffaut also worked intermittently as assistant to the Italian neo-realist director Rossellini, to whom Bazin had introduced him in 1954. Since Rossellini made no films during these years (1954–56), Truffaut gained experience in the preparation of scenarios rather than in the actual process of filming, but the shooting and editing of the brief *Une Visite* (with Rivette and Resnais) in 1955 confirmed his desire to move behind the camera. The problem of financing the production of a film had first to be overcome. By 1957, Truffaut was planning the making of a short film, *Les Mistons*, and was also engaged to Madeleine Morgenstern, daughter of the managing director of the film company Cocinor. On the advice of Marcel Berbert, his father-in-law's assistant (and subsequently Truffaut's production director) he applied for funding to the UFIC bank, which specialised in film investment. Unknown to Truffaut, Berbert guaranteed the loan on behalf of Cocinor, thus ensuring that the film would be financed and enabling Truffaut to set up the independent production company Les Films du Carrosse (named after Renoir's film *Le Carrosse d'Or*) which would produce his films for the rest of his career. From an intensive participation in the history of cinema as spectator, critic and theorist, Truffaut moved on to the role of director.

References

Baecque, Antoine de and Serge Toubiana (1996), *François Truffaut*, Paris Gallimard.

Bazin, André (1957), On the *politique des auteurs* in Jim Hillier (ed.), *Cahiers du cinéma Vol. I. The 1950s: Neo-Realism, Hollywood, New Wave*, London, Routledge & Kegan Paul, 1985.

Bazin, André (1975a), *Qu'est-ce que le cinéma?*, Paris, Editions du Cerf. References here are to this edition. Selected essays in translation can be found in Hugh Gray (ed.): *What is cinema?* Vol. I, Berkeley, University of California Press, 1967, and in Hillier (below).

Bazin, André (1975b), *Le Cinéma de l'Occupation et de la Résistance*, Paris, Union Générale d'Editions, Collection 10/18. Preface by François Truffaut. Translated by Stanley Hochman as *French Cinema of the Occupation and Resistance*, New York, Frederick Ungar, 1981.

Chirat, Raymond (1983), *Le Cinéma français des années de guerre*, Renens, 5 Continents Hatier.

Desjardins, Aline (1993), Aline Desjardins s'entretient avec François Truffaut, Paris, Editions Ramsay.

Gillain, Anne (1988), *Le Cinéma selon François Truffaut*, Paris, Flammarion..

Hayward, Susan (1993), *French National Cinema*, London, Routledge.

Insdorf, Annette (1996), *François Truffaut: Les Films de sa vie*, Paris, Gallimard.

Nicholls, David (ed.) (1976), *Movies and Methods: An Anthology*, Berkeley, University of California Press.

Prédal, René (1991), *Le Cinéma français depuis 1945*, Paris, Nathan.

Siclier, Jacques (1981), *La France de Pétain et son cinéma*, Paris, Editions Henri Veyrier.

Sorlin, Pierre (1991), *European Cinemas, European Societies*, London, Routledge.

Triolet, Elsa (1944), *The Lovers of Avignon* in *A Fine of Two Hundred Francs*, trans. Helena Lewis, London, Virago 1986.

Truffaut, François (1987), *Le Plaisir des yeux*, Paris, Flammarion.

Winston Dixon, Wheeler (1993), *The Early Film Criticism of François Truffaut*, Bloomington & Indianapolis, Indiana University Press.


```
┌─────────┐
│         │
│    2    │
│         │
└─────────┘
```

A career in cinema

Awakening of a passion

'Rien qu'en lisant tes journeaux [*sic*] de cinéma, ça me donne envie d'être à Paris car il y a l'air d'avoir de bons films'[1] (Truffaut 1988: 19). This letter to his friend, Robert Lachenay, written from Binic near St Brieuc in the summer of 1945 when he was only thirteen, reveals the depth and early manifestation of Truffaut's interest in the cinema. Even in a generation which shared a common passion for the medium, his obsession with it, which suffuses these early letters to Lachenay, was exceptional. They are full of references to films he had seen, films he wanted to see, and littered with the names of stars and directors. In the same letter from Binic, he even, in a post-scriptum, sketched out the embryonic scenario of an event (Antoine's running away) and a character (the teacher) which were later to form the basis of an episode in *Les 400 Coups*. In order to be able to persuade his friends that it really happened, he urged Lachenay in his next letter to 'raconte[r] ... mon odyssée nocturne et souterraine dans le métro la cause, l'action, son résultat, raconte exactement comment les faits se sont passés quand j'ai couché au métro quand on était chez Ducornet. Parce que mes cops ne veulent pas me croire'[2] (Truffaut 1988: 20).

1 'Just reading the cinema reviews you sent me makes me want to be in Paris, there seem to be lots of good films on'.
2 'Tell the story of my nocturnal, underground odyssey on the tube, the cause, the action and the outcome. Set out exactly what happened when I slept in the tube when we were at Ducornet's. 'Cos my friends won't believe me.'

Young though he was, he was already instinctively setting life out in terms of a film script. Although the episode was to be much modified by the time it entered the narrative of *Les 400 Coups*, this letter shows how, already, details from his personal experience are being stored for later use. The letter and extensive correspondence with Lachenay highlight a second important characteristic of the young Truffaut, one which was to remain with him throughout his life and have an important bearing on his films: his passion for writing.

The successive steps which led Truffaut from a troubled child-hood and adolescence into a career as a director have been charted above (see chapter 1): his mania for cinema as a boy, his attempts to run a film club, his meeting up with André Bazin, the time spent as an assistant with the Italian director, Roberto Rossellini, his contributions to film magazines, all in retrospect seem to mark out a clearly defined and single-minded ambition. In reality, his progress towards a career as a film director was a little less assured and somewhat more circuitous.

The aim of this chapter is to provide the reader with an overview of Truffaut's films, from a number of perspectives. An initial discussion of critical evaluations of his work is followed by a brief examination of some of the ways in which the films can be grouped and categorised. This leads into a chronological review of the body of work which foregrounds the main themes and discusses Truffaut's working practices as a director, drawing on his own writing about his film-making. The chapter thus serves as a general introduction and provides a framework for the thematic analyses of the succeeding chapters.

Critical perspectives: the question of political commitment

There can be no doubt that Truffaut is a major figure within French and indeed world cinema, the sheer number of works devoted to him, many of them in English, bear witness to that fact. There are, however, a number of competing evaluations. Some critics, while writing positive appraisals of Truffaut's work, resort to descriptors such as 'charming' and 'nostalgic', 'lightness of touch'. Such approaches draw attention to Truffaut's intuitive, nuanced investigation of human, mainly heterosexual, relationships, to his success in handling child actors which enabled him to convey convincingly the experience of childhood, to his somewhat romantic evocation of a recent past. By implication, such critics suggest the lack of an intellectual edge, the failure to inject into the films any form of social or political critique. Truffaut himself appeared to acknowledge the validity of such reservations when he described his work – interestingly, to Annette Insdorf, one of his more perceptive critics – as 'plus instinctif qu'intellectuel' ('more instinctive than intellectual', Truffaut 1988: 505).

In a country which takes the political views of its artists and intellectuals seriously, a frequently made criticism of Truffaut's films is that they do not engage with issues of a social or political order. Whereas many of the greatest French film directors (Renoir, Carné) produced films that were overtly or obliquely committed to the values of the Left, and Truffaut's contemporary Godard made films that became increasingly political and challenged received thinking on virtually every level, Truffaut avoided making political films and certainly making films politically. This does not, however, signify that Truffaut was wholly apolitical: he displayed a clear commitment to broadly left-wing causes both as an individual and, once his fame was established, as a public figure. In 1960, when the success of *Les 400 Coups* had made him a minor celebrity, he was one of the signatories of the *Manifeste des 121*, a document signed by leading left-wing intellectuals expressing opposition to French policy in Algeria, where the army was engaged in a brutal war against the pro-independence National Liberation Front (FLN). Truffaut's reasons for signing were heartfelt but characteristically skewed towards the personal: both in letters written at the time (Truffaut 1988: 173) and in retrospective accounts, he interprets the Manifesto as an expression of loyalty to a colleague – one of his collaborators at the Films du Carrosse had fallen foul of the law by allowing her flat to be used for FLN meetings – and as an expression of support for those French soldiers who deserted rather than fight the FLN. Himself an ex-deserter, Truffaut opposed the Algerian war in a spirit of solidarity with anti-militarist rebellion, rather than as the result of a fully thought-out political commitment. Similarly, in May 1968, Truffaut was passionately involved in the maelstrom of protest and revolt that constituted *les événements*, but for reasons that were again consistent with his abiding priorities. It was the French government's threat to dismiss the co-founder and director of the national film archives (the *Cinémathèque*), Henri Langlois, and to replace this guardian of all that Truffaut held most dear by a more efficient, but perhaps less ardently cinephile administrator, that sparked off Truffaut's fit of activism. From leading the (successful) fight to have Langlois reinstated, Truffaut moved on to the wider struggle, playing a leading role in the closing of the Cannes Film Festival in May in a gesture of solidarity with the striking students and workers. In 1970 he was on the streets with Sartre and Beauvoir selling the banned Maoist newspaper *La Cause du peuple*, not, as he stated in a letter to the presiding judge at the trial of a fellow-vendor, because he was in any way committed to the paper's political views ('je n'ai jamais eu d'activités politiques et je ne suis pas plus maoiste que pompidoliste...'), but because of his love for 'les livres et les journaux' and attachment to 'la liberté de la presse et l'indépendance de la justice'.[3]

As a private individual and as a personality on the public stage, Truffaut's sympathies were, then, with the Left – though he was not, as he stated in an interview in 1978 'de gauche' (of the Left) since he was rarely politically active, he was 'gauchisant', or *on* the Left, and voted accordingly on the grounds that the Left was simply 'more just' (Rabourdin 1985: 34). His politics were essentially emotional and cultural, concerned above all with resistance to any threat to freedom of expression, and with the defence of his beloved cinema. In terms of his cinematic output, the fact remains that the films eschew political commitment. It is difficult, for example, to

3 'I have never been politically active and I am no more Maoist than Pompidolist' [Pompidou was then the President of the French Republic] ... [The letter continues] 'What matters to me is my love for books and newspapers and my attachment to the freedom of the press and the independence of the legal system.'

refute criticism of the way the period of the Occupation is portrayed in *Le Dernier Métro*. On this most sensitive of topics, Truffaut opts for nostalgia and produces a film packed with romanticised reminiscences of everyday life in wartime Paris, accompanied by the richly evocative music of the day, and all filmed in hazy browns, reds and yellows. The effect is to anaesthetise the real trauma of the situation and to sidestep completely the still haunting question of collaboration. This line of criticism inevitably also picks out the 'blindness' of a director who could make a film like *Baisers volés* (1968) as France was taking to the streets in the most significant political upheaval it had witnessed for decades.

There are, however, critics – in whose ranks we place ourselves – who advance more positive readings of the work and who believe that closer scrutiny reveals more than just charm and nostalgia. Such readings present a different picture: that of a remarkable story-teller who, while avoiding direct engagement with contemporary issues and debates, tapped into the collective preoccupations of his public through narratives that are at once everyday and mythic. Truffaut succeeded in straddling the frontier between 'art-house' and popular cinema, consistently achieving a degree of commercial success (chiefly in France, but also abroad) that enabled him to remain an independent film-maker. Part of the territory of popular entertainment is the representation of emotions and experiences shared by its audience, in a manner that is pleasurable because it allows both identification and detachment, both recognition and a cathartic distancing. Though always and inevitably shaped by social context, some of these emotions and experiences are fundamental and recur in popular fiction from the earliest myths to the present: childhood relations with mothers and fathers, love and desire, the fear of death. Truffaut's films deal, at best, compellingly, with these fundamental themes, through narratives that are occasionally historical but are more often set in the recognisably contemporary world of France from the late 1950s to the early 1980s.

The Doinel films, for example, chart the childhood, adolescence and youth of a baby-boomer hero who conspicuously fails to become involved in the grand narratives of his generation –

perceiving the events of May 1968 only as an obstacle that prevents his meeting with the girl he desires, never quite finding a career that will provide a recognised place in society, failing to establish a family – but whose very marginality encourages an enjoyable mix of empathy and critical detachment. The films depict the rites of passage of a young man in a specific social context (echoes of Rastignac, central protagonist of Balzac's *Comédie humaine*), and at the same time evoke some of the most profound conflicts of growing up: the formative drama of maternal/filial love and separation, the contradictory drives towards social integration and anarchic freedom.

Other films strike different chords: *Jules et Jim* (1961), *La Peau douce* (1964), *Les Deux Anglaises et le continent* (1971), *Le Dernier Métro* (1980), *La Femme d'à côté* (1981) – indeed the majority of the films explore the complex territory of heterosexual relationships (and, in some cases and through secondary narratives, gay relationships), skilfully charting the temptations and permutations, joys and traumas of love. Many of the films, and in particular *La Nuit américaine* (1973) and *Le Dernier Métro*, invite the audience to participate in and celebrate the pleasure of storytelling itself, reflecting at the same time on the complex relationship between fiction and a lived experience that is itself mediated through the stories we tell ourselves. And meanwhile most of the films are also shot through with the fear of – frequently tinged with the desire for – the oblivion of death. Truffaut's narratives rarely deal with the major events and issues of French history, but they do address what Anne Gillain has termed 'les structures profondes de l'inconscient collectif'[4] (Gillain 1991: 18), and do so with a suspicion for authority, a persistent empathy for powerless and vulnerable individuals, and a benevolent sense of humour consistent with the broadly left–liberal values the director espoused in his non-professional life. The presence of powerful themes within entertaining narratives, and the humane and flexible 'voice' of the films, help to explain their enduring appeal.

4 'the deep structures of the collective unconscious'

Structural perspectives

Another useful way of approaching Truffaut's work is to attempt to classify the different types of films he chose to make. It is immediately apparent that five of his films can be separated from the rest since they are linked in an obvious way, are distinct from his other films and constitute his main claim to originality. These are, of course, the 'Cycle Doinel' films, in chronological order: *Les 400 Coups, Antoine et Colette, Baisers volés, Domicile conjugal* (1970) and *L'Amour en fuite* (1979). These films cannot be clearly ascribed to any filmic genre, other perhaps than the rather loosely defined one of 'autobiographical' films, though by analogy with the novel they might be described as a filmic *Bildungsroman* or a 'novel of development' in several 'volumes'. Indeed, the literary conventions, and in particular the history of the French novel, with which Truffaut like most people educated in France was familiar, provide a more productive context for categorising these films and above all Balzac's *Comédie humaine* whence came, via Zola's Rougon–Macquart series, the notion of linked texts with recurring characters, settings and situations. Truffaut is probably best known for the Doinel films which articulate most of the principal themes: childhood and adolescence, relationships with parents, love, cinema itself.

A second group of films can be described as genre films. A large number of his works can, at least superficially, be thus defined. However, at this point the problems of attempting classification become apparent: for example, a number of Truffaut's thrillers could also be classified as love stories, or as *films noirs*. The three films generally looked upon as thrillers are *Tirez sur le pianiste* (1960), *La Mariée était en noir* (1967) and *Vivement dimanche!* (1982). Also, on some counts, warranting inclusion in this category, despite affinities with other genres, are *La Sirène du Mississippi* (1969), *La Peau douce* (1964) and *La Femme d'à côté* (1981). The only genre film not to fall in the present category is Truffaut's one science fiction film: *Fahrenheit 451* (1966).

A third set of films can be loosely grouped together on the simple grounds that they are all set in the past: *Jules et Jim* (set in the first thirty years of this century), *L'Enfant sauvage* (end of the eighteenth century), *Les Deux Anglaises et le continent* (1899-1920), *Adèle H.* (second half of the nineteenth century), *Le Dernier Métro* (the Occupation) and *La Chambre verte* (the 1920s). With the possible exception of *Le Dernier Métro* there is, however, no question of these 'historical' films forming part of the 'heritage' tradition which has resurfaced strongly in recent years, with films like *Jean de Florette* (1986) and *Manon des sources* (1986) and *Cyrano de Bergerac* (1990) nostalgically evoking a romanticised vision of France's past. What really links Truffaut's historical films is less the fact that they are set in the past than their sharing of a common style and repeated focus on familiar themes. All but *L'Enfant sauvage* might also be classified as love stories while *Le Dernier Métro* could be seen as a war film, or at least a film about the war, and *Jules et Jim* as an early, French, version of the buddy movie.

Setting or location provides another way of grouping the films. One of the effects of the Nouvelle Vague films was a certain promotion of contemporary France and its culture which countered the increasing dominance of the USA. Images of France and its lifestyle are a key to identity and language and the fact that films shot in France and with a soundtrack in French reached screens throughout the country served to stem the flood of films from across the Atlantic. In this light, it is interesting to note the locations chosen by Truffaut for his films. It is apparent that he was sensitive to the situation and no fewer than ten of his films are shot mostly in the French capital while another ten are filmed mainly in some part or parts of the provinces. He even showed France overseas in the form of a *département d'outre-mer*, namely the island of La Réunion (*La Sirène du Mississippi*). There are glimpses, or supposed glimpses, of other lands: Nova Scotia (in reality, Guernsey) in *Adèle H.*, a futuristic England in *Fahrenheit 451*, an early twentieth-century Wales (in fact Normandy) in *Les Deux Anglaises*. He moved around the provinces from the north (*La Chambre verte*) to the south (*La Nuit américaine* and *Vivement dimanche!*) from provincial towns such as Nîmes (*Les Mistons*) and Thiers (*L'Argent de poche*) to the mountains near Grenoble (*Tirez* and *La Sirène*). In some films, there is considerable movement, an at times frenetic toing and froing as in *Jules et Jim* (between France and Germany, Paris and the Midi), *La Mariée était en noir* (various locations in and near Paris and in Cannes) and *Les Deux Anglaises* (France and, supposedly, Wales). His filming in these many and varied locations no doubt brought a welcome boost to local economies. The wide distribution, in America and England, of a good number of his films ensured that this full picture of France, both past and present, spread beyond the *hexagone*. Part of the appeal of the films was undoubtedly their 'Gallic' charm.

Finally, another productive way of approaching Truffaut's output is to group together films that exploit the same or similar narrative structures. The picture that emerges enables us to identify a central core of themes and ideas. A number of the films introduce and explore triangular relationships, most notably the two films based on Roché novels – one involving two men and a woman (*Jules et Jim*) the other two women and a man (*Les Deux Anglaises*) – together with *La Peau Douce* and *La Femme d'à côté*, which also share with *Jules et Jim* a violent denouement centring on a *crime passionnel*. Structurally speaking, *Une Belle Fille comme moi* (1972) with its five males playing opposite a single female both echoes *Les Mistons* and closely resembles *La Mariée*. The male school narrative, setting the dreams and desires of boys against the demands of school as the agent of social order, appears first in *Les 400 Coups* and is repeated, this time in optimistic mode, in *L'Argent de poche*. The search for love and the desire to write intertwine to drive the stories not only of Antoine Doinel, but also of Claude Roc (*Les Deux Anglaises*), Adèle H. and Bertand Morane (*L'Homme qui aimait les femme*). The 'play within a play' structure recurs from *La Nuit américaine* (where to be more precise there is a film within a film) to *Le Dernier métro* (play within a film). The unstable nature of desire, the close connection between love and death, the importance of the conflict between the will to freedom and the demands of social order, the centrality of the theme of fiction, are all apparent in the recurring structures of the films. Patterns of repetition and variation constitute the arteries that sustain the films and serve to focus attention on the themes and ideas which constitute the fabric of Truffaut's work.

The point has now been reached at which it is appropriate to undertake a brief review of the films themselves.

'The idea was to make a film' (or the first wave)

Truffaut's early attempts at film-making were not very promising: *Une Visite*, a 16 mm short made in 1955, was never shown in public. Until comparatively recently, little was known about the film, in large part since Truffaut himself had little regard for it: 'Tout cela n'était pas très bon. On me demande très souvent des copies, je suis très content qu'il n'en existe plus ... C'est un film perdu'[5] he claimed in conversation with Anne Gillain (Gillain 1988: 81–2). However, when Koichi Yamada, the Japanese writer and critic and an admirer of Truffaut's work, asked for a copy to help in the preparation for his book on Truffaut, it transpired that Lachenay still had a print (Truffaut 1988: 617). In his reply to Yamada, Truffaut enclosed a page of scenario and a list of those involved without which, Truffaut felt, the film would seem 'a bit mysterious'. 'L'idée était de faire un film en 16 mm qui ne ressemble pas à un film d'avant-garde, c'est-à-dire où il n'y aurait pas de morts, pas de flaques de sang, pas d'effets poétiques et qui serait gris clair ... j'avais envie de faire un film en demi-teintes, pas franchement drôle mais un peu étrange et qui plastiquement ressemblerait à des films américains'[6] (Gillain 1988: 81).

Gilles Cahoreau has given a fuller account of *Une Visite* in his biography of Truffaut. The film was shot in the flat of a friend, Jacques Doniol-Valcroze with a 'crew' comprising director Truffaut, cameraman Jacques Rivette, two actors (Jean-José Richer and François Cognani) an unnamed actress and Jacques Doniol-Valcroze's infant daughter, Florence. In all, nineteen minutes' worth of film were shot which, after editing by Alain Resnais, were

5 'It wasn't very good. People often ask me for copies and I'm happy that no copies of it are to be found ... It's a lost film'.

6 'The idea was to make a 16 mm film which would not be avant-garde, that is to say there would be no corpses, no pools of blood, no poetic effects, and which would be light grey [...] I wanted to make a film in muted shades, not really comic but a bit strange and having the texture of American films.'

reduced to a final version lasting seven minutes and forty seconds. Interestingly, given Truffaut's admiration for the era of silent films, this first attempt at film direction had no sound track, though this was possibly due more to the technical problems of recording sound than to an authorial decision on Truffaut's part.

It was some time before Truffaut began work on a second project – filming took place in the summer of 1957. *Les Mistons*, the first public screening of which took place on the fringes of the Tours Film Festival in November 1957, marked Truffaut's real début and established him as a young director of genuine promise. The freshness and spontaneity of *Les Mistons* can be attributed to the fact that it marked, in 1957, a new departure: its setting was contemporary and recognisable as were its characters and themes. It was distinctively French, could not be easily ascribed to any particular genre, and was free of the formulaic characteristics of the *tradition de qualité*. Its bitter-sweet tone, captured in the music, was a first identifying feature of Truffaut the *auteur*. This time, he proclaimed himself satisfied with the outcome and invited Robert Lachenay to a screening at a cinema on the Champs-Elysées: 'Rivette, Rohmer, Godard, Doniol, Bazin, etc. aiment énormément le film, que j'aime aussi de nouveau et presque entièrement. La musique est épatante, tu verras.'[7] (Truffaut 1988: 141).

The twenty-three-minute short was again made with a small crew composed mainly of friends. With funds procured by Marcel Berbert, a company was set up to produce the film. The formation of this company, Les Films du Carrosse, established Truffaut's independence as a director. As he explained in a letter written seventeen years later to another French director, Louis Daquin: 'Ma société, les Films du Carrosse, me permet d'établir des scripts avec mes amis scénaristes, puis de constituer le casting et d'établir le budget; ceci me donne une totale liberté de création, car le film se trouve protégé des influences extérieures'[8] (Truffaut 1988:

7 'Rivette, Rohmer, Godard, Doniol, Bazin etc. really like the film and I've come round to thinking it's OK again, at least most of it. The music's great, you'll see.'
8 'Having my own company, *Les Films du Carrosse*, allows me to produce scenarios with my script-writing friends and then to do the casting and set up a budget; this process gives me complete creative freedom since the film is thus protected from outside influences.'

461). And in a letter to the writer and critic Jean-Louis Bory written a little over a month later, he returned to the same theme: 'Bons ou mauvais, mes films sont ceux que j'ai voulu faire et *seulement* ceux-là. Je les ai tournés avec les acteurs – connus ou inconnus – que j'avais choisis et que j'aimais. Si l'on doit un jour me refuser un projet, je m'en irai le tourner en Suède ou ailleurs'[9] (Truffaut 1988: 467).

Often in collaboration with other producers – TF1, A2, Artistes associés – Les Films du Carrosse contributed to financing the majority of Truffaut's films with receipts from one film helping to finance its successor and provide a consistent measure of artistic freedom. With *Les Mistons*, Truffaut sensed he was on the verge of a breakthrough: 'Je suis évidemment très excité puisque l'heure va sonner où je saurai à quoi m'en tenir pour l'avenir immédiat: d'autres sketches, un grand film ou que dalle?'[10] (Truffaut 1988: 141).

His third foray, *Une Histoire d'eau*, was, however, a false departure. Another short (eighteen minutes), it combines a Godard script with footage shot by Truffaut in and around Paris at the time of flooding in the spring of 1958. In a manner that characterises the close relationships and working methods of those forming the Nouvelle Vague, the project was taken over by Godard and is usually attributed to him since he organised completion of the shooting and editing. With this film, however, a key aspect of Truffaut's work pattern was beginning to emerge: as one project moved to completion he was already working on the next. With success, this process became more complex and at most points several projects were being considered simultaneously.

9 'Good or bad, the films I've made are the ones I wanted to make, I haven't made any others. I made them with actors – known and unknown – I chose and like. If one day one of the projects is turned down, I'll go and film it in Sweden or somewhere.'

10 'Obviously, I'm very excited because the moment is approaching at which the immediate future will become clear: more shorts, a big film or whatever?'

Universal acclaim

Although *Les Mistons* had been well received, it was not a full-length feature and brought Truffaut to the attention of only a comparatively small circle of mainly Parisian cognoscenti. The situation was about to change dramatically. As has been well documented, the year 1959 marked a turning point in French cinema. The Nouvelle Vague which had been in gestation throughout the 1950s, in film clubs and in the pages of the *Cahiers du cinéma* and other reviews, finally burst onto the screen. Truffaut's first full-length feature film, *Les 400 Coups*, was shown in May of that year at the Cannes film festival and was a major success with both critics and public. On one level, the metropolitan nightmare of *Les 400 Coups* was the antithesis of the provincial, pastoral idyll that is *Les Mistons*. On another, the two films are very similar: *Les 400 Coups*, like *Les Mistons*, does not conform to genre expectations, the setting is realist, or neo-realist, and highly recognisable (the Nîmes of the earlier film is replaced by Paris with its apartment life, its streets, schools, monuments). The focus is again on youth, in the form of a loveable rogue, Antoine Doinel, a slightly older version of the brats. Despite possessing a style and flair which are distinctively French, the film's appeal transcended national boundaries, receiving an equally enthusiastic reception in London, at the November Film Festival and, a month later, in New York.

Perhaps the single most significant outcome of the success of *Les 400 Coups* was that it filled the coffers of Les Films du Carrosse and gave Truffaut the confidence to move onto new and different ground. Although he is not generally viewed as an experimental director, the two films which follow in the period 1960–62 can lay claims to a degree of innovation. *Tirez sur le pianiste* (1960), in particular, puzzled critics and audiences alike at the time of its release. P. J. Dyer, writing in *Sight and Sound*, declared: 'It would be much too easy, and absurdly premature, to write off Truffaut purely on the evidence of [*Tirez sur le pianiste*]. Undisciplined, Hollywood-influenced, confused to the point of anarchy ... The film ends, and within hours one realises that nothing has stayed in the mind but the plot (or as much of it as one has managed to follow), which is patently rubbish' (Dyer 1960–61: 18).

Although this critic identified redeeming features, he and others did not acknowledge the film's originality and complexity. Of all Truffaut's films, this is the only one subsequently to inspire two studies devoted uniquely to it (Braudy 1972, Brunette 1993) in addition to a range of articles (for example Thiher 1977, Fairlamb 1996). The film is a complex brew, mixing genres and tones. The claim that the plot is 'patently rubbish' misses the point, since Truffaut attached little significance to plot, seeing it primarily as a vehicle. Although at first sight the film seems a long way removed from the semi-autobiographical world of *Les 400 Coups*, closer scrutiny reveals thematic and formal links with the earlier works. At the heart of the film are human relationships, and again the environment is mainly urban and contemporary (Paris for the most part). Once more the film resists classification but on this occasion this is not due to the absence of generic features – on the contrary, the film abounds in them. It is the presence of more than one genre, the film's seeming inability to stick firmly with any one of them and its unusual structure which underpin its claims to originality. Perhaps partly due to the public sharing the bewilderment of the critics, *Tirez* did not repeat the success of *Les 400 Coups* at the box office.

The film did, however, foreground an element of Truffaut's style which is already apparent in the preceding films: his sense of humour and of play. This is first apparent in the abrupt interruption of the main plot for Boby Lapointe (playing himself as a café performer) to sing the ribald and witty *Avanie et Framboise*. The song's intricate wordplay and *double entendres* are rendered strange – and more comic – by the contrast with Lapointe's deadpan delivery. There are a number of further moments in the film, particularly those associated with the gangsters, which reinforce the rich vein of comedy running through this and other films. The sense of play is also evident in the conspiratorial nods and winks to films of contemporaries and predecessors, for example to Abel Gance's *Napoléon* in the 'triple screen' narration of Plyne's treachery.

Jules et Jim (1961) echoes *Tirez* in that it too is adapted from a novel (though this time a French one) and again experiments with structure, subordinates plot to theme and is shot in black and white. In other ways, however, it marks a new departure: spread over thirty or so years from the turn of the century onwards, it abandons contemporary reality in favour of the historical and dispenses with any recognisable generic codes. Truffaut claimed that it was the first film he had made which was 'délibérément emmerdant' ('difficult to sit through') but nevertheless felt it would do better than *Tirez* at the box office if not as well as *Les 400 Coups* (Truffaut 1988: 195). He was, then, sensitive to his films' reception but clearly did not allow this alone to determine either his subject or his treatment of it. At this stage of his career, he was prepared to take risks and to experiment and *Tirez* and *Jules et Jim* arguably remain his most innovative works.

Working methods

Jules et Jim focuses attention on an important aspect of the director's work: his source material. As a member of the Nouvelle Vague, Truffaut resisted making adaptations of classic texts, an approach to film-making identified with the *tradition de qualité*. As an *auteur*, his aim was, rather, to set out his own world-view. In theory, this would mean that the Nouvelle Vague directors would favour using their own scenarios, the more so since negotiating rights can be a time-consuming affair. As Truffaut himself acknowledged, it is easier to work from one's own scenario: 'Je crois qu'après *Fahrenheit* je laisserai tomber les adaptations au profit des scénarios originaux, tout de même plus faciles à faire!'[11] (Truffaut 1988: 230). Despite this, only eleven of Truffaut's films were based on original scripts. Of the remaining twelve, ten were based on novels, one on a diary (*Adèle H.*) and one on a medical case study (*L'Enfant sauvage*). The important principle to note and the one which distinguishes him from the directors of the

11 'I think that after *Fahrenheit* I'll write original screenplays, which are in any case easier to do, rather than adaptations.'

tradition de qualité is that Truffaut did not seek to capitalise on the established success of the work he was adapting (compare, for example, the James Bond films where it is the author of the book rather than the director of the film who becomes the marketing tool and is the name that is remembered). The novels of American writers David Goodis (*Down There* on which *Tirez* is based), Ray Bradbury (*Fahrenheit 451*), William Irish (*The Bride Wore Black/La Mariée était en noir* and *Waltz into Darkness/La Sirène du Mississippi*), Henry Farrell (*Such a Gorgeous Kid Like Me/Une Belle Fille comme moi*) and Charles Williams (*The Long Saturday Night/ Vivement dimanche!*) were not well known in France (some of them were possibly not all that well known in North America), while Maurice Pons's short stories (*Les Virginales*) were not widely read. Furthermore, Truffaut was only drawn to texts which served his own purposes (e.g. Roché's novels depict triangular relationships; Doctor Itard's report on the 'wild child' privileges the surrogate father/child relationship) and used them simply as a framework-cum-starting point for his films. Although *Les Mistons* includes chunks of Pons's original text, the finished film is Truffaut's to the extent that he asked the writer to recast sections of his text, suggesting key words he should emphasise. 'J'ai très peur de vous montrer *Les Mistons*, car j'ai conscience de n'avoir pas été fidèle à votre récit'[12] (Truffaut 1988: 136). With other texts, Truffaut paid scant respect to the original which was no more than a peg on which to hang his own ideas and structures 'Je vous adresse *Vivement dimanche!* dont mon prochain film est tiré, mais, à l'exception du début et de la fin du livre, nous avons été amenés à tout changer'[13] (Truffaut 1988: 625).

Such had been the success of *Les 400 Coups* that, even after the comparatively limited impact of *Tirez* and *Jules et Jim*, Truffaut was still financially secure and artistically independent. His method of working, broadly speaking, conforming to the Nouvelle

12 'I'm very much afraid of showing you [that is, Pons] *Les Mistons*, since I'm conscious of the fact that I've not been faithful to your story.'

13 'I'm sending you *Vivement dimanche!* [Charles Williams's novel] on which my next film is based. With the exception of the beginning and the ending of the book, we've had to change everything.'

Vague and *auteur* philosophies that had evolved in France as a reaction to the *cinéma de papa* as well as to the big-budget, studio-generated productions of Hollywood, was now well established: comparatively modest budgets, an emphasis on location shooting (though by no means to the total exclusion of studio work), a predilection for improvisation, close control over all aspects of film production from finance and casting to script-writing and editing, a preference for little-known actors rather than stars, but above all a desire to work with a team of actors and technicians whom he knew and trusted. A glance at the credits of his films confirms this last point: the same names crop up again and again: Marcel Berbert (executive producer for fifteen of the films), Suzanne Schiffman ('script-girl' from 1962–69, then assistant director for virtually all the films up to and including the last), Roland Thénot (*régisseur* or production manager for thirteen films), Delerue (composer of the musical score for eleven of the films), Claudine Bouché, Agnès Guillemot, Yann Dedet and Martine Barraqué (Truffaut's film editors), Raoul Coutard (cameraman for five of the first eight films) then Nestor Almendros (cameramen for nine out of the last thirteen, from *L'Enfant sauvage* to *Vivement dimanche!*). The same actors and actresses also reappear from film to film, some little known outside Truffaut's cinema (for example Sabine Haudepin, Richard Saroyan, Albert Rémy, Marie Dubois), others relatively unknown in the early films but with stardom ahead of them (Jean-Pierre Léaud, Jeanne Moreau) and, as Truffaut gains status as a director, a third category of already established stars (Catherine Deneuve, Gérard Depardieu). This notion of family becomes quite literal with names such as Eva and Laura Truffaut, Mathieu and Guillaume Schiffman cropping up in the credits.

Another fairly common feature of Truffaut's film-making was the duplication of functions. Thus several members of the production team pass in front of the camera and become actors: the producer Marcel Berbert appears as the hero's friend and colleague in *La Sirène du Mississipi* and occupies minor roles in *Domicile conjugal*, *La Nuit américaine*, *L'Argent de poche*, *L'Homme qui aimait les femmes* and *Le Dernier Métro*, the script-writer Jean-Louis Richard plays the small comic role of the 'Man in Café' in *Jules et Jim*, Daxiat in *Le Dernier Métro* and Louison in *Vivement dimanche!*, the assistant director Jean-Louis Stévenin plays his real-life role in *La Nuit américaine* and stars as the schoolteacher in *L'Argent de poche*, Truffaut takes the leading role in *L'Enfant sauvage*, *La Nuit américaine* and *La Chambre verte*. To take one film as an example, in *La Chambre verte* Marcel Berbert, Martine Barraqué, Jean-Pierre Kohut-Svelko, Roland Thénot and of course Truffaut himself can all be found in both the production credits and the cast-list. This notion of the 'team', the 'family' is an important and consistent aspect of Truffaut's film-making methods. It is captured, above all, in *La Nuit américaine* and *Le Dernier Métro*, both films which celebrate artistic creation as a shared process. It also constitutes one of the most direct homages to Jean Renoir who, famously, also saw and practised cinema as a collective enterprise, and whose influence is unmistakable.

The questions Truffaut was asking himself at the beginning of the 1960s were the questions that face any successful creator following initial success. In particular, where to go next? For Truffaut, life was rapidly becoming a series of scenarios, each having its own, variable, period of gestation. Not infrequently, ideas, some quite well developed, were abandoned. For example, in 1961 he wrote to Aznavour to discuss a possible musical with him as lead, mentioning at the same time the sketch for Léaud that was to become the second Doinel film: *Antoine et Colette*. A letter to his American friend and collaborator Helen Scott, written three years later, sheds light on his method of planning: always adaptable and flexible, he lined up a number of projects knowing that finances, rights, availability of actors, competition for scripts were so many rocks on which good ideas could founder:

> Comme Resnais et comme les Américains, je vais lancer trois ou quatre scénaristes ... sur des sujets de films que j'ai en réserve ... Voilà quels sont ces projets: 1. *L'Enfant sauvage* (l'histoire de l'enfant-loup que je vous ai racontée); 2. *La Petite Voleuse* (genre *Monika*, d'Ingmar Bergman, naissance de la féminité et de la coquetterie chez une petite délinquante, *400 Blows* femelle); 3. une histoire genre *Pianiste* ou *Bande à part* pour Jean-Pierre Léaud,

peut-être un vieux roman de Goodis; 4. une comédie dramatique sur un couple jeune qui se sépare et se réconcilie, pour, éventuellement, Romy Schneider et Belmondo; 5. et, enfin, le film dont je parle depuis longtemps et dont toute l'action se déroulerait dans une école'[14] (Truffaut 1988: 284).

Although the fourth project bears a faint resemblance to *Domicile conjugal*, only two of the above survived to reach the screen: *L'Enfant sauvage* was completed four years later in 1969; the last became *L'Argent de poche* (1976). The rights to *La Petite Voleuse* were bought by Claude Berri and the film was eventually made, respecting Truffaut's scenario, by Claude Miller. The others, like *Bonnie and Clyde* which was originally written for him and on which he did a good deal of work, simply evaporated as other projects took their place. What is clear is that Truffaut had a kind of 'organic' way of generating ideas for scenarios (Truffaut 1988: 468). This was in stark contrast to his mentor Hitchcock who on one occasion wrote in anguished tones 'What I want to know is how do you find the subject to make into pictures? At the moment I am completely helpless in searching for a subject' (Truffaut 1988: 465). Truffaut's ability to exploit his rich store of cinematic and literary memories seems to have spared him the anxiety of the author in search of a subject.

Maintaining the momentum

In the six years from 1962 to 1968, Truffaut completed five films beginning with the second and finishing with the third of the

---

14 'Like Resnais and the Americans, I am about to set three or four script-writers working on ideas for films that I have up my sleeve. These are the projects: 1 *L'Enfant sauvage* (the story of the wolf-child I told you about); 2 *La Petite Voleuse* (a bit like Ingmar Bergman's *Monika*, awakening of femininity and self-awareness in a young delinquent, a kind of female *400 Blows*); 3 a story along the lines the lines of *Pianiste* or *Bande à part* for Jean-Pierre Léaud, [based] perhaps on an old novel by Goodis; 4 a comedy about a young couple who separate and then get together again, with, perhaps, Romy Schneider and Belmondo; 5 and, the last one, the film I've been talking about for ages where all the action takes place in a school.'

films in the Doinel cycle: *Antoine et Colette* and *Baisers volés*. In between were sandwiched two genre films: one a science fiction film, *Fahrenheit 451* based on Ray Bradbury's novel, and the other a thriller, *La Mariée était en noir*. The fifth film was based on a scenario he wrote with Jean-Louis Richard, *La Peau douce*, a dark story of passion and adultery.

Antoine et Colette (1962) was Truffaut's contribution to a compilation film comprising five sketches – the other contributors were Andrzej Wajda, Renzo Rossellini, Marcel Ophuls and Shintaro Ishihara – which was released with the title *L'Amour à vingt ans*. It takes up Antoine's life in adolescence and follows his first steps in work (manufacturing of records) and in love (with Colette). In neither field is he particularly successful: his feelings for Colette are not reciprocated and she abandons him for a taller, more mature young man, Albert. As with *Les 400 Coups*, the film effectively charts the young male's progress and, adopting a viewpoint that is mainly but not exclusively Antoine's, it deftly traces the erratic mood swings, impulsiveness and self-delusion of the adolescent.

The sombre tone and culminating violence of *La Peau douce* (1964) is probably not unconnected with the fact that Truffaut's increasingly difficult relationship with his wife had at this time reached a turning point. He announced their separation to his American confidante, Helen Scott: 'j'ai pris en horreur l'hypocrisie conjugale; là-dessus, je suis assez révolté en ce moment'[15] (Truffaut 1988: 257). The film is a study of adultery and of the hypocrisy he evokes in his letter; the two lovers it portrays are limited, self-centred and far from sympathetic. However, a few key sequences relieve this mediocrity and one of these, depicting a woman's forthright rebuttal of a man's inopportune advances, signals the ambiguity of Truffaut's position *vis-à-vis* the representation of women.

Fahrenheit 451 (1966) belongs in the category of Truffaut's genre films, though it represents his only attempt at the particular genre of science fiction. Not one of his most successful films, it is somehow weighed down by the idea which inspired it: in order to preserve culture in an oppressive book-burning regime, human

15 'conjugal hypocrisy has become abhorrent to me: right now, I'm pretty appalled by it'.

beings learn books by heart. He had difficulties, as director, with the male lead, Oskar Werner, and the financial problems, which dogged the film virtually from its conception, persisted. His dislike of England and the English meant that he spent virtually the entire period in England, when not actually shooting, in the London Hilton.

The difficulties with Oskar Werner were not the first of their kind. There had been signs of tensions with male leads as early as 1957 with Gérard Blain, the Gérard of *Les Mistons*. Blain found Truffaut's focus on the kids irritating and was further exasperated at Bernadette Lafont's taking centre stage at his expense, a frustration compounded by the fact that Bernadette Lafont was his partner at the time. The problem originates in Truffaut's obsessive fascination with women, an obsession which finds its fullest articulation in the character of Bertrand Morane (*L'Homme qui aimait les femmes*). Whether the women were playing the lead or not – in only a handful of his films did they do so – Truffaut and his camera tended to dote on them with inevitable consequences for the male actors involved. He admitted as much not long before his death 'Je filme préférablement les femmes, les enfants et, à l'arrière-plan, des hommes qui ne s'affrontent pas vraiment'[16] (Truffaut 1988: 622). Perhaps, he added, enigmatically, 'because I'm an only child'. Gender representation is an important and contested aspect of Truffaut's films.

La Mariée était en noir (1967) starred Jeanne Moreau in the central role of a woman wreaking vengeance on the five men involved in the (accidental) killing of her husband. There are echoes of *Les Mistons* – five brats and the couple – and also of *Tirez* which presented three contrasting females as opposed to *La Mariée*'s five stereotypical males. Of all Truffaut's films, it is the one which most obviously reflects the influence of Hitchcock and is one of the four films in which the lead is taken by a woman.

The filming of *Baisers volés* (1968) coincided with the lead up to 'the Events' of May 1968. This third film in the Doinel cycle, with its light-hearted evocation of Antoine's progress towards marriage

16 'I prefer filming women and children with relatively docile men in the background'.

with Christine Darbon, was shot as Truffaut took an active part in the acrimonious campaign to save the Cinémathèque and its director, Henri Langlois. Antoine takes no part in the *événements*, though a conversation with his girlfriend Christine reveals that the film's action is set (in Paris) at the height of the demonstrations. Instead he continues to move between a variety of low-paid jobs (including that of private detective, a narrative device that allows for a number of thematically related sub-plots based on the clients' cases) and pursues his 'sentimental education', principally in relationships with two women. The film ends with the formation of an apparently stable couple, but the promise of unending love is undercut both by the presence of a mysterious second suitor who declares his love for Christine in the film's closing moments, and by the lyrics of the Charles Trenet song that plays over the credits: 'Que reste-t-il de nos amours?' which, loosely translated, mean 'Where has our love gone?'

A moment of darkness

While the above films enjoyed reasonable success and did not harm his reputation, none of them achieved either the success of *Les 400 Coups* or broke new ground in the way that *Tirez* and *Jules et Jim* had done. Truffaut's next project, *La Sirène du Mississippi* (1969), involved location shooting – on the island of La Réunion and in the south of France. The days of using unknown actors were now over (in part at least due to those appearing in his films becoming stars overnight, like Jean-Pierre Léaud for instance) and Truffaut hired two of the French cinema's best-known stars, Jean-Paul Belmondo and Catherine Deneuve. On the surface, the film is another thriller and the influence of Hitchcock is again apparent though Truffaut maintains his individual, not to say idiosyncratic, approach through jokey references to his earlier films, in particular, the last sequence which features the house, woods and mountains of *Tirez* and a laconic but apposite reference to Renoir's *La Grande Illusion* in the last frame.

The same year, 1969, saw the realisation of a long-cherished project, *L'Enfant sauvage*. Of the six historical films, this one is set the furthest back in time – in the late eighteenth century. It breaks new ground in several ways: heterosexual love and the couple/triangle do not feature at all (there is, almost uniquely in Truffaut's work, no major female role); nor does one find the familiar recourse to genre; for the only time in his career the source text is neither an adaptation of a novel nor a scenario of his own making; after four films in colour, he reverts to black and white and, finally and most obviously, Truffaut, as well as directing the film, plays the lead role of Doctor Itard. Based on a real case study, the film traces the attempts to educate a young boy who has grown up in the wild. Arguably, however, this new approach serves only to introduce a number of familiar themes: absence of the father, the role of education, language and communication.

The next two films, *Domicile conjugal* (1970) and *Les Deux Anglaises et le continent* (1971), in some ways echo the dark and sombre mood of *La Peau douce*. Whereas in 1964 this could be attributed to his separation from his wife, at the beginning of 1971 it was a nervous breakdown precipitated by the break-up of his relationship with Catherine Deneuve. The crippling reality of his illness is described seven years later: 'Ces déchirements qui sont comme des morts, la sensation du trou noir, du je n'existe plus, cette irréalité des visages croisés dans la rue, tout cela je l'ai connu, et aussi la certitude qu'on ne peut pas faire comprendre aux autres ce qui se passe en soi, le concret qui se dérobe, ce vide hébété'[17] (Truffaut 1988: 542–3). *Domicile conjugal* was the fourth Doinel film. It was shot in the months leading up to this breakdown and appears in many ways to herald it. It traces the anguish and stress of a couple falling out of love and its most significant feature is the highly unflattering portrayal of Antoine at his most childish, fickle and unstable, a canvas against which Christine as the young wife stands out most positively.

17 'These separations which are like a death, the feeling you are in a black hole, that you don't exist any more, the unreal air of faces you see in the street, I've known all that as well as the sure knowledge that you can't make others understand what's going on inside you, that the physical world is crumbling to pieces, the numbing feeling of emptiness.'

Truffaut had read Roché's novel *Les Deux Anglaises et le continent* as his illness took hold and, as he recovered sufficiently to work, he turned to it for his next film. In its focus on another triangle, this time two women and one man, it is a mirror image of Roché's earlier novel which had been the springboard for *Jules et Jim*. It is no surprise then that Truffaut should be drawn to it as it allowed him again to explore the theme he had defined at the time of *Jules et Jim* which he saw as 'un hymne à la vie et à la mort, une démonstration de l'impossibilité de toute combinaison amoureuse en dehors du couple'[18] (Truffaut 1988: 172).

The return of his sense of humour and zest for life are to be found in *Une Belle Fille comme moi* (1972), shot in the spring in the Midi (he stayed in Béziers during the filming). It is the second film, following *La Mariée était en noir*, to have a female lead – Camille is played by Bernadette Lafont (from *Les Mistons*) – and there are a number of similarities with the earlier film, above all the structure which opposes the single female to a string of contrasting males. The principal distinguishing feature of the film is, however, its tone: comic in large part with a gusto and *joie de vivre* that is reflected in the wide-ranging musical score. With its wry twist at the end and its exploration of a variety of relationships, it nevertheless remains on familiar territory: the conflict between institutionalised authority and the individual rebel reappears in comic mode, and men's tendency to see women through the prism of their fantasies is again central to the narrative.

Year of the Oscar

The following year saw a return to his best form with *La Nuit américaine* which won a Hollywood Oscar, for Best Foreign Film, at the 1973 award ceremony and brought Truffaut worldwide recognition. The film foregrounds an aspect of his work that is present throughout: self-referentiality. As identified earlier,

18 'a hymn both to life and to death, proof that all combinations in love, other than the couple, are impossible'.

Truffaut's sense of play, in both its light-hearted and more serious manifestations, frequently materialises in references to the medium itself. This can take a number of forms, for example allusions or homages to other films, use of film language which draws attention to the medium, and the physical presence, in almost all his films, of a cinema. As discussed above, this self-referentiality is already apparent in *Les Mistons* in ways more complex than the mere presence of the 'cinoche'. The strength of *La Nuit américaine* lies in its successfully combining a rich complex of themes: there is the usual Truffaldian exploration of different types of relationships (here both heterosexual and gay); the fascination with the creative process, above all that of film-making; the recourse to *mise en abîme* which exploits the shooting of the somewhat lamentable *Je vous présente Paméla* within the frame of *La Nuit américaine* in order to demonstrate in loving detail how the work is carried out. The film eloquently displays Truffaut's working methods, in particular his predilection for working in a team, and sets out an approach to film-making which contrasts with the factory style of Hollywood and its big studios.

La Nuit américaine reveals another of Truffaut's working habits: his tendency towards improvisation. The insertion of Julie Baker's words at the moment of her 'crise' into the script of *Je vous présente Paméla* highlights two aspects of this improvisation: first, scripts were rarely adhered to rigidly, the actors were accustomed to receiving their lines on the night before shooting and to further adaptation during the shooting itself; second, those who knew Truffaut became accustomed to excerpts from conversations with him appearing in his films, sometimes years later. Further, the more the shooting advanced and the greater the pressures of time and money, the more improvised all aspects of the film-making became. *La Nuit américaine* demonstrates this as the denouement of *Je vous présente Paméla* is completely rewritten following the death of the male lead, Alexandre.

From a relatively early point in his career, Truffaut had found his way to America: to see Helen Scott and Hitchcock in order to work on what he often referred to as the *Hitchbook*; to attend the New York Film Festival; and for English lessons in Los Angeles.

As his reputation grew and particularly after he won the Oscar, he received invitations, from those 'nice Americans', to make a film in the USA. His reply to these overtures was categorically in the negative.

The Nouvelle Vague might in a number of ways have passed its zenith and observation of its principal tenets by its most fervent disciples might have been on the wane. Truffaut's desire, however, to work within a French cultural tradition and to resist the cultural hegemony of the USA as promulgated by its film industry remained undiminished.

Personal concerns

The group of four films which were made in the five years following this success resemble in a way those made after the success of *Les 400 Coups*. The acclaim and funds resulting from *La Nuit américaine* enabled Truffaut to complete a series of projects which have their origins in personal concerns: absolute love (*L'Histoire d'Adèle H.*, 1975), the desire to make a film focusing on children (*L'Argent de poche*, 1976), the persistent interest in the fetichisation of women (*L'Homme qui aimait les femmes*, 1977) and his own obsession with death (*La Chambre verte*, 1978). Each film in its own way takes up and explores recurrent themes. The first of this cycle of films, *L'Histoire d'Adèle H.*, is interesting in that the central protagonist, present on screen virtually throughout the film, is female, though otherwise the theme of obsession is a reworking of a familiar vein. *L'Argent de poche* echoes *Les Mistons* and *Les 400 Coups*, being in some ways the reverse side of the coin in its positive images of adults generally and teachers and other figures of authority in particular. The film is otherwise little more than a pot-boiler and an indulgence on the part of Truffaut and Suzanne Schiffman who collaborated closely on the scenario and in the shooting. In *L'Homme qui aimait les femmes*, Bertrand, the central character, is an adult Antoine, though he barely qualifies for the description of 'grown-up'. *La Chambre verte* foregrounds what is perhaps Truffaut's greatest obsession: death. His feelings on the subject are set out in a letter explaining why he is unable to attend a funeral

> Il y a beaucoup, beaucoup, trop de morts autour de moi, que j'ai aimés, et j'ai pris la décision, après la disparition de Françoise Dorléac, de ne plus assister à aucun enterrement, ce qui, vous le pensez bien, n'empêche pas la tristesse d'être là, de tout obscurcir pendant un temps et de ne jamais s'estomper complètement, même avec les années, car on ne vit pas seulement avec les vivants, mais aussi avec tous ceux qui ont compté dans notre vie[19] (Truffaut, 1988: 381).

Virtually all his films introduce the theme: most overtly, a few obliquely. This macabre film opens in the trenches of the Great War and focuses on the loss and grief of the protagonist following the death of his wife. The theme of death is linked to that of love, both within this text and in others, for example *L'Histoire d'Adèle H.*, through the obsession of the central characters.

Under pressure from his public to continue with the adventures of Antoine Doinel and fuelled by his own desire to bring the series to a close, Truffaut returned, with *L'Amour en fuite* (1979) to the Doinel story. The film cites numerous extracts from the previous films in the cycle and although this device is potentially an interesting one, the film exudes a tone of weariness and one senses that Truffaut was simply going through the motions and that he now had little more to say on the subject of his most famous creation.

Renewal

At the end of his second decade of film-making, he appeared played out and lacking in inspiration. However, the next group of

---

19 'I am surrounded by far, far too many dead people, people I loved, and I took the decision, after the death of Françoise Dorléac, never to attend another funeral. This does not, as you can imagine, block out sadness or prevent it from turning everything dark for a while. It never fades completely, even with the passing of the years, for we live not only with the living but also with all those who have counted in our lives.'

three films, which were to be his last, demonstrated that he had not lost the capacity to surprise, to renew himself and to make films with wide popular appeal. All three – *Le Dernier Métro* (1980), *La Femme d'à côté* (1981) and *Vivement dimanche!* (1983) – were successful at the box office. The first is generally regarded as one of his best films and the other two, starring Fanny Ardant, his final companion, share a coherence and vitality that were lacking in the films he made in the mid to late seventies. *Le Dernier Métro* brings together two themes which had long been scenarios in embryo: the theatre and the period of the Occupation. The film was criticised for failing to look at the latter in an objective light. Indeed, Truffaut as others before him, sidesteps the difficult issues and concentrates on the nostalgic, and simultaneously patriotic, aspects of those years. Its success lies in its interesting structure (in this way echoing the early films), in the acting of two great stars (Gérard Depardieu and Catherine Deneuve), in the traditional Truffaldian exploration of human relationships and in the complex interplay between the fictional and the real also investigated in *La Nuit américaine*.

La Femme d'à côté – 'une histoire d'amour-passion de nos jours' ('a story of passion for our times') (Truffaut 1988: 610) – is also interesting from the point of view of its structure: the whole film consists of a single, long flashback framed briefly by the sympathetic commentary of an intra-diegetic narrator. The desire for, yet inevitable failure of, the 'solution couple' drives the narrative whilst the triangular relationship and tragic outcome echo previous films – *Jules et Jim* and *Les Deux Anglaises et le continent* in particular. Depardieu, this time with Fanny Ardant, appears in his second successive Truffaut film.

Truffaut's last film deliberately refers back to *Tirez* and a number of parallels can be drawn between the two films.[20] It provides a second vehicle for Fanny Ardant, this time paired with another male star, Jean-Louis Trintignant. As was the case with

20 *L'Avant-scène Cinéma* dedicated a double volume edition in July/August 1983 to 'François Truffaut et la série noire'. It contains the screenplays of both films, an introduction by Claude Guérif, two articles by Anne Gillain and a contribution from Claude Beylie entitled 'L'Homme qui aimait les livres'.

the earlier film, *Vivement dimanche!* exploits, on one level, the rich vein of *film noir* and it is not, therefore, surprising that Truffaut should elect to shoot the film in black and white. This decision, he knew, risked provoking a strong reaction from some critics and the public who by now looked upon black and white as antiquated, a relic of the era of silent movies. He defended it staunchly:

> Chaque année, ici ou là dans le monde, un metteur-en-scène, disposant de sa liberté créatrice, choisit de tourner en *noir et blanc* et, presque chaque fois, le film constitue un événement. Chacune de ces réalisations fait la démonstration qu'un film *en noir et blanc* est, de toute façon, un film «en couleur» puisqu'il présente, entre le noir et le blanc, une infinité de gris qui le nuancent et l'enrichissent ... *Vivement dimanche!* s'efforcera de restituer l'ambiance nocturne, mystérieuse et brillante des comédies américaines policières qui, autrefois, nous enchantaient. Je crois que l'utilisation du *noir et blanc* nous aidera à retrouver un charme disparu, je crois surtout que personne au monde ne réussira à me prouver que le *noir et blanc* est moins *culturel* que la couleur[21] (Truffaut 1988: 625–6).

Truffaut thus turns the anti-naturalist qualities of black and white into a virtue rather than a defect, and points out that the term occludes the rich spectrum of greys in the non-colour image. His defence of his last film emphasises two of the enduring features of his work: the fact that the realist tenor of Truffaut's cinema is regularly undercut by devices and techniques that disturb the fictional illusion, and the emphasis throughout on the pleasure of the visual image.

This chronological overview of Truffaut's cinematic production

21 'Every year, in some country or other, a director, availing himself of his creative freedom, chooses to make a *black and white* film and, almost every time, the film is seen as an event. Every one of these films demonstrates that a *black and white* film is, in any case, a 'colour' film since it produces, between black and white, an infinite number of greys which nuance and enrich it ...
Vivement dimanche! will seek to bring back the nocturnal, mysterious and glossy feel of those American comedy thrillers which so used to enchant us. My belief is that using *black and white* will help us to rediscover a sense of magic that has been lost, above all, I don't think anyone in the world will succeed in proving to me that *black and white* is less *cultural* than colour'.

has served to highlight a number of aspects connected to the evolution of his work: the warp and woof of themes, ideas and formal considerations, the gestation processes of individual films, the working methods adopted, the role of influences such as 1930s French cinema and Hollywood. At the same time it has attempted to make clear the reasons for the wide appeal of the films.

The fact that his work is popular does not, however, mean that it is superficial and banal, as the chapters which follow seek to demonstrate. Carole Le Berre is far from being the only critic to have uncovered a meaningful discourse beneath the surface of the work: 'Il n'y a pas d'image simple chez lui: derrière une image apparemment neutre, évidente, se profile toujours une autre plus violente, plus secrète qui se superpose à la première et la subvertit souterrainement'[22] (Le Berre 1993: 193).

References

Braudy, L. ed. (1972), *Focus on 'Shoot the Piano Player'*, New Jersey, Prentice-Hall.

Brunette, P. ed. (1993), *Shoot the Piano Player*, Oxford, Roundhouse Publishing.

Cahoreau, Gilles (1989), *François Truffaut 1932–84*, Paris, Julliard.

Dyer, P. J. (1960–61), Tirez sur le pianiste, *Sight and Sound*, 30: 1, p. 18.

Fairlamb, A. (1996), *Tough Guys and Fairy-Tales*: a case-study of the influence of the films of Nicholas Ray upon Truffaut's *Tirez sur le pianiste*, *French Cultural Studies*, 7: Part 1: 19, pp. 49–62.

Gillain, A. (1988), *Le Cinéma selon François Truffaut*, Paris, Flammarion.

Le Berre, Carole (1993), *François Truffaut*, Paris, Cahiers du cinéma.

Rabourdin, D. (1935), *Truffaut par Truffaut*, Paris, Chêne.

Thiher, Anne (1977), The existential play in Truffaut's early films, *Film/Literature Quarterly*, 5, pp. 183–97.

Truffaut, François (1987), *Le Plaisir des yeux*, Paris, Cahiers du cinéma.

Truffaut, François (1988), *Correspondance*, Paris, Hatier.

22 'There is no such thing as a straightforward image in Truffaut's work. Underneath an apparently neutral image the meaning of which appears obvious, there always emerges a second image more violent, deeper than the first which it eventually replaces and surreptitiously subverts'.

3

Jules et Jim: anatomy of a film

Jules et Jim, Truffaut's third full-length film, is generally agreed to be one of his greatest. By tracing the film's genesis from little-known literary source to film classic, and by 'reading' the film in terms of structure, signifying techniques and themes, we hope to demonstrate more closely the specificity of Truffaut's method and style, briefly outlined above in the chronological survey of his career.

The source

Henri-Pierre Roché's autobiographical novel *Jules et Jim* was published in 1953, when the author was seventy-three years old. His second novel, *Les Deux Anglaises et le continent*, also based on Roché's youth and also the source of a Truffaut film, was to be published two years later. Truffaut read *Jules et Jim*, by chance, in 1955, having picked it up in a booksale, and was immediately drawn to and moved by the story. First, he was always fascinated by attempts to transpose *le vécu* (lived experience) into textual form (book or film), in a way that combined authenticity with aesthetic pleasure: 'j'aime les récits "vécus", les Mémoires, les souvenirs, les gens qui racontent leur vie'[1] (Gillain 1988: 127). This liking for the autobiographical mode is apparent in many of

---

1 'I like stories based on lived experience, Memoirs, reminiscences, people telling their life stories.'

Truffaut's films, including *Les Mistons*, in which an adult narrator recalls his childhood, *Adèle H.* and *L'Enfant sauvage*, both adapted from the diaries of central characters (Adèle Hugo and Dr Itard), and the Doinel films, *L'Homme qui aimait les femmes*, and *Une Belle fille comme moi*, all of which centre around the theme of self-narration or telling one's own story (see chapter 7). The very fact that Roché had, so late in life, decided to give literary shape to an important part of his experience attracted Truffaut's sympathy.

Second, there was much in Roché's attitude to life, as evidenced by the novel and by the subsequent correspondence between the two men (Roché died in 1959), that struck a sympathetic chord with Truffaut. Truffaut's passion for cinema was never exclusive but went hand in hand with an ardent enthusiasm for books and writing. Roché was a man of eclectic interests, a dilettante who painted, translated, wrote stories and articles, interested himself in all aspects of the cultural life of his age: like Jim in both novel and film he was 'un curieux de profession' ('a man for whom curiosity was a profession'). He was also a man for whom friendship was of great importance, and an *homme à femmes* ('a woman's man') for whom heterosexual relationships were absolutely central to the quality and purpose of life. In 1921 Roché published a collection of stories about Don Juan (a character irresistibly evoked by Truffaut's 'man who loved women'), and *Jules et Jim* the novel begins with its heroes absorbed by a whole series of – often shared – love affairs with a variety of beautiful women.

Roché's closest friend was the German/Jewish writer Franz Hessel, the model for the character of Jules. Both in life and in the novel, this friendship made it impossible to view the 1914–18 war, in which the friends found themselves on opposing sides, in terms of a battle between good and evil, or between 'us' and 'them'. Indeed Roché's novels, like Truffaut's films, systematically refuse to divide the world into the good and the bad: 'J'ai une profonde méfiance', said Truffaut in an interview, 'vis-à-vis de tout ce qui sépare le monde en deux: les bons et les mauvais, les bourgeois et les artistes, les flics et les aventuriers'[2] (Gillain 1988: 135). Truffaut

2 'I deeply mistrust everything that divides the world neatly into two: goodies and baddies, bourgeois and artists, cops and robbers.'

was attracted by the fact that although *Jules et Jim* contains the familiar triangle of husband, wife and lover, each is granted equal sympathy, no one becomes merely the obstacle to the others' happiness. Few characters in Truffaut's cinema (with the possible exception of Daxiat in *Le Dernier Métro*) could be described as unequivocally bad; on the whole, Truffaut observed the principle that he also attributed to Roché: 'On doit laisser aux personnages toutes leur chances de salut et toutes leurs contradictions'[3] (Gillain 1988: 135). And finally, Truffaut was clearly drawn to the central theme and rhythm of Roché's work: the simultaneous longing for and impossibility of a durable, passionate love, articulated through a repeated narrative trope of desire, followed by mutual happiness, followed by separation, and the rebirth of desire.

The method

Truffaut was convinced from his first reading that Roché's novel would adapt well to the cinema, but it was not until 1960 that he was able to start work on the project. His enthusiasm for the book was matched by that of Jeanne Moreau whom he saw, from the start, as his Catherine. He began by re-reading the novel and marking all the parts he particularly wanted to retain for the film, then he passed the annotated text to his co-writer Jean Gruault, who produced a 200-page scenario. Truffaut then went to work 'cutting and pasting' ('travaillant à la colle et aux ciseaux' (Gillain 1988: 128)), modifying Gruault's version and leaving space within it for the on-set improvisation he found essential when filming. The scenario retained the central narrative structure of the novel, though the diverse characters and locations of the original text were condensed and simplified to accommodate both the director's limited resources, and the need for concision imposed by the medium. In the post-war section of the plot, for example, Catherine's many lovers are limited, on screen, to just one (Albert); the two daughters of Jules and Kathe, in the novel, are reduced to

3 'You have to let the characters keep all their chances of salvation, all their contradictions.'

one in the film; whereas in the novel Jim and Kathe travel extensively during their affair, the film limits the variety of locations to Germany and Paris. The voice of the novel's extra-diegetic narrator was retained whenever this was central to meaning, but impossible to transform into dialogue, and whenever the original text was simply, in Truffaut's words, 'trop beau pour se laisser amputer'[4] (Gillain 1988: 128). Here, as in other films based on 'literary' texts (as opposed to the *série noire* thrillers adapted for *Tirez*, *La Mariée*, *La Sirène*) it is Truffaut's respect for the language of the original that leads him to use the device of the voice-over, the narrator whose verbal style – in, for example, *Les Mistons*, or *L'Enfant sauvage* – helps to establish the mood of the film.

However, a literal fidelity to the source text was one of the features of the *tradition de qualité* cinema of the 1950s, in opposition to which Truffaut and his fellow New Wave directors had defined their own cinematic ideals. Truffaut made a deliberate decision to reproduce parts of Roché's text, in the form of dialogues and narrative voice-over, because he felt an affinity with the drily emotional, droll yet passionate tone of the novel. Beyond this, he was not so much concerned with faithful accuracy to the text, rather with the creation of cinematic equivalents for the novel's distinctive style, a style that he described as a 'style invisible, qui n'a l'air de rien' (('unobtrusive style') Gillain 1988: 132). From the scenario to the direction and editing he attempted to create the same understated, discreet quality in the film. Thus Georges Delerue was asked to keep the music restrained, the actor who spoke the narrator's voice-over to use a spare, unemotional style of delivery, the camera work and editing were (with one or two exceptions, see below) complex, imaginative but not spectacular. For reasons that had to do with budget but that also contributed to the film's low-key style, all the actors except Jeanne Moreau (already well known for her performances in Louis Malle's *Ascenseur pour l'échaffaud* (1957) and *Les Amants* (1958)) were relatively new faces, unknown to film audiences (though Marie Dubois would have been recognised by those who had also seen *Tirez sur le pianiste*).

---

4 'just too beautiful to be dropped'.

Shooting took place between April and June 1961, the timing determined in part by the theatrical commitments of Moreau and Oskar Werner (Jules). Location and duration of shooting were determined to some extent by budget limitations, for the financial situation of the Films du Carrosse was far from secure after the commercial failure of *Tirez*, and the death of Truffaut's father-in-law early in 1961 made him the more anxious not to 'foutre en l'air l'argent de sa veuve'.[5] The entire film, including the scenes set in Greece and Germany, was shot in different regions of France, notably Normandy, Paris, Provence and the Vosges. The small crew of fifteen was composed of what was becoming Truffaut's film 'family', and included many members of the teams from *Les 400 Coups* and *Tirez*. Truffaut found both the directing and the subsequent four months of editing arduous, in part because of his anxiety to respect the values and the quality of the Roché novel, in part because he found the film emotionally draining, as the story's 'épouvantable tristesse' ('terrible sadness') gradually became apparent in the course of the film's production, against his original intentions. '*Jules et Jim* m'a véritablement épuisé ... C'est la troisième fois que cela m'arrive: commencer un film en imaginant qu'il sera amusant et m'apercevoir en cours de route qu'il n'est sauvable que par la tristesse.'[6] (Truffaut 1988: 188). Rather than being rigorously determined by a pre-written scenario, the meanings of the film evolved in part from the creative process itself, a feature that was to remain constant throughout Truffaut's film-making career.

Narrative structure

Roché's novel is divided into three sections of roughly equal length: 'Jules et 'Jim', 'Kathe' (who becomes 'Catherine' in the

5 not to 'throw his widow's [i.e. Truffaut's mother-in-law's] money down the drain'.
6 'It's the third time this has happened to me: starting a film thinking that it's going to be light-hearted then realising while I'm making it that it can only be saved by its sadness.'

film), 'Jusqu'au bout' ('Right to the end' or 'to the bitter end'). The film follows the narrative structure of the novel, in the sense that it begins by establishing the friendship between Jules and Jim, is concerned throughout the central section with the three-way relationship between the two men and Catherine, and concludes with the downward spiral towards the end, which is death.

The film opens on a dark screen, as the voice of Jeanne Moreau (Catherine) introduces the theme of the non-coincidence of love, or what Annette Insdorf nicely terms its 'syncopation' (Insdorf 1994: 85): the tendency of mutual desire to occur not simultaneously, but alternately, will remain central to the film's structure and imagery.

> Tu m'as dit: je t'aime.
> Je t'ai dit: attends.
> J'allais dire: prends moi.
> Tu m'as dit: va t'en.[7]

The note of desolation has been sounded, but is rapidly forgotten in the humour, pace and *joie-de-vivre* of what we might term the film's 'prologue'. This opening section is set in Paris at the *belle époque* and introduces us to the friendship between two wealthy, leisured young men – Jules (German Austrian) and Jim (French) – verbally, through the commentary of an unidentified narrator, and visually, through a series of fast-cut vignettes showing them fencing, clowning, deep in conversation, falling in and out of love with women. The musical score is loud and jubilant, with a period flavour that matches the charm of the costumes and sets and reinforces the 'silent movie' overtones of the black and white image. The prologue establishes the bond between small, fair Jules, with his diffident charm and quiet intensity, and tall, dark Jim, more self-contained and socially adept; it also creates a mood of optimism and ludic energy through the combination of image, music and editing. If the spectator gains a sense of sharing in the fun, this is in part due to the active, mobile camera that pans, zooms, glides and even – in the celebrated sequence where Thérèse

---

7 'You said: I love you. I said: wait. I was going to say: take me. You said: go away.'

performs her impression of a steam-train – spins a giddying 360 degrees.

The main part of the narrative begins, however, with the arrival on the scene of Catherine, and the extension of the Jules–Jim couple to the more complex structure of a triangle. Each line of the triangle is important, for both men are irresistibly drawn to Catherine, and she responds to each, though it is Jules who becomes her lover and Jim respects Jules's need, this time, for sexual exclusivity: 'Pas celle-là, Jim, n'est-ce pas?' ('Not this one, Jim, alright?'). The exuberant, playful mood is maintained in games and disguises; Catherine dresses up as a boy and challenges the other two to a race, which she wins (characteristically) by refusing to play by the rules; they rent a house on the coast, go on bicycle rides and imaginary treasure hunts, engage in bantering conversation. The happiness of this unconventionally triangular love affair is underlined visually by the long tracking shots framing – in all combinations – the three bicycles as they glide downhill in the sunshine, musically by the lyrical theme tune that accompanies, for example, the shared hunt for 'traces of lost civilisation'. At one level, this section of the film constitutes an exploration and celebration of an alternative to the couple which, as Jim (and many subsequent Truffaut characters) says, 'en amour ... n'est pas idéal' ('in love ... is not ideal'). But a darker note also sounds: the triangle too will prove resistant to the lovers' quest for durable happiness, and it is in Catherine, the woman who comes both to enrich and to disturb the men's friendship, that the threat of pain, jealousy and disaster is concentrated. Catherine is granted the status of a queen or a deity by both men, and like some archaic goddess her demands are absolute and her vengeance terrible. She is associated with fire (burning some old letters, she almost sets fire to herself and Jim), acid (she carries vitriol 'pour les yeux des hommes menteurs'[8]), and death by drowning (she jumps into the Seine in anger at being excluded from the men's conversation). Yet so far Catherine's potential for destruction is always contained. The fire is extinguished, the vitriol poured away, the leap into the river, since Catherine is a good swimmer, leads only to Jim's admiration and Jules's relieved

8 'for the eyes of men who lie'

silence. Catherine accepts Jules's proposal of marriage. The trio's *belle époque* ends not as a result of their own internal tensions, but because history intervenes in the shape of war.

Truffaut follows Roché in devoting little narrative time to the experience of war, but it nonetheless forms the film's caesura, the turning point after which everything is changed. Jules and Catherine announce their intended marriage to Jim on the telephone from their shared bed, a shot/countershot edit again underlining the warmth and closeness of the triangle as each in turn dialogues with Jim. The sequence closes with Jules comically declaiming in his German accent the words of the *Marseillaise*, the French national anthem, thus accentuating the friends' indifference to national boundaries and nation as source of identity. Immediately the scene shifts to the outbreak of war in 1914, which Truffaut screens by use of authentic newsreel footage intercut with brief sequences shot for the film. Jules is seen in a German dug-out, writing letters home to Catherine and thinking of Jim perhaps in the trenches opposite; Jim is seen on leave in Paris, worrying about Jules. The noise and brutality of shells exploding, soldiers crashing into the mud, the dull tones of the black and white image, the passionate intensity of Jules's letter home to Catherine are all in stark contrast to the leisured playfulness of the preceding scenes, with their exuberant musical accompaniment, high contrast, richly gradated use of black and white, frequent use of humour.

After this brief but striking sequence of war, the triangle resumes, but now a more pessimistic view of love as rarely reciprocal, painfully intermittent, and finally mortal comes to dominate the film. Jim travels through a Germany now scarred by the detritus of battle and by acres of anonymous graves, and is reunited with Jules and Catherine, now married and the parents of a little girl, Sabine. Certain sequences echo the lyrical and ludic qualities of the pre-war period: the couple's rural chalet by the Rhine recalls the house the three shared at the French seaside; the narration of Jim's arrival is momentarily interrupted by a sweeping aerial shot of the treetops, recalling the exuberant camera movements of earlier scenes; the three adults and Sabine run out into the fields that surround the chalet and Jim 'roly-polys' downhill holding the delighted Sabine close to his chest, her shrieks of delight echoing over the theme music. In a later scene the bicycle is again used to signify harmonious pleasure as the trio – with the addition now of another of Catherine's lovers, Albert, and of Sabine – free-wheel down hill, the camera framing them in different combinations but tracking smoothly, sharing the elation.[9]

But the rhythm of this, the longest part of the film (from the war to the second break-up of the trio accounts for approximately two thirds of the film) is profoundly different, as if the war had put an end to utopian dreams and strengthened darker forces. Love and desire are now characterised by discord, despite the mutual tenderness that continues to connect the three protagonists. The Jim–Jules axis never wavers, but despite Jules's continuing devotion Catherine has fallen out of love, and the line between Catherine and Jim now becomes a current of mutual love and desire – almost to Jules's relief, for at least he may thus manage to keep Catherine 'in the family'. The love between Jim and Catherine, at first intensely happy, soon takes on the dislocated rhythm of the film's opening words: Catherine punishes perceived slights by infidelities, Jim retreats to Paris and to his faithful long-term lover, Gilberte, letters cross in the post so that the messages each receives are out of time and out of step; worst of all, their desire to have a child results first only in sterility, then in brief hope destroyed by a miscarriage, and at last the couple separate in bitterness. The crisp pace of the earlier section is replaced here by longer sequences, narrative repetition, an insistent circularity at the levels of plot and imagery; a sense of the awkward and intractable nature of the real is produced by the protracted, sometimes exasperating quality of the film narrative itself.

The film's final, very brief section takes place some years later, in the 1930s. After a long period of separation – curiously unmarked in the film – Jim meets Jules and Catherine by chance, in a cinema, and learns that they have moved back to Paris. The male friends are delighted to see each other again, Catherine retains her enigmatic calm. At a riverside café she invites Jim to take a ride in

9 This scene is affectionately recreated by the trio of central characters in George Roy Hill's 1969 film *Butch Cassidy and the Sundance Kid*.

her car and, as Jules watches, drives deliberately along a ruined bridge to plunge into the river. The film ends with the funeral of Catherine and Jim, at which Jules is the sole mourner.

Truffaut's authorial style

Jules et Jim is, then, a film that tells a story, and engages the spectator in a narrative of friendship, love and loss. Truffaut deliberately seeks a manner of narration that echoes Roché's unobtrusive style, a style that effectively renders the narrative moving and absorbing, without focusing attention on the literary/filmic discourse itself. The understatement, though, and the deployment of film technique to support rather than disrupt the fictional illusion, do not detract from its complexity nor from the aesthetic pleasure the film provides. Though he remains faithful to the story-telling tradition of cinema, Truffaut also follows another line of his inheritance by treating the film as a poetic text. Thus without real interruption of the narrative flow, the spectator is invited to share in the pleasure of the medium itself. Truffaut deploys the New Wave techniques of mobile camera, unexpected point-of-view shots, freeze-frames, fast editing with a variety of transitional devices from lap-dissolves to iris – the iris is a device which ends a sequence by enclosing the image in shadow – and structures the film not only as a linear narrative but also as a text held together by patterns of repetition and variation, both visual and musical. In this, he follows in the footsteps of his cinematic heroes, most notably of Renoir whose 1962 letter from Hollywood, warmly praising the film, Truffaut carried around with him for weeks (Baecque and Toubiana 1996: 263–4).

Truffaut's chief cameraman for the film was Raoul Coutard, who had also worked on *Tirez* and on Godard's *A Bout de souffle* (1959). As in these films, the possibilities of the new lightweight cameras were fully exploited: particularly in the first part of the film, the camera's participation in the action is central to the spectator's sense of physical and emotional energy. When Jules, Jim and Catherine, dressed as Thomas, race across a long railway bridge, the camera first tracks ahead of them, framing all three laughing, panting figures, then focuses solely on Catherine's face and 'runs' alongside her in a jerky, blurring motion that places the spectator in the position of a participant in the race. When the trio wander in the forest, looking for what Catherine terms 'the traces of lost civilisation', the camera focuses on the ground and tracks amongst the undergrowth, adopting the point of view of all three characters. The bicycle rides are filmed both in long shot and in mid-shots that frame the characters alone and in different combinations. The smoothness of camera movement echoes the riders' own gliding motion, and the combination of sustained framing and panning between characters provides a visual metaphor for their shifting degrees of intimacy and separation. One of the film's characteristic camera movements is the fast pan, in which the link between two characters is made not by a shot/countershot edit but by a rapid wheeling of the camera from one to the other. By emphasising the spatial gap between two people, this shot always draws attention to the possibilities of relationship, joyfully in, for example, the 'village idiot' sequence when the camera revolves between successive close-ups of each of the trio and Sabine as they take turns to play the idiot (echoing the 360 degree turn that accompanies Thérèse's steam train impression); signifying the tension of a familiarity not yet refound, when the trio are reunited after the war and the camera pans rapidly from one to the other. When Catherine, now Jim's lover, decides one day to seduce Jules, the camera pans vertically between a quietly distraught Jim, downstairs, and Catherine and Jules tumbling around on the bed laughing, upstairs. Here the choice of visualised movement rather than a cut emphasises Jim's intense awareness of the couple, and implies too that Catherine is equally aware of the listener below. As one of the film's insistent motifs, the fast pan could be linked to the theme articulated in Catherine's song *Le Tourbillon de la vie* ('The whirlwind of life'), for it signifies the speed with which desire and love circulate, change direction, may be transformed from intimacy to a sense of separateness and distance. Visual techniques and soundtrack rhyme here, as they do in the film's representation of intense mutual love through images of flight: at the height of Jim and Catherine's happiness Truffaut's voice-over uses the words of Roché's narrator 'Une fois de plus ils planèrent, comme de grands oiseaux rapaces',[10] and the camera 'flies' over the forest (both crane and helicopter shots were used in the 'German' sequences) in a sweeping aerial shot evocative of fierce elation.

The framing of the image is also central to the film's signifying techniques. The triangle is perhaps the most recurrent visual pattern: Jules, Jim and Catherine are constantly framed together in different combinations and attitudes, of which perhaps the most famous is the shot of the house at the seaside with each standing on a different balcony, Catherine and Jules on the first floor and Jim above, literally forming a triangle. This is echoed later at the German chalet, in a shot framing Catherine and Jim – about to become lovers – standing in front of the house, while Jules looks down from a first-floor balcony. In two scenes in particular Catherine is placed at the apex of a horizontal triangle, outside the foregrounded Jules–Jim axis and struggling to break in. This occurs first at the seaside, with the two men seated in the foreground at either side of an outside table, absorbed in a game of dominoes, whilst in the centre of the screen, further away, Catherine is seated alone against a flat, white background that emphasises her solitude. The visual composition announces and underlines the narrative point, which is Catherine's sense of exclusion from the friendship and her insistence on the men's total attention, which she succeeds in gaining. The scene is echoed at the chalet by the Rhine, when the same visual patterning precedes Catherine's disruption of the men's conversation, and their drinking of German beer, with a litany of names of French wines, before she redraws the triangle by taking Jim off to the garden.

In the second half of the film, characterised by a slower rhythm and a sense of the obduracy of life, the fast-cutting style of the early sections is replaced by a predominance of longer sequences and by relatively long, uncut 'takes'. The introduction of new

10 'Once again they hovered high in the sky like great birds of prey'. [The same line is used in *Le Dernier Métro*.]

characters to a sequence tends here to be achieved by reframing rather than by a cut. The effect of this is particularly clear in the episode of the white pyjamas, when the trio briefly reforms for the second time in Paris, and Catherine takes Jules and Jim to dine at a country hotel where Albert, always held in reserve for purposes of revenge, suddenly appears. The reason for the wrapped pyjamas Catherine has brought with her becomes clear. In terms of framing of the image, the episode begins with a lingering shot of the three principal characters' arrival before the hotel, in close formation, fast-pans to Albert at the door of the hotel and refocuses to include all four as they enter and sit down at table. A dissolve cut marks the passage of time, the door re-opens and the trio separate from Albert, followed by the camera, re-establishing the formation of the opening shot. Catherine now unexpectedly takes her leave of them and returns to Albert, so that successive images frame Catherine and Albert as a couple, then frame Jules and Jim alone together. The triangle has enlarged to include a fourth, as it has before, but the effect of this is to destroy the original structure.

Visual framing is often strikingly beautiful in the film, though never gratuitously so. When Catherine and Jim, despairing of their sterility and resigned to losing each other, spend one last night in a hotel before Jim's departure, the camera frames Jeanne Moreau's lovely, self-absorbed face in an oval mirror as she slowly applies cold cream then wipes the cream away. Jim is seated in the bed behind her, his face at first reflected over her shoulder as he watches silently, producing a dense image of their loss of mutual intimacy and their imminent separation. The camera then refocuses to present Catherine's face reflected alone, to the accompaniment of the theme music that always signifies sadness. There are no images of the two together – only the narrator's voice-over tells us that they made love for one last time but that it was 'comme s'ils étaient morts' ('as if they were dead'). Moreau's expressive face is also filmed in close-up in the preceding sequence, when she leaves Jim's bed and takes refuge with Jules, weeping for the loss of her dream of perfect love and promising, desperately, that she and Jules will grow old together. As the two hold each other the frame is filled with their faces, Catherine's wet with tears, Jules's impassive with pain, in an extreme form of the close-up as signifier of intense emotion. The complexity of that emotion – Jules resigned to the permanent loss of her sexual love for him, suffering but full of tenderness, Catherine aching for the lost love with Jim and willing herself to settle for Jules's devotion – is moving because of subtle and skilful acting (particularly that of Moreau), but its effect is also due to the framing of the image that reproduces the effect of intense emotional pain by shutting out any sense of the rest of life.

Jules et Jim is also a film that freely employs the device of freeze-framing the image. Whilst this is a technique that does interrupt narrative flow and thus invites the spectator to notice, it is used here in a way that has clear narrative and thematic relevance. The early part of the film contains many still images of women: the photos of German girlfriends that Jules shows to Jim, the sketch Jules scribbles on a café table, paintings, the slides of ancient Greek statues that Albert shows the friends and that sends them to the island where they find the statue with the magical smile. All of these images represent men's images of women, or women as men's idealised 'others' placed, through art, safely outside the awkward realities of time and change. When Catherine appears, her resemblance to the statue means that she too has a ready-made place in the men's fantasies. Both the prolonged and repeated close-ups of Catherine's face that recur from her first scene almost to her last, and – more markedly – the freeze-frames that immobilise her in time, link Catherine to the earlier images and make her physical appearance more significant than that of the men. With typical Truffaldian ambiguity (see chapter 5) the device both shares in and draws the spectator's attention to the process of male idealisation of women.

The freeze-frame, as suggested above, momentarily arrests the passage of time, and hence may be used to represent permanence. Thus the freezing of the image of Jules and Jim at the moment of their reunion after the war may imply that their friendship, unlike the shifting, changeable emotion of love, is durable. Freeze-framing is just one option open to the director at the point of editing the film, and clearly editing contributes immeasurably to the final product. The editing of *Jules et Jim*, as we have said, produced the very different rhythmic patterns of parts one and two, part one being characterised predominantly by fast-cutting, the use of lap dissolves, irises and other innovative transitional devices (innovative for the early 1960s – irises, for example, were extensively used in silent cinema), and a high degree of camera movement, part two by longer takes, less cutting and a more static camera.

Editing included the addition of the narrator's voice-over and of the musical score. The intermittent voice-over, which uses the 'literary' past tense of the past historic, gives to the story the distance of retrospection. Stories told by film can engage the spectator totally in what feels like present time; here the narrator's commentaries both add a note of poignancy – for what is happening on the screen is situated in the past, as experience now lost in time – and draws attention to the process of storytelling, which (as in most Truffaut films) is a recurrent theme. Delerue's music is an equally significant element of the film text: several different musical themes rapidly become associated with the film's varying moods, and interact with the narrative either by echoing the action (as in Catherine and Jim's farewell night together, described above) or by counterpointing it. The film concludes with an example of counterpoint: as Jules leaves the cemetery, a solitary and desolate figure, the music swells into the exuberantly lyrical theme that has been associated throughout with Catherine, denying the bleakness of the denouement, suggesting that death has not merely obliterated the trio's attempt at living otherwise, celebrating the capacity of art to recreate what time has destroyed. *Jules et Jim* also contains a theme song *Le Tourbillon de la vie*, which perfectly combines an intra-diegetic function (within the plot, the song expresses Catherine's philosophy of life and, since it is written and accompanied by Albert, serves to arouse the jealousy of Jules and Jim) and an extra-diegetic function (the song resumes the plot and the central rhythm of the whole film).

Truffaut's aim of finding an equivalent in film terms for Roché's 'style qui n'a l'air de rien' was almost entirely successful: analysis reveals the use of a complex set of signifying techniques, but in watching the film a careful balance is maintained between drawing attention to these, thus inviting an intellectual/aesthetic response from the audience, and sustaining the pleasure of narrative illusion. What this story of love, infidelity, jealousy and murder might have been if told with less discretion can be glimpsed in the one sequence that jars with the overall style. It comes towards the end of the film, when the three have met again in Paris and Catherine has attempted to rekindle Jim's love through the 'episode of the white pyjamas'. Catherine telephones Jim and asks him to come to the old watermill house in which she and Jules now live. He finds her in bed, and explains to her that their affair is over, that the brave attempt to 'invent love', to 'refuse hypocrisy et resignation' has failed, that he has committed himself to Gilberte. Catherine reacts at first with a quietly intense 'Et moi, Jim, et moi?' ('What about me, Jim?'), but at this point the whole mood switches inexplicably to one of high melodrama. Loud, staccato chords of music warn of impending violence, Catherine pulls a gun and locks the door: 'Tu es lâche Jim, je vais te tuer'.[11] As the music, thriller style, reaches a climax of tension, Jim disarms her and leaps from the window to the ground below; the music changes to a triumphal fanfare and the camera sweeps up to the lowering sky, panning across to where the rays of the sun strike through. The definitive end of the affair, and Jim's escape from death, are thus treated in full-blown dramatic style, as if Truffaut suddenly (whether deliberately or not it is hard to say) strayed into another, remembered set of generic codes. The importance of deliberate restraint to the success of the whole film becomes the more apparent.

Themes (a conclusion)

What *Jules et Jim* is 'about' has already, inevitably, been suggested in the discussion of the film's narrative structure and signifying techniques. Though the director's lightness of touch extends to

11 'You're a coward, Jim, I'm going to kill you.'

the repeated presence of mild humour (about to sing her song before Jules and Jim, Catherine, for example, comments drily 'je pense que c'est bien trop beau pour eux mais tant pis, on ne choisit pas son public'[12]), the themes are clearly serious and were taken seriously enough in the early 1960s for the film to be given an 'over-eighteens only' rating in France, and to be initially banned (though the ban was later lifted) in Italy. If the film was considered shocking, it was because it is about the search for an alternative to the couple as the sole legitimate form of heterosexual love. The 'eternal triangle' is a familiar theme of fiction, but it does not usually contest the couple as institution, centring rather on a choice between two partners and on the jealousy of the one excluded. Here the excluded partner – moreover a husband, whose property rights over his wife had, until well into the twentieth century, been enshrined in French law – accommodates his wife's lover, because the relationship between the two men is close and loving, and because it seems possible, for a time, to replace the couple with a threesome. In the novel, Jim dreams of forming a household that prefigures the 'commune' of the 1960s, in which he, Kathe, Jules and Gilberte might live together with all the children of their different couplings: 'Peut-être pourraient-ils vivre tous les quatre, avec les enfants présents et futurs, dans la même vaste maison de campagne, où tous travailleraient chacun à sa façon? C'était le rêve de Jim'[13] (Roché 1953: 124). The same dream seems at times to underlie the film.

If the dream is impossible it is in part because the society in which the three live has no place for such experiments – thus war between nation states returns each firmly to their own side of national and gender borders, and Jim and Catherine are 'not allowed' to have their ashes mingled – but also because of the nature of desire itself, which always seeks the unobtainable, refuses to be domesticated or to be fitted into a neat reciprocity. The mobility and intermittence of desire are at the heart of the

12 'I think it's too good for them but too bad – you don't get to choose your public.'
13 'Perhaps they could all four live together, with present and future children, in the same huge country house, each one working in their own way. That was Jim's dream'.

film. Moreover, reality, in the second part of the film, proves obdurately resistant to human desires, as Jim and Catherine's longing for a child is answered only at the nadir of their love and then, once their hope is re-ignited, destroyed by Catherine's miscarriage.

The film also raises important questions about the relationship between the sexes, as Jean Renoir pointed out in his letter to Truffaut ('Vous aidez à dissiper le brouillard qui enveloppe l'essence de cette question'[14] (Baecque and Toubiana 1996: 264)), though this will be studied in more detail below (chapter 5). Catherine, as a character, struggles to become a 'subject' rather than the mysterious *femme fatale* of male fantasy, though she is helped in this by the fact that Jeanne Moreau's acting, and especially her face, express an irreducible depth and range of subjective feeling. Relations between men are also central, for friendship does not entirely take second place to love here but endures separation and jealousy to emerge as an important and lasting emotion.

Like *Les 400 Coups* and many subsequent Truffaut films, *Jules et Jim* is also about the significance and the joy of telling stories. All the central characters experience the need to shape and recount their experience to willing listeners, and to tell other tales that function more obliquely to make sense of their own lives. Jules and Jim are both writers, and exchange with each other accounts of their lives and loves. Jim also tells the story of the soldier who conducted an entire love affair through letters, dying before he was ever reunited with the object of his love. The affair between Jim and Catherine begins with mutual storytelling, as each recounts the plot so far from their own perspective. Thérèse, the 'steam train', meeting up again with Jim after a long absence, comically recounts her entire intervening history at breakneck speed. It is significant, and entirely in keeping with the rest of Truffaut's cinema, that the film's final sequence is located in time by a clip from a 1930s newsreel showing the Nazis burning books in Berlin. It is this desecration of the book, the tangible form of the

14 'You help to see through the fog that surrounds this question.'

story, that stands here for the brutal inhumanity of Nazism, just as in *Fahrenheit 451*, it represents the ruthless powers of the totalitarian state.

Finally, and again typically, the film is about death. Death is intermittently present throughout, in Catherine's threats of fire and vitriol and her premonitory plunge into the Seine, in the carnage of World War I, in the miscarriage of the child and Catherine's second attempt on Jim's life, finally in the last plunge into the river, and the visual precision and detail with which the cremation of the bodies and the grinding of the bones to ashes is observed. The film ends on a stark reminder of the material reality of death and the fragility of life, though what remains with the spectator is also the film's exhilarating creativity, celebrated in the closing, orchestral rendition of *Le Tourbillon de la vie*. Critical reception was almost unanimously positive, and has remained so.

References

De Baecque, Antoine and Toubiana, Serge (1996), *François Truffaut*, Paris, Gallimard

Gillain, Anne (1988), *Le Cinéma selon François Truffaut*, Paris, Flammarion.

Insdorf, Annette (1994), *François Truffaut*, Cambridge, Cambridge University Press.

Roché, Henri-Pierre (1953), *Jules et Jim*, Paris, Gallimard Collection Folio.

Truffaut, François (1988), *Correspondance*, Paris, Hatier.

4

The genre films

A first statement: *Les Mistons*

Truffaut's attitude to genre and the questions it posed for French film-makers is neatly summed up at a very early point of his career in the juxtapositioning of two short sequences in *Les Mistons*. Unobtrusive and understated, these sequences nevertheless eloquently express the views of the Nouvelle Vague directors on the subject of the future direction of French cinema and its relationship with its American counterpart.

The first of the two sequences shows the kids at play: conventional boys' shooting games with dramatic, tumbling 'deaths'. The second recounts a brief narrative: gardener waters lawn, boy steps on hose, flow of water stops, gardener inspects hose by looking down nozzle, boy releases foot, gardener is well and truly doused. Neither sequence makes a direct contribution to the 'narrative' of *Les Mistons*, indeed, initially, the sequences appear quite gratuitous. However, it is evident that this short film is as much about cinema and what cinema should be as it is about the two young lovers and the uncomprehending behaviour of the pubescent males who torment them. Once seen in the context of a film about film, the two sequences take on an unmistakable relevance. The boys' games are polyvalent: they are playing at gangsters or at soldiers or at cowboys and Indians. The allusion to genre films, the gangster/thriller, the war film, the western and thus Hollywood and American cinema, is unambiguous. The homage sequence juxtaposed with the games sequence is instantly identifiable to those familiar with the origins of (French) cinema: it is a remake of the Lumière Brothers short film: *L'Arroseur arrosé* (1895). Thus, deliberately placed side by side are a reference to Hollywood genre films and a reference to a classic of French cinema. The interplay is rich in implications: silent film (with piano accompaniment) alongside talkie (sound effects); the very first narrative film as opposed to its modern descendent; violence, action and gimmicks in contrast to a story in which the interest is focused on the characters.

On another level, this brief sequence from a short, début film spelled out the stance adopted by the Nouvelle Vague *vis-à-vis* American cinema. For polemical reasons – any new movement has to portray the 'opposition' in a negative light – genre films are evoked here by Truffaut as violent, undemanding intellectually and dependent on special effects. French cinema, in contrast, is presented as slower-paced, humorous, reflective. Truffaut's article *A Certain Tendency of French Cinema* demonstrated the other main butt of Nouvelle Vague scorn: the classic adaptations of the likes of Aurenche and Bost and the 'psychological realism' their screenplays generated. Truffaut's films can be seen as predicated on two basic principles: first, a return to the classic 'Golden Age' French cinema of the 1930s, to the films of Vigo and Renoir and, second, the need simultaneously to acknowledge and 'recuperate' the contribution of Hollywood. In retrospect, the dual influence of Renoir and Hitchcock, each emblematic of the influence of others, is one of the more readily identifiable traits of Truffaut's films.

The Hollywood of the 1940s and 1950s was geared to the production of genre films: westerns, World War II films, science fiction films, musicals, thrillers. A highly sophisticated industry based on the major studios, some of which specialised in certain genres, churned out a profusion of genre movies in response to the demands of the domestic and European markets. Truffaut and his colleagues found themselves at the receiving end of this invasion from their childhood days onwards. Fuelled by a genuine passion for the cinema, they built up during this time a comprehensive knowledge of genre films and a detailed understanding of how they were put together. The balance of input between studio/company on the one hand and *metteur-en-scène* on the other and the degree of independence afforded the latter were crucial, and were factors to which the young enthusiasts were sensitive, quickly learning to identify those films in which the *metteur-en-scène* had played more than a purely executive role. The direct consequence of this familiarity with genre films was a certain ambivalence in attitude. On the one hand, the Nouvelle Vague directors sought to challenge the American dominance of cinema worldwide. On the other, their respect and affection for these films were genuine and lasting, a fact to which the studies of Hitchcock by Chabrol and Rohmer on the one hand and Truffaut on the other, bear eloquent testimony. An appreciation of these apparently contradictory views is the key to understanding Truffaut's genre films. The solution was, on the surface at least, simple: in each of his genre films he borrowed the framework offered by the genre and used it as a vehicle to convey his own themes and ideas. The reality was, as might be suspected, not quite so straightforward. However, before looking more closely at Truffaut's approach to making genre films, it is helpful to dwell briefly on the subject of genre and the problems of definition.

Definitions of genre

Much work has been done on genre, with specific focus on the topic in the 1960s and 1970s as the impact of the *politique des auteurs* began to mutate. A particularly cogent definition of genre and a concise summary of the evolving theory surrounding it can be found in *The Cinema Book* (Cook 1985: 59–112). The first step in defining the concept is relatively uncomplicated: the naming of the different genres and listing of the codes and conventions associated with each of them can be quickly and clearly achieved e.g. westerns evoke guns, horses, saloons, shanty towns in wide-open spaces; stetsons, chaps, spurs; law-enforcing sheriffs defending law-abiding citizens, lawless outsiders, demure, hard-working wives and game, warm-hearted prostitutes. Further reflection on the topic, however, reveals the complexities: which film(s) does one take as the basis on which to form a definition and at what point in the history of the evolution of the genre? Pam Cook talks of 'sets' or 'runs' of films and at the same time draws attention to the way genres evolve over time: Clint Eastwood's *Unforgiven* (1992) is a good illustration of such evolution: the film is in part a critique of previous westerns and in particular those in which Eastwood had starred as actor or himself directed. When analysed, many films resist classification: a western may well have elements of the thriller, aspects of the musical can invade almost any genre. Moreover, genres splinter into sub-genres: war films embrace spy movies, escape movies, air force/navy/army movies. Still further examination reveals that the vast majority of mainstream genre films share the same basic structures: e.g. simplistic, Manichaean struggles between the forces of good and evil, stereotypical representation of the sexes, classic progression from order to disorder to neat and ordered closure.

Although Truffaut made his first genre film – the *film noir*, *Tirez sur le pianiste* – in 1960, some time before the main debate took place, he was undoubtedly sensitive to the problematics of genre. His knowledge of genre films, as he had seen them in the cinemas of Paris, was extensive and varied. Thus, it was on the basis of knowledge and experience that he made the decision, at various points in his career, to adopt a specific genre as framework for his film. Cook is again helpful here in spelling out the possibilities open to an *auteur* seeking to make a genre film. She lists three approaches

> In one view there can be a coincidence between genre and author which enables the director to use its conventions as a kind of shorthand, enabling him or her to go straight to the heart of his/her concerns and express them at a formal level through the interplay of genre convention and motif ... In another view the author works in tension with the conventions; attempting to inflect them, so as to express his/her own vision in the differences set up between the expected playing out of the convention and the new twist s/he develops – vision expressed in counterpoint ... A third view posits genre as a beneficial constraint which provides a formal ordering

and control over the drive to personal expression, preventing its dissolution in an excess of individualism and incomprehensibility, but at the same time capable of containing a certain non-naturalistic dimension – the theatricality or expressionism of a baroque sensibility (Cook 1985: 63).

In his genre films, Truffaut could be said to adopt a combination of all three of the approaches identified above: he certainly uses the conventions as a shorthand, a convenient medium for his own themes; at the same time, there is a discernible intent to inflect the conventions in the form of an ironic parodying of them; finally, he could also be deemed to exploit genre as a constraint, though it is questionable whether all his critics would agree, in a case such as *Tirez* in particular, that this prevents dissolution into 'individualism and incomprehensibility'.

The debt to Hitchcock

As suggested above, Truffaut's exploitation of genre is not as straightforward as it at first appears. If his genre films are, with one exception, *films noirs* or thrillers, this is attributable in large part to the influence of the films of Alfred Hitchcock. Analysis of the latter's work reveals that Hitchcock himself was already exploiting genre conventions in the ways identified by Cook and that Truffaut took not just the conventions but also the ways of subverting them and inflecting them to his own ends. That Truffaut was fully aware of this process is evident from his writings. He acknowledges Hitchcock's popular appeal – based on adoption of the thriller genre and his knack of creating and sustaining fear and suspense – but notes the paradox: 'Alfred Hitchcock, le cinéaste le plus accessible à tous les publics par la simplicité et la clarté de son travail, est en même temps celui qui excelle à filmer les rapports les plus subtils entre les êtres'[1] (Truffaut 1983: 13).

1 'While, due to the simplicity and clarity of his films, Alfred Hitchcock is the most accessible of all directors, for all types of audiences, he is at the same time the most successful in filming the subtlest nuances of human relationships.'

It is not surprising that Truffaut so much admired Hitchcock and that he should have adopted, for a number of his own films, the latter's strategy of combining genre with investigation of human relationships Watching a series of over 100 clips from Hitchcock's films, spread over the three hours of the New York Film Club's annual gala which in 1974 was held in his honour, Truffaut realised the full extent to which Hitchcock's work focuses on love and death and, thus, by implication, resembles his own

> Je connaissais cette œuvre, je croyais la connaître très bien et j'étais sidéré devant ce que je voyais. Sur l'écran, ce n'étaient qu'éclaboussures, feux d'artifices, éjaculations, soupirs, râles, cris, pertes de sang, larmes, poignets tordus, et il m'apparut que, dans le cinéma d'Hitchcock, décidément plus sexuel que sensuel, faire l'amour et mourir ne font qu'un[2] (Truffaut 1983: 294).

Truffaut, then, in the manner of Hitchcock, successfully married genre with the *auteur* approach. It is evident, however, that a certain tension exists between these two concepts and that the debate involved is of primary relevance. The Nouvelle Vague won respect and credibility for the notion that a film is as much the product of one person as is a novel, a play or a poem. The concept of genre films suggests the opposite: genre films are collective enterprises, literally the product of a company, assembled by a team of producers, script-writers, technicians and actors. In this kind of set-up, the *metteur-en-scène* is no more than an agent, the person who turns the script into images. The finished product is then marketed through its genre ('the greatest western ever') and stars ('John Wayne at his best'). In some ways, the *politique des auteurs* merely perpetuated a long-established literary tradition, that of the individual creator, no more than another manifestation of the Platonic notion of the gifted few scattering pearls of wisdom to the many. Genre films, in contrast, offered a much more egalitarian approach, not just in terms of production but, more

2 'I was familiar with these films, I thought I knew them very well, but I was astonished at what I was seeing. The screen was full of splashes of blood, fireworks, ejaculations, sighs, groans, cries, bleeding, tears, wrists being twisted in torment, and it came to me that, in Hitchcock's films, which are definitely more sexual than sensual, love and death are inseparable.'

importantly perhaps, also in terms of evaluation. To examine genre films critically was to open up a whole range of films that previously had not been deemed worthy of critical appraisal. Following this new approach, the full range of cinematic production, and not just its masterpieces, could be considered on an equal footing and popular culture could be treated seriously. Truffaut recognised this quality in Hitchcock's work: 'Son œuvre est à la fois commerciale et expérimentale, universelle comme le *Ben Hur* de William Wyler et confidentielle comme *Fireworks* de Kenneth Angers'[3] (Truffaut 1983: 14), and made clear the strength of his commitment to this approach in an article which first appeared in *Esquire* in 1969:

> On discute souvent à propos de ce que doit être le contenu d'un film, doit-il s'en tenir au divertissement ou informer le public sur les grands problèmes sociaux du moment, et je fuis ces discussions comme la peste. Je pense que toutes les individualités doivent s'exprimer et que tous les films sont utiles, qu'ils soient formalistes ou réalistes, baroque ou engagés, tragiques ou légers, modernes ou désuets, en couleurs ou en noir et blanc, en 35 mm ou en Super 8, avec des vedettes ou des inconnus, ambitieux ou modestes ... Seul compte le résultat, c'est-à-dire le bien que le metteur en scène se fait à lui-même et le bien qu' il fait aux autres[4] (Truffaut 1987: 271).

He returned to the same idea ten years later, this time in the preface to a *Book of the Cinema*: 'Or, je crois fermement qu'il faut refuser toute hiérarchie de genres et considérer que ce qui est culturel c'est simplement tout ce qui nous plaît, nous distrait, nous intéresse, nous aide à vivre "Tous les films naissent libres et

---

3 'His films are both financially successful and experimental, universal like William Wyler's *Ben Hur* and intimate like Kenneth Angers' *Fireworks*.'

4 'The debate over the content of films is a common one and one I avoid like the plague, should films aim only to entertain or have they a duty to keep the public in touch with the big social problems of the day. I believe all types of people should express themselves, all kinds of films are useful whether they are formalist or realist, baroque or committed, tragic or light-hearted, modern or old-fashioned, in colour or in black and white, in 35 mm or Super 8, with stars or unknowns, ambitious or modest. The only thing that counts is the outcome, i.e. the good the director does himself and the good he does others.'

égaux" a écrit André Bazin[5] (Truffaut 1979: 40).

Truffaut's approach to genre was, then, uncluttered by any cultural or social bias or snobbishness. At the same time, as a founding member of the Nouvelle Vague and one of the leading exponents of its aims, he was committed unambiguously to the *auteur* approach. How then is this apparent contradiction between the genre and *auteur* approaches resolved in Truffaut's case?

Auteurism and genre

The solution is to be found first in the evolution of film theory. Cook draws attention to the work of Tom Ryall who, in 1978, posited a progression from 'an earlier tradition which saw films as providing social documents' to auteurism and finally to genre (Cook 1985: 58). In the course of the late 1960s and 1970s, the genre approach gained ground, gradually supplanting auteurism which was increasingly perceived as outmoded. However, while the theorists waged their battles in academic journals, others, in particular the media in film reviews, persisted with the *auteur* approach: 'the latest Spielberg'; 'From the director who brought you *Towering Inferno*'. Academics too continued to write and present analyses of films in the form of monographs on directors. As a result, something of a compromise position was reached in which a maker of genre films could nevertheless be treated as an *auteur*, an acknowledgement that the directors of such films did not necessarily have to be the hired lackeys of a studio or a company, agents executing the orders of those above them and sacrificing creativity and personal views in the process. Hitchcock is a primary example of precisely such a director – one who by and large dictated his terms to the company rather than vice versa – just as Truffaut's study of his work combines an evaluation of genre and popular culture with an analysis of Hitchcock the

5 'I strongly believe that all attempts to create a hierarchy of genres should be resisted in favour of the notion that what constitutes culture is everything which pleases us, amuses us, interests us, helps us to survive. As André Bazin wrote "all films are born free and equal".'

auteur. As made clear earlier, it is perfectly possible for a film-maker to use genre as a vehicle for communication of a personal world-view. Hitchcock, and Truffaut in his genre films, provide evidence for the legitimacy of this fusion.

Truffaut had firm views on genre as on most other aspects of cinema. As demonstrated above, he made no qualitative distinction between a film such as *Jules et Jim* which, on the surface, dealt with the complexities of a triangular relationship and a thriller like *La Mariée était en noir*, ostensibly dealing with a multiple murder. He made a significant number of genre films, though just how many is dependent on how his films are classified. 'I hate war films' (Truffaut 1987: 201), he wrote and, despite authentic newsreel footage in *Jules et Jim*, *La Chambre verte* and *Le Dernier Métro*, he never planned a film of that genre. *Films noirs* or thrillers were however, a different matter and at least six of his films can, with greater or lesser justification, be placed in this category: *Tirez*, *La Peau douce*, *La Mariée*, *La Sirène du Mississippi*, *La Femme d'à côté* and *Vivement dimanche!* all bear the imprint of the genre and most of them, inevitably, of Hitchcock. The science fiction film also appealed to him and he not only made his own, *Fahrenheit 451*, but made an appearance in another, as an actor in Spielberg's *Close Encounters of the Third Kind*. For obvious reasons westerns are not part of French film culture, and musicals appear to be inimical to it. This did not, however, prevent him making numerous allusions to both genres at various points in his work. A further six of his films fall into the category of 'historical' films (see chapter 2). Since a film set in the past can adopt any genre – the majority of westerns, for example, are historical, as are many thrillers and musicals – it is probably safer in this instance to regard the historical factor as secondary and not a determinant of genre. Certainly, Truffaut's six historical films have widely differing subjects and themes and have no more than superficial ties to the 'heritage movies' that re-emerged in the 1980s. For these reasons, Truffaut's historical films are not considered in this chapter under the heading of 'genre'.

Truffaut's genre films

While Truffaut adopted specific genres, he inflected them to his own purposes, maintaining his status as *auteur* not only through the content of the films but also through their formal aspects. The first two films, *Les Mistons* and *Les 400 Coups*, although they contain references to genre, are resistant to classification by genre. They are, rather, personal statements, as close to autobiography as they are to fiction. It was with his third film that Truffaut had the confidence and the finances to experiment. *Tirez* is the first of his genre films, it is equally one of his most artistically successful and one of his most innovative.

Tirez sur le pianiste

Story and genre are, almost inevitably, closely linked. Truffaut took his inspiration for his film from an American novel, *Down There*, by David Goodis. The story, setting and iconography of the film are consistent with the *film noir* genre and in a broad sense are faithful to the book, although Truffaut transposes the events from an American to a French setting. It quickly becomes apparent, however, that the gangster story is of minimal significance and that the codes and conventions of the genre are being treated in an ironic manner. Details are only revealed fully on one occasion – when Chico rapidly recounts his story to Charlie as the latter prepares to perform at the start of the film. This genre element of the plot can be summarised in two or three sentences. Two of the Saroyan brothers, Chico and Momo, have taken part in a robbery with two other gangsters. On successful completion of the job, they decide to double-cross their accomplices and divide the proceeds between themselves. They split up and Chico is pursued by the gangsters he has deceived.

Most of this 'action' has taken place before the film begins (the first shots are of part of the pursuit of Chico) and it surfaces thereafter only intermittently. Truffaut claimed he wrote stories with beginnings, middles and endings even though 'Je sais bien que, finalement, l'intérêt est ailleurs que dans l'intrigue elle-même'[6]

6 'I know very well that, in the long run, the interest lies elsewhere and not in the plot'.

(Truffaut 1988: 465). In the case of *Tirez*, the interest lay in another 'plot', the life and loves of Charlie, but this is less the plot of a thriller than a rich seam of human relationships of the kind frequently exploited in Truffaut's films.

There are parallels here with Hitchcock which are of interest in the context of genre and adaptation. Writing of Renoir, Rossellini and Hitchcock in *Le Plaisir des yeux*, Truffaut pointed out their preference for writing their own scenarios: 'Quand même s'inspirent-ils d'un roman, d'une pièce, d'une histoire vraie, le point de départ n'est qu'un prétexte'[7] (Truffaut 1987: 234). It is clear that both Truffaut and Hitchcock demanded of genre no more than a framework within which to work. This framework would ideally provide a cinematic form – the genre – and a storyline. It was important that the novel or work chosen for adaptation (whatever the subject matter) leave them space to impose their own authorial intentions. Hence Truffaut's hesitation over, and ultimate rejection of, the producer Nicole Stéphane's invitation to direct an adaptation based on Proust's *Du côté de chez Swann* (Truffaut 1988: 278) and the search for less well-known writers whose works reached restricted, even specialised, audiences. In conversation with Hitchcock, Truffaut drew attention to the large number of adaptations in Hitchcock's work: many of his films were based on popular novels which the director freely rewrote, ignoring advice to adapt classics such as Dostoevsky's *Crime and Punishment*

> Oui mais je ne le ferais jamais parce que 'Crime et Châtiment', c'est l'œuvre de quelqu'un d'autre justement ... Je lis une histoire seulement une fois. Quand l'idée de base me convient, je l'adopte, j'oublie complètement le livre et je fabrique du cinéma. Je serais incapable de vous raconter 'les Oiseaux' de Daphne du Maurier. Je ne l'ai lu qu'une fois, rapidement[8] (Truffaut 1983: 55–6).

7 'Even when their films are based on a novel, a play or a true story, the starting point is only a pretext.'

8 'Yes, but I shall never do that, precisely because *Crime and Punishment* is someone else's work. I only read a book once. If the basic idea appeals to me, I adopt it, forget the book completely and make my film. I'd be totally incapable of telling you the story of Daphne du Maurier's *The Birds* since I read the book only once and then very quickly.'

One senses that Truffaut sympathised with this approach and that he followed the same process in his own work. His instructions to Maurice Pons – for instructions are what they are – to re-write parts of *Les Virginales* certainly appear to confirm this (Truffaut 1988: 136-7). This attitude to adaptation is far removed from that of the Aurenche and Bost school of adaptation and from their theories of *équivalence* by which they even sought to 'improve upon' the original text, which in their case was frequently one of the classics, precisely the kind of work which Hitchcock and Truffaut shunned. Where the latter tended to read their source texts swiftly and probably only once, the former polished the scenario which then became untouchable during the shooting of the film, leaving the *metteur-en-scène* with little room to make a personal statement.

The two directors shared a predilection for writers whose works offered themes, characters and settings broadly congruent with their outlook, writers such as David Goodis, Charles Williams, Henry Farrell and William Irish, alias Cornell Woolrich, two of whose novels were adapted by Truffaut and one by Hitchcock (*Rear Window*). In Truffaut's case, it was an additional attraction that these writers' work was further distanced from his audience by language and culture.

Truffaut's adaptation of *Down There* is very much a free one. It is not solely a switch of countries that is involved, but a switch of societies, of cultures and of languages. He similarly takes considerable liberty with the storyline and above all shifts the emphasis from thriller to an analysis of the central character and his relationship with three women. The iconography of the *film noir* is retained: from cars and trenchcoats with upturned collars, to guns and shoot-outs, from car chases to voice-over narration. Truffaut's ironical intentions are, however, apparent from the outset. From virtually the first frames, it is clear that the director is parodying *film noir* rather than recreating it. This was a fact of which Truffaut was at least partly aware at the time, 'I would call the film a respectful pastiche of the Hollywood B-film, from which I have learned such a lot' (Houston 1961: 64). His reference to pastiche is modest understatement since it is evident that the irony is intentional and the interplay between the original form and the critique of it much closer to parody than pastiche, and is itself productive of meaning in the most vigorous of ways.

The opening sequence of the film presents the viewer with a juxtaposition that recalls *Les Mistons'* juxtaposed allusions first to Hollywood, then to French cinema. On this occasion, initial shots of a man on the run are followed immediately by a relatively lengthy conversation between the same man and a stranger. The first indications are that this is a *film noir*: the wet sidewalk glistens in the dark as a man, in the obligatory raincoat, scuttles down the street pursued by a car, its headlights searching threateningly, engine revving noisily. That this is an action movie is underscored on the formal level by the rapid cutting from prey to pursuer and the metonymy of car chases: close-ups of headlamps, running feet, a desperate face, pools of light. Expectations are raised and fulfilled, but only briefly, for almost at once they are ruptured and on every level. The tone of mystery, suspense and danger is punctured by a moment of farce as the man careers into a lamp-post, as if deliberately. The car mysteriously disappears and a second man comes on the scene bearing flowers. The next two minutes are given over to a discussion of love, marriage and children as the newcomer unburdens himself of the most intimate of details to his new-found acquaintance. The pace also alters radically: gone are the rapid cuts, to be replaced by a single tracking shot with a minimum of reframing within it. More apparent now is the direct filming – sound and lighting – typical of the early days of the Nouvelle Vague. Although nothing is made explicit, Truffaut could not have made a clearer statement of his intentions: the *film noir* is no more than a vehicle, the plot is of secondary importance, the film is to revolve more around affairs of the heart than investigate a dispute among criminals, the real theme is cinema itself. This is, moreover, only the first of three occasions on which the camera abandons the 'chase' – staple diet of the *film noir* – at the moment it begins. The second occurs almost at once as Chico, the man chased by the car in the opening shots, is tracked down in the bar where Charlie (his brother) works by the two men pursuing him. He has to implore Charlie to help him which he eventually does. But as the pursuers scramble over the cases which Charlie has brought tumbling down in their path, the camera quits the chase in order to focus on Charlie and the bar's resident singer, played by Boby Lapointe. The latter launches into the hilarious *Avanie et Framboise* which, on closer analysis helped by the sub-titles of the original version, deals with sex. The third occasion occurs at the end of the film when the archetypal car chase is abandoned in favour of the final moments of the Léna–Charlie relationship. On each of these occasions the audience's attention is diverted from genre and plot and made to focus on other concerns: love, human relationships, death.

The detached, ironical handling of genre is undisguised and is reinforced throughout the film in a number of ways. One of the most striking, and that which most confounded the critics on the film's début in 1961, is the constant change of tone. This is connected in part to genre, since the film does not restrict itself to the conventions of the *film noir*. Also evident are allusions to the musical (the songs of Boby Lapointe and Félix Leclerc which feature as more than just background music, the latter in particular being linked thematically to Charlie's love affair with Léna); to the western (Clarisse's undressing behind the screen in Charlie's room, the smashing of windows and the twirling of the gun in the shoot-out at the end of the film); to the comedy (in a number of sequences, but most humorously the conversation between Fido and the gangsters in the car on the subject of watches and the now famous 'dead granny' insert shot). There is even a moment when the Brothers Grimm seem to intrude upon the film as we are brought to the little house in the forest which bears no small resemblance to that of Hansel and Gretel in the famous fairy tale. Such light-hearted moments, like the comic ones, are offset by the juxtapositioning of moments of genuine tragedy in the form of the dramatic and violent deaths of Thérésa and Léna and the dominant and pervasive melancholy of the central character.

The subverting of genre conventions is also apparent in Truffaut's representation of his male and female characters. In *Tirez*, as elsewhere in his work, his predilection for weak heroes and strong females is manifest. This runs counter to Hollywood's robustly masculine stereotypes but conforms with deep-rooted feelings and attitudes in Truffaut on which he commented on more than one occasion:

> Je déteste avant tout les durs, les casseurs et, d'une façon générale, tous les personnages a priori prestigieux, qui dominent l'action et que rien ne peut atteindre. Ce n'est pas une question de format car le grand Sterling Hayden par exemple est aussi fragile que le petit Charles Aznavour; on devine leur cœur avant de voir leurs muscles. En effet, on peut être faible, fragile, vulnérable sans être une victime[9] (Truffaut 1987: 187).

Aznavour is well-suited to the role of Edouard Saroyan/Charlie Kohler, his slight physique and troubled expression evoke precisely the vulnerability that Truffaut sought and which situates this character alongside Antoine Doinel, Julien Vercel, indeed the majority of Truffaut's male characters. Hollywood's macho male simply did not fit with Truffaut's vision and it is not surprising that he rejected its offers: 'Il arrive bien souvent que ces généreux Américains me proposent de venir tourner chez eux, je leur fais presque toujours la même réponse "Avec mon goût pour les anti-héros et les histoires douces-amères, je me sens capable de réaliser le premier James Bond déficitaire"'[10] (Truffaut 1987: 37).

Conversely, there is considerable evidence to suggest that the female characters are frequently the opposite of their male leads: strong, determined, decisive. In *Tirez*, both Thérésa and Léna take the initiative and generally shape and lead the relationship. Only with Clarisse does Charlie show any initiative of his own and then only because, with a prostitute, he feels himself freed of the

---

9 'I hate hard, violent men and generally speaking all self-important characters who dominate the action, who are invulnerable. It's not a question of size since the tall Sterling Hayden is, for example, as frail as the short Aznavour. You can read their heart before you see their muscles, i.e. you can be weak, frail and vulnerable and not be a victim.'

10 'You big-hearted Yanks often make me offers to go and make a film in the States, I usually reply "Given my liking for anti-heroes and bitter-sweet stories, I feel I'd probably succeed in making the first James Bond film to fail at the box office".'

requirement to observe those rituals of courtship which in other relationships cause him to freeze.

Another form of subversion occurs in the way Truffaut handles suspense, an aspect of his work in which he was again influenced by Hitchcock. He comments on suspense on several occasions in his writings and it is clear that he did not conceive of its use in a conventional sense. The main dramatic ingredients of the *film noir* are normally suspense and curiosity, sustained throughout the film by the audience's desire to 'uncover the mystery' and 'find out who did it'. Neither Truffaut, nor his mentor, had much regard for the 'whodunnit'

> [A. H.: Effectivement, [Murder] c'est un des rares whodunits que j'aie tournés, car généralement l'intérêt réside seulement dans la partie finale.]
>
> [F. T.: C'est le cas de tous les romans d'Agatha Christie, par exemple. Une enquête laborieuse, des scènes d'interrogatoire les unes derrière les autres...]
>
> [A. H.: C'est pourquoi je n'aime pas beaucoup les whodunits; cela fait penser à un puzzle ou à une grille de mots croisés. Vous attendez tranquillement la réponse à la question: qui a tué? Aucune émotion[11] (Truffaut 1983: 59).]

Hitchcock and Truffaut prefer to create, and then sustain, suspense by using it within a shot, within a sequence. As the former points out, suspense can be created simply, without having to resort to the cumbersome paraphernalia of the whodunnit: 'C'est le moyen le plus puissant de soutenir l'attention du spectateur, que ce soit le suspense de situation ou celui qui incite le spectateur à se demander: "Et maintenant que va-t-il arriver?"'[12] (Truffaut 1983: 59). Both instinctively link suspense with emotion:

---

11 'A. H.: You're right [Murder] is one of the few whodunnits I've done, the interest lies mainly in the last reel. F. T.: That's how most of Agatha Christie's novels work, for example. A long-winded enquiry, a series of interrogations, one after the other. A. H.: That's why I don't really like whodunnits; they remind you of a puzzle or a crossword. You're waiting, calming, for the reply to the question: who did it? There's no emotion.'

12 'It's the most powerful way of sustaining the spectator's interest, whether it be suspense stemming from the situation or the kind of suspense which makes the spectators ask themselves "What's going to happen next?"'

'Le whodunit suscite une curiosité dépourvue d'émotion; or les émotions sont un ingrédient nécessaire au suspense'[13] (Truffaut 1983: 59).

Tirez provides a good demonstration of application of these principles, namely the sequence, towards the beginning of the film, in which Charlie tries to pluck up the courage to invite Léna for a drink. The sequence is structured so as to oblige the audience to ask the question 'what will happen next?'. Its interest is sustained by the fairly complex web of emotions involved: uncertainty as to whether Charlie is capable of overcoming his chronic shyness, hesitation as to Léna's state of mind, attributable to the lack of access to her feelings (the point of view, via the voice-over, is Charlie's). Having thus skilfully manipulated the spectator's emotions, Truffaut playfully makes the suspense evaporate by having Léna simply disappear: when Charlie finally puts his question she is no longer there.

A final way in which *Tirez* subverts the conventional genre film can be located in the foregrounding of the theme of cinema itself. As demonstrated earlier, this film is only superficially a *film noir*. If it is, rather, an exploration of the complex terrain of heterosexual relationships, it is equally a statement on cinema and on French cinema in particular. The self-referential aspects of the film are communicated through a variety of techniques. One of the first indications comes at the beginning of the film when the audience, already alerted by the abrupt changes of tone and form, is made aware of the independence of the camera. As Chico leaves the stranger with the flowers and, suddenly remembering he is being chased, darts off into the night, the camera momentarily loses him and swings back and then forward again before catching up with him. The significance of this tiny movement is out of proportion to the second or so that it occupies on screen. It represents a fracturing of the narrative, a stepping aside, a wink to the audience that this action is fiction, part of a film, cinema.

There are numerous other such moments, among the most noticeable being the camera's preoccupation with the female cello

13 'The whodunnit arouses a form of curiosity void of emotion when emotions are a vital ingredient in creating suspense.'

player at the crucial moment Charlie enters the room for his audition with Lars Schmeel; the triple-screen allusion to Abel Gance (narration of Plyne's taking the bribe); moments of humour such as Fido and his companion further undermining the credibility of the gangsters by attacking them with milk bombs and Charlie's covering of Clarisse's breasts while making a direct reference to cinema: 'au cinéma c'est comme ça et pas autrement' ('that's what they do in films'). In this assault on the conventions of genre, *Tirez* signalled a re-appraisal of form and, in the context of the film industry in France, a re-evaluation of what films should be and do. In this light it can be seen that Truffaut's second feature-length work was, first and foremost, a film about film.

La Peau douce and *La Sirène du Mississippi*

After a gap of four years during which he made *Jules et Jim* and his third Doinel film, *Antoine et Colette*, Truffaut returned to genre films, making three in succession between 1964 and 1967. Of these, the first, *La Peau douce* is a tale of (misplaced) passion and adultery, a *crime passionnel* culminating in a violent murder. While it is true that the film again owes much to Hitchcock – tension and suspense, often with nightmarish overtones, pervade many of the sequences, even the seemingly banal such as the race to the airport; the film is shot in black and white and is mostly situated in an urban environment – it is less easy to ascribe it to a particular genre and the framework within which Truffaut is working only thinly disguises another exploration of a triangular relationship. In this, *La Peau douce* is closer to *Jules et Jim* than to *Tirez* or *La Mariée*, the genre films which precede and follow it.

The iconography of the thriller genre, to which it might be claimed it loosely belongs, does not have the same prominence as in the other two films and the analysis of Pierre Lachenay's clumsy, self-centred attempts at communicating with wife, lover (and conference audiences) and the tragic outcome of his inability to do so lie at the heart of the film. There is no plot here involving gangsters, no mystery to be solved. Although the race to the airport (like that of Renoir's Amédée Lange to the Belgian frontier) is accompanied by many of the signifiers of the thriller, appropriate music, shots of tense hands, rapid cutting, it is simultaneously apparent that the race is purely one against time and there are no other 'enemies' in pursuit. The three central characters – husband, wife and mistress – form between them virtually the only source of interest. This is sustained, perhaps not as effectively as in other Truffaut films, by the spectator's desire to learn how the developing triangular relationship will resolve itself. However, given the decidedly unattractive personalities of Pierre, Franca and Nicole, this curiosity is never a particularly keen one.

Any suspense is, then, created not through any overarching 'whodunnit' factor but, as usual, within sequences, for example will Pierre abandon the provincial welcoming committee and save Nicole from the prowler? The characters are not cast in the habitual Truffaldian mould. Pierre is more decisive than most other Truffaut males despite his moral vacillation in the relationships with Nicole and Franca. Nicole is not typically strong, indeed she comes across as rather empty-headed and easily-led, attracted to the macho male. Only Franca, in her splendid exposure of the man who importunes her in the street and in the decisive action she takes to put an end to her husband's philandering, confirms the usual pattern of weak males/strong females.

Truffaut himself believed *La Peau douce* to be a failure (Truffaut 1988: 465) and this is perhaps due to its unrelenting portrayal of human nature at its worst. With the delightful exception of the sequence just mentioned, the film lacks humour, a fact perhaps attributable to analogous events taking place in the director's personal life at the time of shooting (Truffaut 1988: 257). One senses that Truffaut sympathised with Hitchcock who recognised that the kind of thrillers he made owed their success, in part at least, to the mixing of humour and seriousness. Some of his English films were, Hitchcock believed, too light-hearted, some of his American ones too serious. It was 'the mix of these two ingredients which was the most difficult thing to control' (Truffaut 1983: 168), and which in *La Peau douce* Truffaut simply got wrong, a criticism which it would be difficult to level at *Tirez*.

La Sirène conforms more closely to the thriller format although once again Truffaut parodies rather than imitates the genre. Where *La Peau douce* focuses on analysis of the three protagonists and scant effort is placed in elaborating a generic framework, *La Sirène* is closer to *Tirez* in its exploitation of the trappings of the thriller. Impersonation and deception underpin the story and mystery shrouds the sudden appearance and identity of 'Julie'. When her true credentials and motives are, at least partly, revealed (her real name – an allusion to *Psycho* – is Marion), the story takes off, in a style typical of Hitchcock, in another direction. In this, *La Sirène* bears a strong resemblance, structurally, to *La Mariée* (see below). Louis is transformed from planter to sleuth and, following his journey from La Réunion to France, the estate, mansion and trappings of wealth are replaced by seedy night clubs, prostitution and hotels. Murder, money and the pursuit (of Marion by Louis) now dominate the plot. However, any suspense generated by Louis's desire to locate Marion and uncover the full truth concerning her identity and intentions is attenuated by the unrealistic ease with which he locates her. As in Truffaut's other films of this type, it becomes clear that the generic conventions lie only on the surface of the film, the main theme of which is the conflict between 'absolute' and 'provisional' attitudes to love and relationships. The lack of a clear resolution of these opposing ways of conducting life and relationships is neatly reflected in the Renoirian final sequence which, in its open-endedness, is diametrically opposed to the normal neat tidying up associated with mainstream genre films.

La Mariée était en noir

The last of the three genre films which Truffaut produced between 1964 and 1967 was another *film noir*, *La Mariée était en noir* (the second film in the group, *Fahrenheit 451*, is a science fiction film which will be considered separately in a moment). The plot line is strong and clear, qualities which derive from its simplicity: Julie Kohler's husband is shot at their wedding as they emerge from the church; one by one, Julie seeks out the five men collectively responsible for his death and in turn kills them. Similarly, the plotting and execution of the murders, the eventual presence of the police, are further aspects of the film to have affinities with certain forms of the *film noir*. However, the parallels that can be drawn do not extend any further and even the police presence, on closer examination, is unconventional: they appear only at a late stage and are not the focalisers for the pursuit and the bringing to justice of the murderer.

Truffaut is again exploiting the genre for his own ends even if, on this occasion, the reasons are somewhat different. Of all Truffaut's films, *La Mariée* most clearly bears the imprint of Hitchcock and, although a number of familiar themes are in play, the main theme is again cinema itself. One of the areas for investigation is that of suspense and how a director can use it. The pattern of the film is clear from the outset and this lends a robust structure to the film which is thus neatly divided into five acts. The spectator's interest is initially sustained through curiosity: the desire to discover who killed Julie's bridegroom, David. This sets up a classic 'whodunnit' situation and it appears that the film will lead to a denouement in which all is revealed and the killer is brought to justice. Truffaut, however, sidesteps established conventions. Preferring to imitate Hitchcock, he uses a device similar to the one used by the latter in *Psycho*, namely that of subverting expectations dramatically at an early point in the film. In Hitchcock's film, the heroine Marion, is killed (in the famous shower scene at Bates's Motel). Since she had been the sole focal point of the film up until this moment, the purpose and direction of the film are no longer clear: her crime, the motive for it and her love affair cease to hold interest when she dies. As pointed out above, the spectator's interest in *La Mariée* seems to centre on the identity of the killer. Truffaut, however, in a manner similar to Hitchcock, reveals how David was killed at a relatively early point in the film and the audience is thus deprived, for the remainder of the film, of the traditional source of suspense and curiosity. It is typical of Hitchcock and Truffaut's manipulation of genre that the established conventions are treated in this way. Interest, from the point at which the manner of the murder is revealed, is sustained in a way that is more reminiscent of the tragedies of Racine than of twentieth-century film. Suspense within each 'act' stems from the desire to know how Julie will carry out her revenge and the form the murder will take. For a moment, in the last but one encounter – with the artist Fergus – suspense is heightened with Julie apparently vacillating and becoming attracted to him. However, just as with Racine, the outcome (i.e. successful completion of her mission of revenge) is certain and is a 'given' factor, virtually from the outset. Truffaut was simply experimenting with the dramatic device of suspense and in retrospect it is clear that nothing would have led Julie to abandon her task.

Hitchcock demonstrated with *Psycho* how easily a director could lead an audience to identify with a character on screen, even a morally dubious one and this is another point on which his influence on Truffaut is apparent. Despite the fact that Marion stole a large sum of money from her employer, the audience's sympathy is unmistakably on her side. The same identification, with the same attendant sympathy, occurs in the case of Truffaut's Julie Kohler: although she kills five men, using methods that are violent and clearly premeditated, the spectator supports her in her mission and wills her to wreak her 'just' revenge. Ambiguous presentation of morally suspect characters has in more recent times tended to become the norm but, in the majority of genre movies of the kind on which Truffaut was weaned, the lines between good and evil were more clearly drawn. Truffaut, after Hitchcock, was working against rather than with the conventions.

Where normally the conflict in a genre film tends towards the Manichaean in its pitting of good against evil, Truffaut presents us with, on the one hand, a highly ambiguous central protagonist and, on the other, with villains who scarcely live up to the name. Although Julie Kohler is the innocent victim of a bizarre accident, this does not excuse her subsequent actions and her adoption of the Old Testament 'eye for an eye and tooth for a tooth' philosophy. She simply cannot be considered as the just righter of wrongs. At the same time, the sequence in which the killers are introduced, reveals that the 'murder' was a stupid albeit tragic accident and that the men involved, while weak and reprehensible, were far from the customary cold-blooded psychopaths associated with the conventional thriller.

As in *Tirez*, there is a strong female whose actions determine the direction of the narrative. However, on this occasion, the nuanced analysis of male–female relationships is conspicuously absent. Given her murderous task, Julie forms no more than brief and superficial ties with her victims. Her personality is barely developed beyond exposition of the single force which drives her: the need to avenge the death of her husband. The male characters are again weak, displaying, in varying degrees, vanity, lechery, pomposity, self-centredness and, in the case of Coral, pathos and loneliness. They are no match for Julie and fall easy prey to her manœuvrings. If there is thematic content in the film, other than the exploration of the formal aspects of film itself, it is to be found here, in the presentation of five male stereotypes. In this sense, Julie is no more than a device facilitating this analysis. Once again, therefore, Hollywood conventions are undermined by the choice of a positive heroine who dictates the plot, by the presence of a series of decidedly unheroic males and by the abandonment of the usual focus of thrillers – the 'whodunnit' factor.

There is, finally, another significant aspect of *La Mariée* which marks a deviation from convention: that of verisimilitude. This was a topic much discussed by Truffaut in his conversations with Hitchcock. It is evident that, contrary to the established norms of genre films which sought to ensure watertight credibility in terms of aspects such as characters, motives, setting, plot and theme, neither was willing to make particular efforts to achieve and maintain realism, their aims lay elsewhere. For Hitchcock, realism was not a challenge: it was too easy to achieve; it was for people without imagination. As far as Truffaut was concerned, ultimately it led only to the documentary – and he had scant regard for that form of the medium (Truffaut 1983: 81–2).

Just as Hitchcock did not feel it worth the trouble to shoot the three sequences that would have been necessary to 'explain' the presence of the female ornithologist in the diner in *The Birds*, so Truffaut had little inclination to show how Julie Kohler identified and located her victims or to explain why the police did not pick up her trail earlier or, when they eventually did, arrest her. The spectator concerned with verisimilitude is not wholly convinced by Morane's death by asphyxiation or by the ease with which Julie is able to procure and use a knife while in prison in order to kill Delvaux. The need to persuade the audience that what they are watching is 'real' leads to varied degrees of contortion on the part of most directors. Truffaut, like Hitchcock, simply did not waste time on aspects of film-making which he considered banal.

Fahrenheit 451

Of Truffaut's essays in genre, *Fahrenheit 451*, a science fiction film, is the only one that is not a *film noir*. Adapted from Ray Bradbury's novel of the same name, it endured a lengthy and difficult period of gestation: there were problems with the rights to the novel, with finance and, once shooting began, with Oskar Werner who played the lead role. A first viewing suggests that on this occasion Truffaut set out to make a genuine science fiction film, thus compromising his *auteur* status.

The iconography of the genre is more prominent than in the preceding films. Like the novel, *Fahrenheit* is set in an unspecified future in which a highly impersonal, totalitarian regime – there are historical (book-burning during the Third Reich) and literary (Orwell's *1984*) allusions – is in power. Truffaut sets out to evoke this society in the ways familiar to science fiction *aficionados*: through clothes, transport (the monorail), anonymous concrete apartment blocks, the interactive, wall-to-wall television.

Further evidence of *Fahrenheit*'s adherence to the genre lies in its adoption of a number of innovative concepts of the kind that constitute the *sine qua non* of science fiction films: the notion that firemen start rather than put out fires, that the state is present in the home through interactive television, that people can literally 'become' books (book-people). Moreover, the fact that Truffaut is adapting quite faithfully the novel from which these ideas are taken reinforces the notion that he is abdicating his role as *auteur*. Inevitably, the closer a film is to its source, the less space there is for its director to develop his or her own world-view.

Another indication that *Fahrenheit* observes the conventions of the genre more closely than its predecessors can be found in the film's thematic core. Normally, this is the area in which Truffaut, in his genre films, most strongly asserts his individuality as an *auteur*. However, while the deep-seated love of literature and books which sustains the film thematically is one which Truffaut undeniably shared, it is equally apparent that the expression of it is, in this instance, Bradbury's and not his own. In this sense, this film is one of the least personal of Truffaut's works. The central tenet that the spirit of a society will survive any attempt to crush it through the eradication of its culture is one that most educated people would share. The concept itself, however, conveyed through the rather laborious metaphor of the 'book-people', weighs the film down and deprives it of life. Significantly perhaps, there is a marked absence of humour, or at least intended humour, in *Fahrenheit*.

As a consequence of this attenuation of his *auteur* status, some of the familiar components of a Truffaut film function only imperfectly. The normally fertile ground of male–female relationships yields little on this occasion: Montag's wife Linda is so impregnated with state propaganda that she is no more than a zombie; his relationship with Clarisse, the woman who befriends him, is so narrowly focused on their overriding aim of preserving the content of books that this relationship also fails to develop in any meaningful way. Montag himself is, at least in the long run, an untypically strong male. Once Clarisse has awakened his curiosity and overcome his doubts, his dedication to books is absolute and his willingness to risk his job, marriage and even his life for them quite unshakeable.

Fahrenheit, then, subscribes to many of the conventions of the science fiction film. In following the source text more closely than in other films, Truffaut has inevitably yielded a degree of authorial independence. A second viewing, however, reveals that, although he has made significant concessions to the genre at the expense of his *auteur* status, the final product is not wholly authentic. In spite of the greater prominence attached to the iconography, the usual irony is apparent in the rather half-hearted and detached way in which it is presented. Close observation of the monorail suggests carriages move in both directions despite the fact that it is a single-track system! The clothes and uniforms are bizarre rather than consistently futuristic while the fire engine is positively old-fashioned, and the blocks of flats, albeit modernistic, are recognisably those of a present-day city. Furthermore, there is a comparative absence of one of the staples of the science fiction film: special effects, unless, that is, one counts the unremarkable use of reverse motion which enables the fireman to move up as well as down their pole.

In the final analysis, Truffaut does not fully sacrifice his *auteur* identity. He is more interested in what constitutes a science fiction film than in the realisation of a convincing example of the genre. It is the notion of pure cinema that attracts him and, on this occasion, the aim of narrating the story through images rather than dialogue – there are long sections of the film from which the human voice is absent, for example the lengthy opening sequence which sets up much of the plot. Such is the coldness of the characters – with the possible exception of Clarisse (played by Julie Christie who struck up a good working relationship with Truffaut) – and the automated world they inhabit that the spectator does not really care whether or not Montag and Clarisse survive. Suspense is thus sacrificed and the importance of the outcome diminished.

Vivement dimanche!

If *Fahrenheit* represented compromise of *auteur* status, *Vivement dimanche!*, more than any of its predecessors, succeeds in fusing genre and *auteur* elements. On the one hand Truffaut, with painstaking care, produced an authentic *film noir*, on the other his integrity as *auteur* remained robustly intact.

On one level, the final product appears closer to pastiche than to parody as Truffaut incorporates numerous aspects of the B-movie version of *film noir* in an attempt to recreate rather than subvert the genre. The unfashionable and commercially risky choice of black and white film stock was undoubtedly driven by the desire to reproduce the chiaroscuro ambience of the genre. The prevalent low-key lighting reinforces this as does the underground, urban world of club, brothel and gambling which the film, in large part, inhabits. No coincidence (other perhaps than the convenient proximity of the Studio Victorine) that the film is set on or near the Provençal coast, whose cities (Marseille, Nice) have long been associated with crime. Other aspects of the décor similarly serve to recreate the ambience of the *film noir*: dark streets, pools of light, a police station, a red-light district, a night club. And the iconography of the genre is present too: guns, knives, corpses, false identity, finger prints, revolving panels, private detectives, uniformed police, lawyers, police interrogations. Flashback, a frequent signifier of the genre, is used twice in the film: to narrate Julien's discovery of Marie-Christine's body and Barbara's uncovering of the link between Maître Clément's office and Marie-Christine's beauty parlour. Binding these elements together and bringing the film closer than any of its predecessors to the actuality of *film noir* as opposed to parody of it, is the fact that Truffaut, working against one of his established principles, constructs his film unambiguously as a 'whodunnit'. It is only in the last but one sequence that the identity of the killer is revealed. Even the idea of drawing the villain from the ranks of the least likely suspect – a close friend of the protagonist and one of society's most respected upholders of order, the lawyer Clément – is one common to many a Hollywood B-movie.

In many respects, then, this film echoes *Fahrenheit* in that Truffaut appears to have allowed the balance to tip in favour of the vehicle – the *film noir* frame – and away from his own world-view. However, unlike the science fiction film, *Vivement* is as much a Truffaut film as is *Tirez*, or even a Doinel film. On this occasion, although the scenario is based on Charles Williams's *The Long Saturday Night*, Truffaut's adaptation of it is much freer than was the case with Ray Bradbury's novel, allowing him the space to express his own concerns. It is in the subversion of one of the genre's staple roles, the *femme fatale*, that his ironic intention is made clear.

The two female leads both qualify, though in different ways, for the role of *femme fatale*. The decidedly vampish and deceitful wife of Vercel, Marie-Christine, emerges early on in the film as a primary candidate although it very quickly becomes clear that she is a caricature of the type, above all in the scene in which she somewhat absurdly seeks to seduce her husband while reading the newspaper and, while the accompanying music is appropriately moody, her make-up and manicure, hairstyle and to some extent clothing are anachronistic in their attempt to ape the archetype. She is unrelievedly evil but it quickly transpires that hers is only a minor role and she is killed off violently and rather abruptly before the plot is really underway, thus clearly signalling subversion of both role and genre.

Barbara, Vercel's secretary, now moves to centre stage. Although her job as demure secretary, together with some aspects of her character, are not those of the conventional *femme fatale*, particularly as evidenced by Marie-Christine, she nevertheless possesses a number of the essential characteristics. 'Film noir gives a very central role to the *femme fatale* and privileges her as active, intelligent, powerful, dominant and in charge of her own sexuality' (Hayward 1996: 119). Barbara is all of these and Truffaut would therefore appear to be conforming to the stereotype in his depiction of his central female.

However, at this point, his persistent presentation of females as the stronger of the two sexes comes into the equation. Susan Hayward identifies the struggle for control of the narrative: 'In the end, film noir is about which voice is going to gain control over the story-telling ... This struggle occurs both between men and between the man and the woman, but more importantly, what this struggle foregrounds is the fact that the woman's image is just that: a male construct' (Hayward 1996: 120). The struggle for control between Barbara and Julien is frequently at the centre of the action as they vie for the right to conduct the investigation. Barbara wins the majority of these tussles, often by outwitting and out-manœuvring Julien. This is in marked contrast to the conventional *film noir* in which the *femme fatale* is in the end eliminated by the male, and the threat she poses is thereby removed. 'There has to be closure ... And in the end, closure does occur, but at a price. It is the male voice (that of the Symbolic Order, the Law of the Father) that completes the investigation' (Hayward 1996: 120). Not only is Barbara not eliminated but it is she who solves the mystery, persuades the police of her interpretation of events and gains their collaboration in the final setting up and unmasking of the killer.

In accomplishing this, she appropriates the male's clothing (his mac), his car and for a time even that archetypal symbol of male power, his gun. The mystery is solved by the female, with only minimal assistance from the mesmerised Julien and the ineffectual police.

There are a number of other signs that Truffaut *auteur* is alert and functioning. As in *Tirez*, there is an important and delightful sense of humour, generated in this film by Inspector Santelli with his curious and constant preoccupation with age and his accident-prone behaviour (for example the episode of the malfunctioning tap), and also by the very amateur amateur dramatics. The lampooning of the police recalls the similar gentle mocking, of the gangsters, in *Tirez* and serves at the same time to remind the spectator of the presence of the *auteur* behind his 'genre' mask. There are also a number of irrelevancies which no tautly structured B-movie would have tolerated, for example the interview with the new secretary and Barbara's play rehearsals. Such scenes, while having no place in a *film noir*, certainly have a function in a Truffaut film and closer inspection reveals that once again, riding on the 'genre' vehicle, are a number of familiar Truffaldian themes. Julien, in his fascination with women and particularly with their legs and whether they are blonde or brunette (the new secretary), is very obviously a brother of Bertrand Morane, 'the man who loved women'. The presence of the theatre is also familiar terrain (cf. *Le Dernier Métro*) – the play chosen and the scenes used in rehearsal are not without a certain ironic relevance to the film's themes. So too is the sense of play involved in the numerous intertextual references (another echo of *Tirez*): the private detective agency is closely modelled on the Blady Agency from *Baisers volés* to the extent that the *mise-en-scène* of one sequence in *Vivement* – the agency staff being briefed by its head – is almost a reshooting of the original in *Baisers volés*. The shot of Massoulier's brother – the priest – reflected and distorted in the car's wing mirror is an echo of the shot of the gangsters, Ernest and Momo, in Léna's hand mirror in *Tirez*.

Finally, Truffaut's authorship is apparent in his subversion of another staple element of American cinema, this time the 'mismatched couple' of comedy films of the Cary Grant–Doris Day variety, examples of which can be found in the Hitchcock repertoire. In the classic scenario, the couple are, for most of the film, at odds with one another, engaging in a war of wit and words, before finally and inevitably falling in love. Barbara, as a typically independent Truffaldian heroine, gives as good as she gets in her clashes with her boss. In this she confirms the stereotype and, following in the footsteps of many a Hollywood heroine, finally falls into the hero's (Julien's) arms. However, whereas Barbara may be a good match for Doris Day and any of Hollywood's other spritely, witty females, Julien more closely resembles the typical frail male of Truffaut's previous films and is far removed from Hollywood's macho male as typified by Cary Grant. Further, although the suspense-generating device of focusing the whole film on an innocent man falsely accused of murder is unquestionably attributable to Hitchcock, Truffaut does not wholly forfeit his identity as *metteur-en-scène* and the ambience of guilt and fear which permeates Hitchcock's films is most notable for its absence here. The heavy moral overtones and sense of anguish are simply not part of Truffaut's world-view and, in the context of the debt to Hitchcock, it would appear that while the borrowing was substantial, it remains on the level of a homage and the essential qualities of Truffaut the *auteur* are not seriously called into question.

In the final analysis and in what was to be his last film, Truffaut marries, then, almost perfectly the two concepts of genre and *auteur*. The film has the poise, elegance and humour of Hitchcock at his best. It is a 'whodunnit', it is a *film noir*. But these goals have not been achieved at the expense of Truffaut's identity as *auteur*. The frequent privileging of references to process, culminating in Barbara's bold declaration to camera which closes the flashback in the beauty parlour, reinforce the ever-present Truffaldian theme of cinema itself, a theme on which he here imposed a neat conclusion by resolving the genre/*auteur* debate and showing that the two approaches need not be in opposition but could exist together in balanced and productive harmony. It also centres on a couple and on the gradual formation of a relationship between them. In this, it was, of course, on central Truffaut ground.

References

Chabrol, Claude and Rohmer, Eric (1957), *Hitchcock*, Paris, Editions universitaires.
Cook, Pam (ed.) (1985), *The Cinema Book*, London, British Film Institute.
Hayward, Susan (1996), *Key Concepts in Cinema Studies*, London, Routledge.
Houston, Penelope (1961), Uncommitted artist?, *Sight and Sound*, 30, pp. 64–5.
Ryall, Tom (1979), *Teachers' study guide 2: The Gangster Film*, London, British Film Institute.
Truffaut, François (1966), *Le Cinéma selon Alfred Hitchcock*, Paris, Robert Laffont.
Truffaut, François (1979), *The Book of the Cinema*, ed. D. Allen *et al.*, London, Mitchell Beazley.
Truffaut, François (1983), *Hitchcock/Truffaut*, Paris, Editions Ramsay.
Truffaut, François (1987), *Le Plaisir des yeux*, Paris, Cahiers du Cinéma.
Truffaut, François (1988), *Correspondance*, Paris, Hatier.

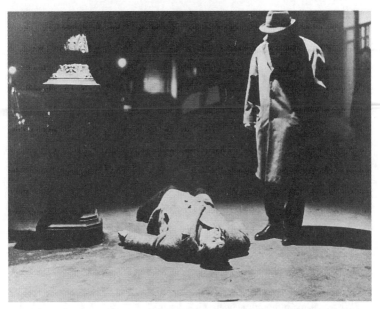

1 The first indications are that this is a *film noir*. Albert Rémy as Chico in *Tirez sur le pianiste*, 1960 (photo: Pierre Zucca)

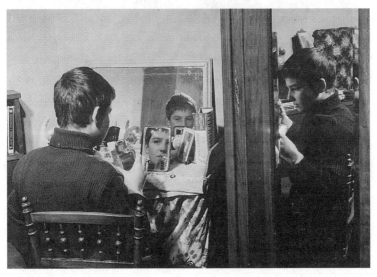

2 The absent mother is evoked as her son sits at her dressing table. Jean-Pierre Léaud as Antoine Doinel in *Les 400 coups*, 1959 (photo: André Dino)

3 Truffaut's filming of sex is generally discreet and elliptical and features the recurring image of the man's hand caressing stocking tops. Catherine Deneuve as Marion and Jean-Paul Belmondo as Louis in *La Sirène du Mississippi*, 1969 (photo: Léonard de Raemy)

4 Big women/small men. Jean-Pierre Léaud as Antoine Doinel in *Baisers volés*, 1968 (photo: Raymond Cauchetier)

5 The thwarted desires of mothers to abort their sons are realised on screen through the murders of men by women. Jeanne Moreau as Julie Kohler in *La Mariée était en noir*, 1967 (photo: Marilu Parolini)

6 Vercel's wife is an almost parodic version of the *film noir* woman. Caroline Sihol as Marie-Christine Vercel and Jean-Louis Trintignant as Julien Vercel in *Vivement dimanche!*, 1982 (photo: Alain Venisse)

7 and **8** [below and facing, at head] Both sides of paternity – the acquisition of language means both joy and loss. François Truffaut as Dr Itard and Jean-Pierre Cargol as Victor in *L'Enfant sauvage*, 1970 (photo: Pierre Zucca)

9 Film-making methods and the *provisoire*: Julie's own words are re-presented to her as dialogue in a shot where visual framing foregrounds the constructed nature of the image. Jacqueline Bisset as Julie Baker, Nike Arrighi as Odile and David Markham as Dr Nelson in *La Nuit américaine*, 1973 (photo: Pierre Zucca)

5

Magic mothers: the sexual politics of Truffaut's films

'Are women magic?'

One of the authorial signs that circulates from one Truffaut film to another is the question (sometimes formulated in the affirmative, as a statement): are women magic? Though enunciated, for the most part, by characters with whom we are not invited to identify or sympathise, such as the surly bar-owner Plyne in *Tirez sur le pianiste* or the spoilt, petulant Alphonse in *La Nuit américaine*, the notion that there is something inherently mysterious and wonderful about women also seems to drive the narratives of more positive heroes, beginning with the *mistons* whose adoration of Bernadette depends upon belief in her radical otherness from themselves, continuing through the stories of Antoine Doinel, Charlie Kohler, Jules and Jim, all the way to Julien Vercel, in the last film, *Vivement dimanche!* gazing up enraptured at the window through which he can observe the legs of female passersby. The title of the 1977 film *The Man Who Loved Women* might be used to define if not all, at least the majority of Truffaut's heroes.

To the spectator who has even a glancing familiarity with feminism, the question 'Are women magic?' is immediately suspect. To define woman as magic is, as Simone de Beauvoir observed half a century ago, to define her 'exclusively in her relation to man ... not ... positively, such as she seems to herself to be, but negatively, such as she appears to man' (Beauvoir 1949: 174–5). In other words, the idealisation of women, like their demonisation, functions to deny them the status of human subject. Truffaut's sexual politics – or more accurately those of his films – have been condemned by more than one feminist critic. Françoise Audé calls him 'le cinéaste de la haine de la mère'[1] (Audé 1981: 49) and describes his attitude to women as 'defensive and vengeful'. Susan Hayward proposes that the liberal, nice-guy Truffaut of popular fame is an 'imposter' who serves to conceal the 'suppressed misogyny' of filmic scripts which repeatedly 'punish the (m)other for the absence of the father' (Hayward 1994: 50, 52). Other critics sensitive to issues of gender politics offer dissenting views: Annette Insdorf argues for a progression in Truffaut's work towards the representation of 'a whole and modern woman' (Insdorf 1989: 148); Anne Gillain agrees with Audé and Hayward on the centrality of the mother–son relationship in Truffaut's work, but finds in his films a sustained attempt to explore the aggression this contains and to 'restaurer avec (la mère) une situation d'échange et de compréhension'[2] (Gillain 1991: 22). We will return to the case for the defence, but first we need to explore the case for the prosecution of Truffaut as the author of misogynist films.

Films that hate women?

Truffaut's first feature film, *Les 400 Coups*, is the most directly autobiographical of his works. It follows a few months in the life of Antoine Doinel, a twelve-year-old boy growing up between unloving parents and a repressive, uninspiring school, from which he takes refuge in truancy, petty crime, and the cinema. Audiences and critics responded warmly to the film – and still do – because with great narrative and aesthetic economy, and without sentimentality, it gives to Antoine's story both the awkward texture of personal experience, and the mythic resonance of fundamental emotional drives: the desire to be loved, contradictory impulses toward social integration and anti-social revolt, the need to order the world through stories. With very few exceptions (such as the visit of the

1 'the director who puts mother-hatred on the screen'.
2 'rebuild (with the mother) a situation of exchange and understanding.'

class tell-tale to Antoine's parents, and Madame Doinel's interview with the judge when she asks for her son to be sent to a young offenders' institution – both scenes which confirm sympathy for Antoine) Antoine is present in all sequences: he is the pivot of the narrative and of the film's thematic concerns. The spectator's access to information sometimes exceeds that of Antoine, but the predominant perspective is a subjective one, that of the adolescent male hero.

Antoine inhabits a social world that is almost entirely male: the school is single-sex, the cafés and amusement centres he frequents with his friend René are predominantly male spaces, the institutions that represent the State's authority – school, police and youth detention centre – are staffed by men. Women appear only in highly sexualised roles: the schoolboys pass around a pin-up photo; a dinner-table conversation reveals that women at work are subject to sexual harassment and assumed to gain promotion solely in exchange for sex; the only women in the police station are prostitutes; as Antoine is driven away from Paris the police van passes through the streets of Pigalle emblazoned with neon signs advertising 'the most daring nudes in the world'. At one level, the sense of a city run by men and catering to male desires is part of the film's mimetic representation of contemporary life, for the society depicted here – which is both that of Truffaut's childhood, and that of the 1950s – defined authority and sexuality in masculine terms. The absence of women, though, also has the effect of intensifying and generalising the significance of the film's one major female protagonist, Antoine's mother. Given the structures of spectator identification built into the film, it is almost impossible to see the sole female protagonist other than through the desires and the hostility of her son – for whom she is a powerful and magical figure, albeit an almost wholly negative one.

Antoine's feelings for his mother are rapidly established in the film as both intense and ambivalent. The opening schoolroom sequence demonstrates the bleakness of Antoine's life outside the home; the second sequence shows him alone in a small, shabby flat, where the absent mother is evoked as her son sits at her dressing table, looks at himself in her mirrors, smells her perfume – the

emotional implications of the scene reinforced by the soundtrack's reprise of a few bars of the film's poignant musical refrain.
Desire for the mother precedes her arrival on the screen: when
she appears, strikingly blonde and glamorous against the
shabbiness of the apartment, an economical scene establishes the
key features of the mother–son relationship. With scarcely a
greeting, she rebukes Antoine for failing to do his chores, sends
him to fetch her slippers, and removes her stockings, displaying
her legs with complete disregard for his awakening sexuality.
When Antoine leaves on an errand to the local shop, the camera
lingers on the mother's narcissistic gaze at her own reflection in
the mirror. Madame Doinel is the archetypal 'bad mother', refusing
to provide the maternal warmth and protection associated with
breast and womb, self-absorbed and indifferent to her son's
emotional and confusedly erotic desires. When, with Antoine, we
overhear a conversation revealing that he was illegitimate and that
his mother would have preferred an abortion, the sense of his
maternal deprivation is complete – though in narrative terms it is
still to be worked out as Madame Doinel succeeds in expelling
him from her life into the care of a State institution. A different
film might have situated the mother's lack of maternal feeling in
the context of poverty, the illegality of contraception and abortion
and the stigma of unmarried motherhood in post-war France, but
here only a reading against the grain – one that would explicitly
ignore the film's own signifying mechanisms – could make these
factors relevant.

Antoine is thus both repelled and fascinated by the maternal;
he both longs for and hates his mother – an ambivalence represented
through a series of apparently unconnected episodes. Antoine
gags on hearing a conversation about childbirth as he waits in the
shopping queue; when he runs away from home and sleeps
overnight in a deserted printworks, the camera dwells on him
alone in the deserted city streets, breakfasting on a stolen bottle of
milk, which the poignant music links to the absent mother; when
Antoine needs an excuse for having missed school he produces a
spontaneous and emphatic 'She [i.e. his mother] is *dead*, sir' – and
the cinema audience often laughs, so enormous is the lie, and so

striking the emotional truth. Although the society that fails to integrate Antoine Doinel is an essentially male society, his downward trajectory is linked more persuasively to his desire for and lack of maternal love – so that when, in the closing sequence, he escapes and runs doggedly toward the sea (which he has never yet seen), it does not seem far-fetched to read beneath the French *la mer* (the sea) its homonym *la mère* (the mother). In the light of the preceding narrative it is not surprising either that the sea/ mother presents no escape, so that Antoine turns back towards the camera and ends the film on a freeze-frame of irresolution. In Truffaut's first full-length film, the mother is seen only through the eyes of her son – as intensely desirable, emotionally and sexually, and as cruelly unattainable. As the only woman on screen for most of the film, she inevitably comes to stand for women in general – and the spectator is firmly positioned with the film's male subject.

The structure of male subjective viewpoint and women characters seen externally, through the lens of male desire, is one that recurs in Truffaut's work. It is powerfully at work in *Jules et Jim* where the mysterious, enigmatic Catherine is visually and diegetically at the heart of the film – but Catherine's seductive power depends upon a refusal to see her as subject, on the insistence that she transcends (and therefore lacks) normal humanity. The film opens with an energetic and humorous collage of short sequences (fast-cutting, mobile camera work, exuberant musical score) which situates the two heroes, Jules and Jim, in the Paris of 1912 and foregrounds their close friendship against a background of cultured leisure, free and easy sexual relationships, cosmopolitan fun. Catherine, significantly, appears in the heroes' fantasies before she appears in person: the friends see a slide of a beautiful statue on a distant island in the Adriatic, and travel there. The statue's mysterious smile enchants them: they experience their discovery as a 'revelation', and agree that if ever they meet such a smile in life, they will follow it. Catherine appears in their lives in the following sequence, smiling the irresistible smile, and for the rest of the film characters and camera follow the vision they have created. Catherine, played by a compellingly beautiful

Jeanne Moreau, is seductive, unpredictable, unfaithful, the embodiment of that 'whirlwind of love' of which she sings – in short, she corresponds to a conventionally masculine view of woman as delightful enigma. The dark side of the 'woman is magic' syndrome appears when she also becomes murderous – the *femme fatale* is literally fatal, and after a failed attempt to shoot Jim she ends the film by enacting a simultaneous murder and suicide. Catherine remains the creature of the male friends' fantasies, the larger-than-life projection of their desires and fears. The film, like the novel on which it was based, and like the majority of Truffaut's subsequent films, positions the spectator with its male heroes.

The attribution of the subject-position to the male protagonist produces one of the most conventional aspects of Truffaut's filming: desire is always represented through shots of the semi-naked female body, never the male. The ubiquitous shots of female legs are a well-known Truffaldian motif ('are women's *legs* magic?' wonders a character in *La Nuit américaine*), generally signifying both the desire of a male character and the camera/film's complicity with this desire. Thus *L'Homme qui aimait les femmes* contains numerous shots of women's legs, seen through the eyes of Bertrand Morane for whom 'les jambes des femmes sont des compas qui arpentent le globe terrestre en tous sens, lui donnant son équilibre et son harmonie',[3] but the camera repeats this partial framing of the female body after Bertrand's death, when a point of view shot is no longer logically possible. Similarly, although Truffaut's filming of sex is generally discreet and elliptical, this ellipsis characteristically takes the form of a shot of bared female flesh: a fleeting image of the man's hand caressing stocking tops and the skin above recurs in several films including *La Peau douce, La Sirène du Mississippi, Le Dernier Métro, La Femme d'à côté*. In a bedroom scene of *La Femme d'à côté*, the fact that Mathilde and Bernard have just made love is signalled visually by the semi-nudity of Mathilde (Fanny Ardant), Bernard (Gérard Depardieu) is fully dressed throughout. In his visual representations

3 'women's legs are compasses that measure out the globe, bringing balance and harmony'.

of sex, Truffaut maintains a solely male (heterosexual) perspective, thus following the normal conventions of a cultural medium so far dominated by men.

As spectators then, we are on the whole positioned by script, *mise-en-scène* and editing to share a male-subjective viewpoint and to see women as 'other'. However, the heroes whose view of the world we are invited to share are far from conventionally masculine or macho figures. Truffaut's choice of actors here is significant, in that it reveals a marked preference for men whose small stature, slight build and delicate facial features disqualify them from the robustly virile roles of a John Wayne or even a Jean Gabin. Jean-Pierre Léaud, the child actor who starred in *Les 400 Coups*, brings to the part of the adult Antoine Doinel a face and body that connote vulnerability and an anxious, nervous energy; his relative smallness and air of fragility are shared by Charles Aznavour (*Tirez sur le pianiste*), Charles Denner (*La Mariée était en noir* and *L'Homme qui aimait les femmes*), Truffaut himself (acting in *L'Enfant sauvage* and *La Chambre verte*) and (though he can look quite different in the films of other directors) Jean-Louis Trintignant (*Vivement dimanche!*). In three films, Truffaut employs male actors whose physical appearance connotes the strength, assertiveness and emotional control of the orthodox hero, but these qualities are undercut by script and direction, bringing Jean-Paul Belmondo (playing a shy and inexperienced lover in *La Sirène du Mississippi*) and Gérard Depardieu (in both *Le Dernier Métro* and *La Femme d'à côté* a confident, successful man whose assurance is severely shaken by a woman) closer to the diffidence and emotional helplessness of the standard Truffaldian male.

Small men/big women

Truffaut's men, then, rarely possess the advantages of greater size and sense of socially conferred authority granted to the more orthodox hero. This departure from the conventions of gender representation is visually underscored in many Truffaut films by scenes which emphasise the discrepancy between small man and tall woman – most famously in comic mode in *Baisers volés*, when Antoine's explanation to a friend that he prefers tall girls is accompanied by a shot from behind of Antoine walking down the street accompanied by an elegant woman who towers head and shoulders above him. When Charlie is wounded in *Tirez sur le pianiste*, their relative sizes mean that Léna can virtually carry him to safety; visiting a brothel in *Domicile conjugal*, Antoine selects the tallest of the prostitutes, a woman considerably larger than himself. The size relationship here recalls that between the children of *Les Mistons* and the taller, adult Bernadette, and that between the adolescent Antoine and his mother. Truffaut's heroes in fact bear less resemblance to standard patriarchal representations of the adult male than they do to those of the male child – they are timid, uncertain of their own abilities, tend to idealise or demonise women whom they experience as quite foreign to themselves. They also display the least attractive characteristics of the immature: egoism, failure to recognise the needs of others, an obsessive concern with the absolute gratification of their own desires – here largely figured as *sexual* desires.

Truffaut's men can, in fact, usefully be read in psychoanalytical terms, as cases of failed Oedipal development – a fact which has not escaped the attention of critics (Gillain 1991; Hayward 1994). This is not the place to discuss in detail the problems raised by Freud's model of the Oedipal complex – deeply inflected as it is by patriarchal assumptions – nor the nature of subsequent feminist revisions; suffice it to say that the model proposed here draws on feminist re-readings of Freudian theory (notably that of Jessica Benjamin) which emphasise, much more than the original, the importance of intersubjectivity and of reciprocal relations with the mother. According to this model, the male infant begins life (at least under normal Western child-rearing arrangements) in close relationship with the mother, who fulfils his needs and is virtually indistinguishable from himself. In order to negotiate the passage to individual identity, he must separate, a process both painful and pleasurable. To separate or individuate successfully, he needs to internalise a sense of the mother's love, thus maintaining a connection with the earliest experience of desire and satisfaction, and to see himself as distinct from her, as a separate subject both like her and different from her. The intervention of a father figure plays a crucial role here, representing an alternative source of identification based on what differentiates son from mother. If the process fails, if the delicate but necessary tension between separation and connection breaks down, then this produces idealisation of the mother (she is all that he has desired and lost) or demonisation of her (she threatens his autonomy, she threatens to re-engulf him if he is not careful). The adult male who has failed to negotiate this process successfully will carry this attitude into relations with women: women will appear either desperately desirable (the lost mother) or terrifyingly powerful (the threatening, re-engulfing mother). Either way, his inability to see in the (m)other another subjectivity, both like himself and different from himself, will ensure that the relationship can not work.

This model helps to explain why so many of the films are driven in narrative terms by the hero's serial quest for love and sex. In both the Doinel cycle, and in *L'Homme qui aimait les femmes*, the narrative makes an explicit link between the unsatisfactory relationship with the mother, and a subsequent near-obsessive search for elusive satisfaction in heterosexual relationships. In the sequels to *Les 400 Coups*, Antoine Doinel pursues a series of women (of whom the most significant are Colette, Christine Darbon, Fabienne Tabard, Kyoko and Sabine), passionate in the quest, but losing interest once his affections are returned. Like Antoine, Bertrand Morane, or 'the man who loved women' grows up with a mother who is both sexually desirable and emotionally cold: in a flashback to Bertrand's adolescence, the mother is shown walking along the street, in a series of shots framing face and legs that connect her directly to all the women Bertrand pursues in adult life. Bertrand's voice-over tells us that she often expresses the wish that he had never been born; her facial expression as she speaks to him is cool, impassive, in contrast to the hesitant, eager-to-please smile of Bertrand's younger self. Bertrand spends the rest of his life, and the rest of the film, in pursuit of an endless series of women whose unattainability is the condition of his desire. Though the film is at pains to emphasise Bertrand's 'love' for women as a sex, and their collective affection for him, several episodes also make it clear that his serial promiscuity is at the expense of many of the partners he abandons on the way.

From the perspective of the childlike hero, the mother/woman has the power to satisfy all his needs, and is thus overwhelmingly desirable and 'magic'. Her power may also, however, make her frightening – the son's inability to transcend his yearning for the mother, thus to fully enter the men's world, makes her a castrating figure. We have already seen how this translates visually into a reversal of the usual-size relationships; it also produces a number of female killers in Truffaut's films. The thwarted desires of Madame Doinel, Madame Morane (and possibly Madame Truffaut?) to abort their sons are realized on screen through the repeated murders of men by women: Catherine (*Jules et Jim*) threatens to put out the eyes of faithless men with vitriol, tries to shoot Jim and finally drowns him; Franca (*La Peau douce*) shoots Pierre; Julie Kohler (*La Mariée était en noir*) coolly and efficiently murders five men; the *Mississippi Mermaid* tries to poison Louis (and murders the woman whose identity she steals); Camille Bliss (*Une Belle Fille comme moi*) merrily kills the men who get in her way; Mathilde (*La Femme d'à côté*), like Catherine, closes the film by killing herself and the man she loves but cannot have. Seen only in terms of their (in)capacity to satisfy the emotional and erotic needs of the son/lover, women in Truffaut's films are both magical and murderous.

We hope to have shown that accusations of misogyny and mother-hatred in Truffaut's cinema are in many respects well founded. The surface impression of a cinema that is unusually 'feminist' in its portrayal of passive men and strong, active women cannot survive closer analysis of how the films work: the reversal of gender stereotypes does not necessarily disturb the basic structure of a male-subjective viewpoint that constructs women as the fantasised objects of desire or as the castrating, death-dealing 'bad mother'. And yet we have been conscious, in setting out the case for the 'prosecution', of the need to be selective in the choice of evidence, and of a disquieting mismatch between the coherence of the reading offered above, and the more ambivalent and contradictory responses both of ourselves and of many students – particularly female students – to the sexual politics of Truffaut's films. The case outlined above is true but it is also incomplete, and we would like now to marshal the counter-evidence, the aspects of Truffaut's cinema that argue against their straightforward relegation to the (crowded) ranks of misogynist cinema.

Undermining misogyny

From his early days as a film critic, Truffaut displays contradictory attitudes to the medium's tendency to present the world from an androcentric point of view. On the one hand, his film reviews share many of the complacently patriarchal assumptions of the 1950s: he mocks the moralists' objections to the display of Brigitte Bardot's body in Vadim's *Et Dieu créa la femme*, but apparently fails to see that this might also raise questions about the objectification of women, and many of his reviews reveal 'a fetishistic obsession with the details of constructed sexuality' (Wheeler Dixon 1993: 5), lingering over Monroe's underwear, for example, in a review of *Niagara* (1953). On the other hand, he consistently takes Monroe, Bardot and other female stars seriously, in terms of their acting skills rather than their bodies alone. A 1960 article 'Cinéma, univers de l'absence' ('Cinema, a world of absence') suggests some awareness of the problems raised by a medium totally dominated by men at the levels of production and direction, but consumed by a mixed audience in which the majority of spectators (at least according to Truffaut) were female. Truffaut states his belief that in a couple it is usually the woman who chooses which film to see, not only because women go to the cinema more often, but also because female spectators are *better* spectators, 'particulièrement sensibles à ce mode d'expression qu'est un film' and '*plus* vivement intéressées que les hommes par la personnalité de l'œuvre'.[4] And yet 'jusqu'à présent les films ont été faits par des

4 'particularly sensitive to film as a medium' [and] 'more interested than men in the personality of the work.'

hommes *pour* des hommes';[5] Truffaut finds *Hiroshima mon amour* (made by Alain Resnais in 1959 from a script by Marguerite Duras) to be 'le premier film véritablement fait pour des femmes, en tout cas le premier à nous montrer non une poupée charmante ou une vamp, mais une vraie femme'.[6] 'Pour la première fois au cinéma', he concludes, 'l'égalité de la femme est évidente dès la première image jusqu'au mot Fin'[7] (Truffaut 1987: 15).

Authorial intention is never a sure guide to the meaning of a completed work, but we can posit some awareness on Truffaut's part of the sexual politics of his films – even in the conservative 1950s/early 1960s. In fact from the outset his films reveal the same ambivalence as his writing: running alongside the script of misogyny are indications of a more self-critical approach, invitations to the spectator to see the gender relations on screen not as natural but as problematic and open to question. Inevitably these signs partially destabilise the main script – indeed, as we shall see, in some films they take over and become the main script.

The *mise en abîme*

One such sign is the inclusion of *mise en abîme* scenes, brief, condensed, often humorous moments that mirror and foreground the gender dynamics at work in the film. This occurs as early as 1961 in *Tirez sur le pianiste*: whilst the main narrative follows a likeable hero through a repeated cycle of relationships in which his emotional inadequacy leads to the death of the woman, minor characters draw attention to the underlying misogyny of the prevailing culture. The film's duo of comic gangsters offer a meditation on the nature of women composed of familiar clichés: 'They all want it really'; 'I'm not against women I love them all – it's just having to talk to them before and after that gets me', the hostility and ill-founded arrogance of these sentiments pointed up

5 'up till now, films have been made by men *for* men' [authors' italitcs].

6 'the first film really made for women, at any rate the first to show not a pretty doll or a vamp but a real woman.'

7 'For the first time, the equality of women is apparent from the first shot to the words "The End".'

by the gangster's buffoonish appearance and professional incompetence – the dialogue takes place in the car as they kidnap Charlie and Léna, and ends when Léna outwits them and the two escape. Within the film's overall logic, Léna and Charlie form a couple opposed to the gangsters' crudely instrumentalist view of human relations – yet Charlie briefly joins in the misogynist litany, contributing 'Mon père disait toujours: quand on a vu une femme on les a vues toutes'.[8] Léna – who will re-enact the story of Charlie's first wife by loving him and dying for him – looks briefly taken aback, then joins in the laughter. *Tirez* also contains the first of Truffaut's proponents of the view that women are magic: the misanthropic, wife-beating bar-owner Plyne chooses the moment before he attempts to kill Charlie to articulate his belief that 'La femme est pure, délicate, fragile – la femme est suprême, la femme est magique',[9] and that therefore the forthright Léna, who has rejected his advances in robust language, is simply not a woman. Truffaut's second film invites sympathy with its hero's uncomprehending (and twice fatal) fascination with women, but it also puts on the screen 'a spectrum of distorted perceptions of women' (Insdorf 1989: 107) that throw a critical light on the hero and the cultural assumptions he shares.

Similar *mise en abîme* scenes occur in many of the films. *La Peau douce*, for example, a story of male infidelity, contains two scenes in which *dragueurs* (English has no neat translation – men who try to pick up women) accost unknown women in the street and harass them, enacting in miniature the hero's desire for a woman sufficiently unfamiliar and different (Pierre Lachenay and Nicole are separated by generation, lifestyle – and, since she is an air hostess, geographical distance) to sustain the fantasy of perfect sexual love. In a nightmarish sequence, the hero, a writer, invited to give a lecture in a provincial town and secretly accompanied by his mistress, finds himself trapped in a café in the company of a bore, unable to rescue Nicole as she wanders helplessly round the dark streets beyond the cafe window pursued by a relentless *dragueur*. The stranger offers a mirror image of Pierre Lachenay

8 'My father always said: when you've seen one woman you've seen them all.'
9 'Woman is pure, delicate, fragile – woman is supreme, woman is magic.'

himself: an older man, obsessively desiring, blind to Nicole's own feelings. The second *dragueur* approaches Lachenay's wife, Franca, in the moments after she has discovered her husband's infidelity. Smug, self-assured, indifferent to her refusals ('Wouldn't you like to go for a little walk with me? go back to my place?'), this *dragueur* gets his come-uppance in a scene that prefigures Franca's subsequent murder of Pierre. With a violence positively cathartic for women spectators who have been the victims of similar approaches, Franca grabs the embarrassed stranger by the throat and forces him (along with amused passers-by) to hear her anger. The humiliation of the situation is turned on the aggressor.

The unwanted seducer also appears, and gets his come-uppance, in that hymn to male seduction, *L'Homme qui aimait les femmes* – introducing a brief and humorous note of female resistance. A customer at a restaurant persistently unties the apron of the waitress as she passes, with an expression that makes it clear he finds himself both funny and charming – until on the fourth occasion she loses patience and judo-throws him over her head. Scenes such as these work by caricaturing attitudes to women which in their more fully-drawn and nuanced form are treated sympathetically by the films – they undermine the seamlessness of the films' men-only perspective.

Narrative irony

Truffaut's characteristically romantic, egotistical hero is the central focus of both narrative interest and spectator identification in thirteen out of the twenty-three films, but even here techniques which establish critical distance at times disturb the sense of complicity between film and protagonist. Although in *Les 400 Coups* the world is seen unequivocally from the point of view of Antoine, in the four sequels that complete the Doinel cycle, narrative sympathy with Antoine is frequently qualified by irony.

In the 1962 short film *Antoine et Colette*, Doinel's story resumes at the age of seventeen: he is shown enjoying the independence of working and living alone, but coming to grief in his attempts to seduce the more sophisticated Colette. Although the film's sympathy with Antoine never wavers, both the use of an extra-diegetic narrator (i.e. an unidentified voice-over) and certain techniques of editing and camerawork establish a critical space, from which we can observe not only the clumsiness of Antoine's tactics, but also the myopic nature of his desire which renders him blind to Colette's indifference. All of these elements come into play when Antoine moves into a rented room directly opposite the flat inhabited by Colette and her parents: the camera first pans back and forth across the space that separates Antoine's window from Colette's, emphasising their proximity, then cuts between Antoine and Colette's parents, as they converse across the gap. A downwards shot to the street indicates Antoine watching as Colette leaves the building; the narrator confirms that whilst the parents have 'adopted' Antoine, he has gained only a position as *voyeur* in relation to their daughter who 'treated him as a friend, exactly as she did before the move'. Two sequences later, Antoine and Colette are at the cinema: the scene cross-cuts between the newsreel they are watching and the couple themselves, juxtaposing a French skier stylishly descending the *piste* with Antoine hopefully taking Colette's hand, then the skier falling and losing the competition, with Antoine clumsily trying to kiss Colette, being rebuffed, and crossly admitting defeat. In each of these instances, the spectator sees Antoine's self-absorbed misreading of the situation more clearly than he can himself, and this creates space for a degree of identification with the exasperated Colette.

The extent to which Antoine Doinel is treated ironically varies between the films, but after *Les 400 Coups* the identification with his viewpoint on the world is always tempered to some degree by techniques which underline the partiality of his vision and illuminate (albeit briefly) the opposing vision of the women he encounters. If the Antoine of *Baisers volés* elevates Fabienne Tabard, the wife of his employer (played by Delphine Seyrig), to the status of magical 'apparition', and the lighting and *mise en scène* in early shots of her endorse this, she is nonetheless given a whole scene in which to refute Antoine's dehumanising romanticism. Antoine has written to her, declaring his love and comparing her to the virtuous, self-sacrificing heroine of Balzac's romantic *Le Lys dans la vallée.* Madame Tabard responds not by letter but by arriving early in the morning at Antoine's rented room where, in a now famous monologue, she explains the difference between an 'apparition' and a woman, and demonstrates her argument by proposing a contract between them, a contract that will be 'equitable for us both': she will join Antoine in bed for a few hours of pleasure, then they will part and agree never to see each other again. A contract, in other words, based on mutual desire and liking and the assumption that each can be sufficiently mature to limit their emotional investment. Although this enjoyable assault on his view of the world has no noticeable effect on Antoine's later behaviour, it makes it impossible to read the film as an unrelieved endorsement of his vision.

Scenes in which the female objects of Antoine's dreams, desires and selfish neglect articulate their own responses also occur in *Domicile conjugal.* Antoine's affair with a Japanese woman, Kyoko, leads to his departure from the marital flat he shares with Christine and their baby, but once at liberty to spend all his time with Kyoko he rapidly tires of her and punctuates their dinners at a restaurant with phonecalls to Christine. Kyoko finally leaves the restaurant, Antoine and the film with a farewell note that says simply (in Japanese) 'Go fuck yourself'. The indulgent Christine also adopts a more acerbic tone, responding to Antoine's litany of praise 'Tu es ma femme, ma petite sœur, mon amie...'[10] with a wry 'J'aurais aimé aussi être ta femme'.[11] In *L'Amour en fuite,* Colette reappears in Antoine's life and after a reunion in which he talks of himself to the total exclusion of any interest in her life, berates him for his self-centredness and dishonesty. Colette later forms an alliance with another Doinel 'ex' in conversation with Christine (who is interested in her story, though they have never met before). The attitude of the two women towards Antoine is maternally indulgent rather than hostile, but it emphasises the inadequacy of his emotional behaviour. The weight of narrative sympathy remains with Antoine Doinel, but the films contain the possibility of a counter-identification with his idols and victims.

10 'You are my mother, my little sister, my friend....'
11 'I'd like to have been your wife too.'

The special relationship between Truffaut and his alter ego, Doinel, more or less determined that the films would be told predominantly from his point of view until the cycle ended. In *La Nuit américaine* (1973), however, Truffaut invents a Doinel-like character outside the semi-autobiographical framework of the Doinel story. Alphonse, played by Jean-Pierre Léaud who was by now thoroughly identified with the Doinel role, is a selfish, immature young actor with a strong tendency to idolise women (and to ask the question 'are women magic?'), who almost manages to wreck the project which the film presents as the *summum bonum* of human endeavour, namely the making of a film. Alphonse is Antoine viewed with minimal sympathy: in a scene that seems to refer directly to Doinel rather than to a character of whose background we know nothing, his lover explains her decision to leave him, and articulates the feelings of most of the film crew: 'c'est pas parce qu'il a eu une enfance malheureuse qu'il a le droit d'emmerder tout le monde'.[12] Later in the film the same point is comically made through visual narration: deserted by his lover, Alphonse in turn deserts the film but is found, after much searching, by the assistant director – driving a toy go-kart at the track. The camera zooms in as Alphonse brakes and comes to a halt face to camera, his helmet perched absurdly above a peevish face, the picture of a cross and stubborn child.

We have already seen that *L'Homme qui aimait les femmes* contains a *mise en abîme* scene that introduces a discordant note of female anger at male complacency. This film – which in many respects seems to endorse the hero's conviction that serial seduction constitutes an almost spiritual project – undercuts its own phallocentrism in a number of ways. Bertrand's desire for women takes the initial form of scopophilia or pleasure in looking, the same pleasure that contributes to the experience of film-watching. When he sees a woman for the first time his eyes are drawn to her legs, and the camera mirrors his gaze: the body on the screen is fragmented, the attraction of the woman is first

12 'the fact that he had an unhappy childhood does not give him the right to be a pain in the neck to everyone he meets'. [The French *emmerder tout le monde* is marginally ruder.]

signalled by repeated shots of the lower half of her body. Although Bertrand's self-appointed mission as a seducer is treated seriously and sympathetically, the obsession with legs and with the endless pursuit of new conquests means that he objectifies his partners, reducing them to erotically charged bodies (or parts of bodies), with the charge dependent on their unfamiliarity. In a striking episode towards the middle of the film, the objectifying power of the gaze is foregrounded through a reversal of roles: Bertrand meets and fails to seduce the proprietress of a women's *lingerie* shop; that night, he dreams that he is displayed in her window as a dummy. In the dream, the shop-owner runs her hands down the dummy's legs, then lifts one trouser leg to reveal black sock suspenders; on the other side of the window a crowd of women – Bertrand's lovers – strains to see the exposed leg. He wakes sweating and panic-stricken as from a nightmare. To be the passive object of the other's desiring gaze is explicitly equated here with humiliation, which suggests a more critical reading of Bertrand than the central narrative would seem to allow.

The scene of Bertrand's death confirms the ambivalence of perspective. The film has followed its hero through multiple episodes of attraction, pursuit and seduction, mostly presented as stages in a legitimate personal quest ('la compagnie des femmes m'était indispensable,' says Bertrand solemnly 'sinon leur compagnie, du moins leur vision'[13]). The spectator has been positioned with Bertrand throughout, though the scenes referred to above have inserted a critical space between spectator and hero. Walking down a city street at night, Bertrand sees a beautiful woman – or rather a beautiful pair of legs – on the other side of the road and moves to follow them, whereupon he walks in front of a car and is knocked over. Cut to Bertrand in hospital, attached to a drip. A shot/ countershot sequence shows a nurse standing by the window, and from Bertrand's perspective her legs silhouetted against the light. He reaches out to touch this vision of all he has desired – and falls out of bed, detaching the drip and causing his own death. Bertrand's story ends with an unintended suicide that repeats the

13 'The company of women was indispensable for me, or if not their company, at least the sight of them.'

reflex that has governed his life: it is irresistibly comic, and the laughter it provokes undercuts the film's endorsement of its hero's values.

L'Homme qui aimait les femmes ends not with Bertrand's death but with his funeral, for the main narrative takes the form of a flashback, framed within opening and closing scenes of his burial attended by all the women he has 'loved'. In one sense, the framing device works to make Bertrand a worthy hero, not only 'the man who loved women' but also 'the man whom women loved': if they all mourn him, how can his Don Juanism have been damaging to women? The funeral, however, also introduces another significant element in the film's structure: a female narrative voice. Because Bertrand writes an autobiographical novel in the course of the film (a point to which we will return in chapter 5), he narrates a considerable part of his own story, reinforcing the centrality of his point of view. But Geneviève, the editor of his novel and his last lover, encloses his narration within hers, observing his funeral and reflecting on the sense of his life just as she has judged and edited his novel – and provided its title with its prescient past tense. In their relationship, Geneviève is seen to take control: it is she who drives the car, she who declares sexual interest in him (in terms similar to those he has used elsewhere in the film), she who points out to him that the rules of heterosexual relationships have evolved and that he must learn to play on equal terms. Geneviève's role as 'master' narrator does not negate the phallocentric tone of much of the film, but it does confirm that the film is also about the problematic nature of conventionally androcentric sexual relations.

Female voices

Geneviève demonstrates that despite the preponderance of a male viewpoint in Truffaut's films the expression of female subjectivity has a place. In the films structured around the story and the perspective of a male protagonist, a contestatory female voice may be heard, disturbing (though sometimes briefly) the overall narrative endorsement of the hero. What female subjects contest is, precisely, the tendency of men to fix them in the roles of idealised mother figures or objects of desire: Fabienne Tabard provides the most fully articulated rejection of this role, but she is echoed by Christine Darbon (*Domicile conjugal* 1970 and *L'Amour en fuite*, 1979) by Geneviève in *L'Homme qui aimait les femmes*, (1977), and by two characters in *La Nuit américaine* (1973). Joelle, the 'script-girl', disconcerts a habitual *dragueur* by taking his advances literally and asserting her own (transient) desire. Finding himself alone with Joelle on the river bank after he has stopped to help change her flat tyre, Bernard the props man finds a nudge and a wink fit the occasion: 'You know Joelle if you ever fancied it...', and is disconcerted to receive the brisk reply 'OK then. Let's do it' as Joelle starts to remove her clothes. The laugh his discomfiture gets from the audience is a laugh against casual verbal sexism (though he recovers sufficiently to accept her invitation). In the same film the actress Julie Baker echoes Fabienne Tabard's kindly but deflating reply to the question of whether women are magic: if women are, then men are too, 'tout le monde est magique ou bien personne ne l'est'.[14]

Female stories

Beyond the inclusion of female voices though lies the surely not insignificant fact that four of Truffaut's films tell a woman's story largely from a woman's point of view (*La Mariée était en noir, Une Belle Fille comme moi, Adèle H.* and *Vivement dimanche!*) and that a further two divide narrative focus fairly evenly between male and female protagonists (*Le Dernier Métro* and *La Femme d'à côté*). The argument for Truffaut as misogynist would oppose to this the fact that of the six women characters involved here, two are ruthless murderers (Julie Kohler and Camille Bliss) and two are obsessed with the man they love to the point of madness or suicide (Adèle H. and Mathilde of *La Femme*), confirming Truffaut's tendency to construct women as idols or monsters. To this we might reply that the remaining two (Marion Steiner in *Dernier Métro* and Barbara

14 'either we are all magic or nobody is'.

in *Vivement*) are neither idealised nor demonised, and that the stories of the 'monsters' are told from their own point of view, significantly undercutting the notion of monstrosity.

In *La Mariée*, Jeanne Moreau, the enigmatic Catherine of *Jules et Jim*, plays another avenging woman, but one whose motivation is more transparent. The film follows the story of Julie Kohler (the name is close to the French *colère*, anger) as she seeks out and murders five men, each of a different type and living in a different town. Through successive flashbacks we gradually learn the reason for her desire to kill: on the day of Julie's wedding to her childhood sweetheart, the five men were engaged in a drinking session in the hotel opposite the church, and a foolish game with a rifle led to the accidental shooting of her husband as the couple emerged from the ceremony. The men fled the scene; Julie was left widowed before the marriage was even consummated. Given the unintentional nature of the killing, her decision that each of the five deserves to die may seem excessive, but as Julie encounters each man and efficiently disposes of him it becomes apparent that she is also implicitly avenging another crime, that of men's distorted perceptions of women and inability to see them as fellow human beings. If we fail to be shocked by Julie's ruthlessness, it is because the film operates both as a thriller, positioning us with the murderer so that we will her not to be caught, and as a sequence of semi-comic sketches in which the five men are recognisable types but sufficiently caricatured to resist our sympathy. Each caricature amplifies an aspect of Truffaldian man, so that a critique of the model of masculinity that underpins most of Truffaut's cinema becomes a central focus of the film.

The first victim, Bliss, is a complacent Don Juan who sees women as desirable but interchangeable prey: Julie lures him to his death by appearing as a new and possibly difficult conquest, a challenge he cannot resist. The second, Coral, as Julie rapidly surmises from the pictures on his walls, idolises women as 'magic', 'distant princesses', 'inaccessible dreams'; it is an easy matter for Julie to charm him as the apparent embodiment of his fantasies, then poison him. The third, Morane, is a self-important, smugly phallocratic politician, whom Julie entraps by playing the role of surrogate wife and mother and adoring listener. The fourth, played by Charles Denner who was later to become 'the man who loved women', is a sort of early sketch for this part, an *hommes à femmes* (women's man) who lives surrounded by representations of female bodies (including a carpet of false breasts), and dies pierced by the arrow he has Julie carry as he paints her in the pose of Diana the Huntress. The fifth is a car-dealer and a criminal, whom Julie intends to attract to his death in the guise of a prostitute, but whom she finally kills in prison, thus completing her mission and closing the film. The flashback reveals that what connected this disparate group, and thus indirectly ruined Julie's life, was their shared taste for 'la chasse et les femmes' ('hunting and women'): in hunting them down, Julie Kohler uses their inability to see beyond their own fantasies of women to lure them to their deaths.

La Mariée repeats the structure of Truffaut's first film *Les Mistons*. Again a group of five male protagonists, linked by desire, confront one woman – but this time she is the one in pursuit, she is the active subject who both uses and avenges the male tendency to reduce her to object. In *Une Belle Fille comme moi*, the structure recurs again, this time with the actress who played in *Les Mistons*, Bernadette Lafont, in the central role. *Une Belle Fille* is very different in tone from *La Mariée*, mingling the genres of farce and musical where the earlier film worked between those of thriller and comedy, centring on a heroine who is noisy, vulgar and exuberant where Julie Kohler is silent, sophisticated and deeply sad. What Camille Bliss (eponymous heroine of *Une Belle Fille*) and Julie Kohler have in common is that they are the active agents in their own stories, that despite their willingness to lie and kill in pursuit of their goals, the film's sympathies remain with them, and that they make use of what the films present as men's distorted and self-interested attitudes to women to achieve their ends. Where Julie's aim is revenge for a lost love, Camille's is freedom and wealth.

The film establishes sympathy with Camille first by the technique of contrast: just as Antoine's humourless, pedantic teacher in *Les 400 Coups* places the spectator with the children against authority, so the earnest sociologist, Stanislas Prévin, interviewing Camille in prison for a thesis on female murderers and determined to fit her into his theoretical frameworks, makes us enjoy Camille's verbal energy and her largely mendacious, but colourful, storytelling. In flashback, much of it narrated from Camille's point of view and showing some comic discrepancies between visual evidence and Camille's words, we learn that she was responsible for the death of her violent father, that she escaped (further echoes of Antoine Doinel) from a reform school, and that thereafter she had four men in her life each of whom wanted, as Camille puts it, 'the same old thing', and each of whom she manipulated in her pursuit of a more comfortable life and of her ambition to be a singer. Stanislas, whose infatuation develops throughout Camille's story, becomes her fifth victim and ends the film in prison in her place convicted of the murders she has committed, while Camille ends the film affluent, free and happy. As with *La Mariée*, the male protagonists resemble caricatures rather than characters in the realist mode – the dim-witted boozer Clovis, the smooth club-singer Sam Golden with his fetishistic need to accompany sex with the soundtrack of car-races, the wheeling-dealing lawyer Murène, the devoutly Christian rat-exterminator, Arthur, and the humourless romantic Stanislas – so that it is difficult to take their fate seriously, and none of them is innocent of the desire to exploit Camille. The vital, truculent amorality of Camille overrides any serious concern with her thoroughly anti-social behaviour.

In the light of *Les 400 Coups* and of what we know of Truffaut's own life, it is possible to read the films' preoccupation with strong women who manipulate and murder weak, romantic men as a masochistic preoccupation with the bad mother who withholds her love and destroys her child. But in the two films which most clearly follow this narrative line, it is the heroine's viewpoint which predominates and the representation of her male victims discourages sympathy with them: Julie and Camille belong not in the category of castrating mothers, but rather with the women in Truffaut's films who present a critique of the dehumanising tendencies of male romanticism. Nor should their roles be seen as wholly defined by gender: it makes as much sense to connect Julie to Julien Davenne in *La Chambre verte*, whose life is equally dominated by a dead love (see chapter 6), as it does to link her to other women characters, and Camille Bliss enacts in comic mode the 'script of delinquency' (in Anne Gillain's phrase) begun by Antoine Doinel. In her resistance to the rational, categorising discourse of the sociologist (for whom she is a classic case of 'sublimated penis-envy'), and in the triumph of her lawless will-to-survive over all attempts to contain her, she also reverses the process of subordination to the civilising Law of the Father depicted in *L'Enfant sauvage* (see chapter 5).

The last films

There is a degree of development in the representation of women in Truffaut's films – not in any straightforwardly linear sense, since his characteristically ironic treatment of male romanticism, and an intermittent attempt to deal with women as subjects, are present almost from the start, but in the sense that the last three films each make female desire and female subjectivity central to the narrative.

In *Le Dernier Métro* (1980), Catherine Deneuve plays Marion Steiner, the leading actress and (in the absence of her husband) director of a Parisian theatre in occupied Paris. Marion's need to maintain secrecy – she is hiding her Jewish husband in the cellar – combined with the plotline of her concealed attraction to and for her new leading man, furnish the conditions for Deneuve to resume a role with which she had already become identified through earlier films (most famously Buñuel's *Belle de jour* in 1967), that of 'the ice-maiden whose intimidating beauty both covers and suggests intense sexuality' (Vincendeau 1994: 43), linking her too to Truffaut's magical but dangerous *femmes fatales*. But Marion is more than an iconic object of male desire. Beautiful, mysterious and enigmatic in the opening scenes, when she is viewed solely through the eyes of the newcomer to the theatre, Bernard, her motives and the complexity of her emotions become apparent once the film reveals her secret. From that point (only a sixth of the way into the film) Marion becomes the spectator's principle point of identification, both because only she and the audience share the knowledge of Lucas's presence, and because she is at the heart of each of the film's interwoven plots. As defender of the integrity of the theatre against the collaborating Daxiat, she saves her husband's life and symbolically preserves French honour; as a woman in love with both Lucas and Bernard, she represents the film's central enigma (who will she end up with?) and in a happy ending that befits the scenario of the Liberation, concludes the film at the centre of a triumphant triangle, one hand in her husband's, the other in Bernard's.

In the last film of all, *Vivement dimanche!* (1982), Fanny Ardant plays another capable and energetic woman who leads the narrative, and whose actions at once save her man and fulfil her own desires. *Vivement*, the most light-hearted of Truffaut's late films, deals playfully both with the conventions of the *film noir* genre, which it self-consciously evokes, and with conventional gender roles. In *film noir* the woman is a powerful figure, both visually and within the narrative, but she is so because female sexuality represents a threat to patriarchal order and 'the work of the film is the attempted restoration of (this) order through the exposure and then destruction of the sexual, manipulating woman' (Kaplan 1980: 3). In *Vivement*, Vercel's wife is an almost parodic version of the *film noir* woman, slinky, manipulative, unfaithful and visually and musically coded as a 'vamp' (painted eyes and lips, black stockings, high heels, sultry music) – but her exposure and destruction occur before the plot really gets underway. The central female part falls instead to Barbara, whose very 'feminine' job as Vercel's secretary is gradually replaced by her self-accorded role as detective and righter of wrongs: as the narrative progresses Barbara appropriates all Vercel's symbols and tools of masculine power, from his wallet and car to his gun. Though Vercel shares the Truffaldian passion for women's legs, Barbara's legs 'stride across the world' ('arpentent le monde' in the phrasing of *The Man Who Loved Women*) not merely for his delectation but for the very practical purpose of proving his innocence. The film's final scene – a church wedding, with

Barbara dressed as a bride and hugely pregnant – may seem to restore the order of fixed gender roles, but it is Barbara's desire for Vercel, and not the reverse, that has driven the story and led to this conclusion. Moreover, the camera rapidly loses interest in the happy couple and focuses instead on the choir of children kicking a photographic lens around the church floor, suggesting that this ending functions more as an affectionate, ironic nod to a familiar formula than as a real denouement – and that the film is more concerned with modes of cinematic storytelling than with romance.[15]

The last two films make paradoxical use of genre signs: *Vivement dimanche!* uses the black and white image, high contrast lighting and narrative preoccupation with murder and detection of the *film noir*, but is one of Truffaut's lightest and most optimistic films. *La Femme d'à côté* (1981), on the other hand, has the setting and appearance of a light social drama, but deals with love so passionate it can only lead to death. Here Fanny Ardant plays Mathilde, a woman who has been deeply damaged by her relationship with Bernard, eight years before the action begins. Having suffered a breakdown after their separation, she has recently married the gentle, devoted Philippe. They move into a new house, and Mathilde discovers that Bernard, now married to Arlette and father of a small son, Thomas, lives in the house opposite. Neither of the ex-lovers reveals the past to their partners; though they both resist the reawakening of desire, the relationship resumes. At first it is Bernard who is unable to maintain the veneer of normality over his desperate desire for Mathilde; when he recovers, after an explosive scene that reveals the truth to Philippe and Arlette, it is

15 In his article 'Truffaut's *Vivement dimanche!* (1983) or, How to take away with one hand what you give with the other', Phil Powrie argues that despite the central and active role of the Barbara character, she is constantly relocated within a partriarchal framework by, for example, episodes of male violence towards her, her dressing up as a prostitute, a *mise-en-scène* that carefully frames her beneath a naked female figure – and finally the highly conventional wedding scene. Persuasive and closely argued as this case is, what predominates in watching this film still seems to be Barbara's mobility, competence and determined desire – and clearly we are reading the concluding scene rather differently.

Mathilde who breaks down and eventually kills both Bernard and herself.

Mathilde is clearly characterised in some senses as the archaic mother, she whose womb connotes not life but death, she who, in Truffaut's work, is both infinitely desirable and mortally dangerous. Mathilde first appears on the screen descending a flight of open stairs as Bernard waits below, unaware of the identity of his new neighbour's wife: the first shot is of her legs, recalling the son's troubled desire in *Les 400 Coups*. The shot of legs recurs in the closing scenes of the film, as Bernard hears a door banging in the empty house now abandoned by Philippe and Mathilde, and a low-angle shot reveals Mathilde's approach to the spectator. Mathilde has also had an abortion, at Bernard's insistence, again recalling the mothers of both Antoine and 'the man who loved women'. Bernard's first memory of seeing Mathilde was at a children's party, as she buttered bread, 'and that was why I fell in love with you immediately'; she illustrates and writes children's books. In the end Bernard dies lying between her legs, in the position not only of coitus but also of birth.

But what invalidates this reading of the film is the fact that we are given as much access to Mathilde's point of view as to Bernard's, unlike, for example, in *Jules et Jim* where we never see Catherine apart from the two men. Mathilde does not simply arouse in Bernard the mingled terror of and desire for an impossible return to the mother, she also experiences an equivalent intensity of passion. The film constructs both lovers as subjects. Like *L'Homme qui aimait les femmes*, this story is framed by the narration of the wisest character who directs spectator sympathies and articulates the film's implied values. The fact that this narrator is a woman, Odile Jouve, and that she is strongly linked both through mutual sympathy and through their shared experience of destructive passion to Mathilde, supports the view that Mathilde's drama is as central to the film as is Bernard's. Though the opening scenes of the story itself are focalised from the viewpoint of Bernard, establishing the pleasant domestic normality of his life and thus its disruption by Mathilde's arrival, the perspective soon begins to alternate between the lovers. Covert telephone conversations re-establish their relationship, a series of shot/ countershots switching between the speakers and revealing the tension provoked by the other's voice. Once they become lovers again, sequences of their meetings alternate with sequences of each back in their everyday lives, but the camera displays most concern with the increasingly taut and anguished face of Mathilde. After his explosion of angry desire at the party, Bernard retreats into the security of the family and departs on holiday with his wife and son. The narrative follows Mathilde into the breakdown already prefigured by physical collapse – two scenes have shown Mathilde fainting to the floor – returning to an alternation of perspectives on Bernard's return.

The relationship between Bernard and Mathilde, as Anne Gillain points out (Gillain 1991: 48–9) is frightening and incomprehensible to them both, a desire for that total fusion with the other that precedes the formation of individual, gendered identity and resembles death rather than life. Mathilde explains Bernard's previous withdrawal from her as an inability to live 'sans sa carapace' ('without his shell'), in the intense intimacy they shared; as the film progresses her 'shell' breaks too, and the elegant, well made-up face of Philippe's wife becomes the bleak, grief-stricken mask of the scenes in the clinic. The pleasant, affluent surface of the film (the rural commuter village, the suburban tennis club) is disturbed by evidence of a more violent and uncontrollable realm beneath: the noise of cats not fighting but 'making love like savages' (as Arlette says) and of motorbikes roaring off into the night penetrate the safe space of domestic interiors; the manager of the tennis-club has lost a leg twenty years before, driven by despairing love to a suicidal leap that resulted only in her mutilation; Bernard repeats the story of a woman who feared being held by men and of the lover who cut off his arms for her; when Bernard and Arlette go to the cinema the film is a tale of infidelity and murder. Although a superficial air of realism prevails as the film begins, the images on screen are not naturalistic but constantly tinged with a blue that comes to signify both desire and emotional pain – until the final death scene is wholly shot in a deep indigo.

The film strongly suggests that at the extremes of love and

desire both sexes may experience the impossibility of maintaining a rational order, and a longing for the total fusion of pre-individuation that amounts to a death wish. Mathilde is no more monstrous here than is Bernard; their final love-making is instigated by her return to the place of their reunion, and it is she who pulls the trigger, but the passion is mutual and its conclusion in death seems less an act of aggression than the only and inevitable resolution.

In conclusion, then, Truffaut's films undoubtedly do contain a script of misogyny which both idealises and demonises the mother, fetishising her body as a means to gain control, and employing a repertory of familiar patriarchal images to do so. Yet his films are also shot through with an ironic awareness of the emotional drives that produce misogyny, thus with techniques that undercut identification with his (often highly sexist) heroes, and introduce the counter-perspective of the female subject. In the final films, the pain or pleasure of the woman protagonist becomes a central focus, and reconciliation between the sexes is effected in jubilant (*Le Dernier Métro*), tragic (*La Femme d'à côté*) or comic (*Vivement dimanche!*) mode. In the next chapter, we turn to the equally vexed and closely connected question of masculine identity.

References

Audé, Françoise (1981), *Ciné-modèles Cinéma d'elles: situation de femmes dans le cinéma français 1956–1979*, Lausanne, Editions de l'Age d'homme.

Beauvoir, Simone de (1949), *The Second Sex*, trans. H. M. Parshley, Harmondworth, Penguin, 1972.

Benjamin, Jessica (1990), *The Bonds of Love. Psychoanalysis, Feminism and the Problem of Domination*, London, Virago.

Gillain, Anne (1991), *François Truffaut: Le Secret perdu*, Paris, Hatier.

Hayward, Susan (1994), *Truffaut auteur ou imposteur*, in G. Harris (ed.), *Truffaut Ten Years On*, Salford, ESRI Conference Proceedings.

Insdorf, Annette (1989), *François Truffaut*, New York, Touchstone.

Kaplan, E. Ann (ed.) (1980), *Women in Film Noir*, London, BFI.

Powrie, Phil (1990), Truffaut's *Vivement dimanche!* (1983) or, How to take away with one hand what you give with the other, Modern and Contemporary France, 43, October 1990, pp. 37–46.

Truffaut, François (1987), *Le Plaisir des yeux*, Paris, Flammarion/Cahiers du cinéma.

Vincendeau, Ginette (1994), Catherine Deneuve and French womanhood, in Pam Cook and Philip Dodd (eds), *Women and Film a Sight and Sound Reader*, London, Scarlet Press, pp. 41–9.

Wheeler Dixon, Winston (1993), *The Early Film Criticism of François Truffaut*, Bloomington and Indianapolis, Indiana University Press.

6

'Where is the father?' Masculinity and authorship

The last chapter argues for a fundamental ambiguity in Truffaut's representation of gender relations: on the one hand an all too familiar denial of female subjectivity and reduction of women to the roles of desirable enigma or castrating mother, on the other hand a deliberately critical display of the dynamics of misogyny and an attempt – particularly in the later films – to screen women as subjects. Underlying this argument is the assumption that the Oedipal scenario – the process whereby individual identity is shaped and gendered through a combination of identification with and separation from each parent – is a fundamental human story, and that where the films engage effectively with the complexities and tensions it contains, this contributes to the spectator's interest and pleasure. So far, though, we have only dealt with two of the players in the Oedipal triangle: the mother and the child. The father also plays a role in the construction of identity, representing, in a culture where the public domain is gendered masculine, the intervention of society's laws and codes into the mother/child duo.

Truffaut's cinema is frequently concerned with the role of the father, both in the literal sense of the male parent, and in the wider figurative sense of the older male figure who represents a model, a teacher, an initiator into the social world – and whose authority may need to be contested if the son (or daughter) is to forge an individual identity. The director's own life predisposed him to a concern with the question of paternity: François Truffaut learnt of his own illegitimacy around the age of twelve, the identity of his biological father remained a secret, never openly discussed between himself and his mother, and he seems to have lacked any satisfactory relationship with the man who was legally and nominally his father. As a young critic, Truffaut's virulent rejection of the dominant French tradition of the 1950s – significantly referred to as the 'cinéma de papa' – suggests filial revolt, whilst the pleasure Truffaut took in identifying and imitating his cinematic heroes – particularly Renoir and Hitchcock – implies an equally strong desire for surrogate, good father figures. In the person of André Bazin, the young Truffaut found a model of benevolent paternity who not only protected and cared for him, but also introduced him to his eventual career (through the *Cahiers du cinéma*) and represented an attitude to life and to cinema that Truffaut would continue to admire. Not only was Bazin an 'être d'exception' whose generosity and respect for others was infectious ('tout le monde se comportait bien avec André Bazin, chacun s'améliorait à son contact'[1] (Truffaut in Bazin 1975: 16)), he was also the finest post-war critic to whose intelligent and humane writings Truffaut attributes the best developments in French cinema: 'le cinéma français d'aujourd'hui ... est né de la pensée et de la réflexion d'André Bazin'[2] (Truffaut in Bazin 1975: 30).

In the films too, a preoccupation with the father's absence or inadequacy co-exists with an attempt to cast the paternal role as a positive and creative force. As so often in Truffaut's cinema, an apparently incidental scene played in comic mode announces one of the questions that underpins his fictional world: the English teacher in *Les 400 Coups* teaches his class some of the complexities of English pronunciation by having them repeat the telling question 'where is the father?'

1 'everybody behaved well with André Bazin, everyone improved through knowing him.'
2 'the French cinema of today ... was born out of Bazin's thought and reflexions.'

Paternity in the Doinel films

As in the case of the idealised or castrating mother, it is *Les 400 Coups* that sets up the basic scenario of paternal/filial relations that will recur, with variations and developments, throughout Truffaut's cinema. Locked into a relationship with his mother that is both nostalgic (though for a lost closeness that is fantasised rather than remembered) and embittered, Antoine needs a point of contact with the extra-familial world that will allow him to develop a separate sense of identity, and find a path into adult life. Psychoanalytical theory allots this function to the father, whose role it is to separate son from mother, and to introduce the repression of desire which is fundamental to the social order. In the film, the first candidate for the paternal role in the film is Antoine's stepfather, and some of the early scenes sketch in the possibility of a father/son comradeship formed against the mother. When she claims to be working late, Monsieur Doinel proposes a 'dîner entre hommes' ('dinner for the boys') and they fry eggs together, amicably, as the father asks Antoine about his day at school and gives him advice: 'You have to push yourself forward in life, take some initiative'. But Monsieur Doinel is also an ineffectual father, cuckolded by his wife, inconsistent in his treatment of Antoine towards whom he is sometimes kindly, sometimes neglectful, and sometimes harsh. The double slap to the face he delivers in front of Antoine's classmates, after learning of his son's truancy and lies, is one of the film's most brutal moments. It is he who, when Antoine's theft of a typewriter is discovered, hands his son over to the police on the grounds of loss of parental control. Monsieur Doinel turns out not to be Antoine's father in the biological sense, but this only confirms his failure to fulfil a paternal role. Lacking both sexual potency and effective authority, he appears in the film to be an insufficiently masculine figure, who offers no route out of Antoine's private miseries into the adult realm.

Beyond the home lies a masculine world, represented initially by the school, that could also provide Antoine with a pathway into adult independence. However, if Monsieur Doinel lacks virility, the institutions that govern Antoine's life outside the home could be described as phallic in the word's most negative sense: they are rigid, authoritarian, and controlling, offering no bridge between Antoine's emotional needs and the demands of adulthood. Social institutions impose repression, but offer little compensation in the form of entry into a new and exciting social order. The school has barred windows, visually connoting imprisonment rather than the free exchange of knowledge, and the syllabus appears dry as dust, not so much intellectual exploration as the imposition of order through rote-learning. The reform school operates on a system of strict regimentation, the boys identically dressed in semi-military uniform and marched from place to place, punished by slaps and imprisonment if they contravene the rules. The film contains a number of images of pleasure, mobility, imagination and emotional warmth, but these are all situated outside the institutions that shape future citizens. When Antoine and his friend René play truant from school and spend the day loose in the city, both the active, mobile camera and the joyful musical score emphasise the pleasures of friendship and freedom of movement, and Antoine's dizzying ride in the rotor is partly shot from his point of view so that we share the elation of spinning, safe but out of control. The rotor powerfully evokes the zoetrope, that pre-cinematic cylindrical container of static images whose whirling action produced the illusion of movement. The allusion to cinema is not gratuitous: all forms of fiction – Antoine's reading of Balzac, his family's one scene of shared happiness at the cinema, the puppet play shot largely through the happy, absorbed faces of the watching children – represent joy. There is a clear opposition between the repressive (phallic) social order, which Antoine will nonetheless have to enter if he is to survive, and the pleasurable, creative domain associated with transgressive behaviour and with fiction.

Les 400 Coups deals with the confrontation between Antoine's desires and society's imperative to conform and obey. If the other films in the Doinel cycle are less emotionally compelling, this is partly because they circumvent the social theme by situating their hero comfortably on the margins of society, sufficiently integrated to survive but avoiding either assimilation to or confrontation with the paternal authority of the State and the normative model of masculinity. Antoine duly negotiates progression into male adulthood, observing the major rites of passage (employment, marriage, fatherhood), but although he is fascinated by the stability and benevolence of successful family units like those of Colette (in *Antoine et Colette*) and Christine (in *Baisers volés* and *Domicile conjugal*) – each of these, like Antoine's family, composed of mother, child and stepfather – he himself never achieves the role of the orthodox paterfamilias. Antoine does not settle into a career, but changes jobs frequently, becoming, in the course of the Doinel cycle, a worker in a record factory, a night porter, a private detective, a television repairman, a flower seller, a trainer of tanker drivers whose job bears a remarkable resemblance to playing with toy boats (Truffaut has two other heroes who make their living in this way, Bertrand in *L'Homme qui aimait les femmes* and Bernard in *La Femme d'à côté*) and finally a proof-reader in a printing company – jobs that are either casual and unskilled, or (more happily) in some way connected with the privileged domains of play and artistic expression. His marriage to Christine founders on his egoism and infidelity, and Christine expresses anger at his paternal posturings once their son is born on the grounds that 'De toutes façons, cet enfant je l'ai attendu toute seule'[3] (*Domicile conjugal*). As the divorced father of Alphonse, he is loving but unreliable, too concerned with his own emotional tangles to remember appointments with the child (*L'Amour en fuite*).

Surrogate father figures enter the plots from time to time: Monsieur Henri, the old detective who teaches Antoine the trade in *Baisers volés*, the kindly stepfathers of Colette and Christine, even – in *L'Amour en fuite* – the lover of Antoine's mother, glimpsed only once in *Les 400 Coups*, and now an elderly man, but none of these plays a major role in Antoine's story. Monsieur Henri dies suddenly halfway through the film; the fathers of girlfriends and wives disappear once Antoine's relationship with their daughter fails; given the starkness of the emotions evoked in

3 'In any case I've been on my own during this pregnancy.'

Les 400 Coups, the reappearance of the mother's lover and his attempts to persuade Antoine that 'elle t'aimait vraiment, mon petit' ('she really loved you, lad') seem both trite and sentimental. Although Antoine ends the final Doinel film *L'Amour en fuite* in an apparently successful relationship, the film, like its title, puts the emphasis on its hero's propensity for flight and evasion, and it is hard not to read the final sequence as simply the first stage in another cycle of desire, fulfilment and separation. As Truffaut himself commented, the last glimpse of Antoine shows him still 'trying to find a way into society' (Gillain 1988: 383). Antoine remains fatherless, apparently destined to repeat endlessly the emotional cycle that began with his mother, and himself scarcely able to assume a paternal role.

Paternal absence: *Les Deux Anglaises et le continent*

The dilemma in the Doinel films is that absent or weak fathers leave the son unable to invent for himself a viable role as a man (hence Antoine's liking for surrogate fathers) but that a powerfully authoritative paternal presence (school, police, army) represents the very opposite of all that Antoine (and the film) values: rigidity versus mobility, conformism versus a mild delinquency, order versus creative disorder. The 1971 film *Les Deux Anglaises et le continent* is also concerned obliquely with the absence of fathers. The hero, Claude, is the only child of a widowed mother: from the opening sequence, in which his attempts to swing high on a trapeze end with a fall to earth, and his broken leg places him firmly in his mother's care, it is apparent that her involvement in his life, though benevolent, is itself crippling. He is, she later explains, 'her monument, built stone by stone', and the film's powerful evocation of enclosure, oppression and sterility is created in part by the intensity of this central, controlling relationship, from which the father is missing. Claude travels to Britain to stay with the 'two English girls' of the title, Anne and Muriel Brown, and falls in love with the latter, but his mother insists on the unsuitability of the match. Mrs Brown is also widowed, and enlists the help of a male friend, Mr Flynn, to 'arbitrate' in the matter. Mr Flynn is kind and ineffectual, proposing a compromise solution that separates the lovers for a year and returns each to their mother, thus initiating the series of withdrawals, separations and renewed advances that will constitute the plot of the film and end in Claude's childless solitude.

Though the film's décors are varied and often beautiful – the rugged coast of Wales (actually shot in Normandy), the parks and monuments of Paris, and a riverside location in rural France – *Les Deux Anglaises* is shot so as to almost totally exclude the sky. The frequent use of the iris adds to the sense of entrapment. Though the possibility of a generous, comradely and happily erotic love appears through Claude's affair with Anne, the love relationship that dominates the film is that between Claude and Muriel, a blocked, obsessive and finally fruitless love signified by the failure of their long-delayed sexual union to produce a child. Each remains locked in childhood patterns of dependence, fantasy and profound egoism, represented by Muriel's guilty preoccupation with masturbation and her often hidden, bandaged eyes, as by Claude's exploitation of her most personal letters for his own artistic ends. The resistance of Muriel's hymen when they finally make love, in the most explicit and violent of all Truffaut's erotic scenes, signifies the difficulty each has in emerging from narcissistic self-absorption, but leads to no lasting union. *Les Deux Anglaises* is a film that combines many Truffaldian themes – obsessive love and desire, the relative importance of life and art, maternal/filial relations – but which is also marked by the absence of fathers and the attendant difficulty for sons and daughters of establishing adult identity. The character of Anne – sculptor, emancipated woman, generous friend and lover – suggests that successful separation may be achieved by the daughter, but Anne's life (in a departure from the novel on which the film is based) is terminated abruptly, leaving the film to focus solely on the blocked relationship between Claude and Muriel.

The oppressive father: *L'Histoire d'Adèle H.*

Conversely, *L'Histoire d'Adèle H.* is a film dominated by the father, paradoxically a father who never appears, not even in the title. Based on the journal of Adèle Hugo, second daughter of one of France's most celebrated men of letters, the film follows its heroine's desperate and self-deluding attempts to recapture the heart of her ex-suitor, Lieutenant Pinson, whom she has followed to Canada from the family home in Guernsey, where Hugo spent the years from 1851 to 1870 in political exile. By his own account, Truffaut's fascinated sympathy with Adèle arose both from her pain at the lack of paternal love and attention, and from her struggle to extricate herself from the crushing weight of her father's name and authority. Whereas Adèle Hugo was a little-known figure in France, at least before Truffaut's film, Hugo's eldest daughter, Léopoldine, has been a familiar name since shortly after her death in 1843. Drowned in a boating accident with her new husband shortly after their marriage, Léopoldine became the subject of some of her father's most moving poetry. In the film, Adèle suffers from a recurring nightmare of drowning, represented visually by the superimposition of the drowning figure over that of Isabelle Adjani as Adèle, and an alternate merging and separation of the two figures. The image conveys both Adèle's terror at loss of identity, and her desire to be her father's most beloved daughter. 'En faisant ce film' wrote Truffaut 'j'ai l'impression de lui faire prendre, enfin, sa revanche sur Léopoldine ... car je suis persuadé qu'Adèle a beaucoup souffert d'avoir été la moins aimée. Elle se sentait de trop. Elle n'avait même pas un nom à elle: elle portait le prénom de sa mère et le nom d'Hugo l'écrasait'[4] (Gillain 1988: 327).

Though Adèle's pursuit of Pinson forms the narrative thread of the film, it is apparent that the pursuit is also a flight from the father. Living under an assumed name, Adèle is horrified when her identity as Hugo's daughter is discovered: in what is intended

4 'In making this film I feel that I am letting [Adèle], at last, take her revenge on Léopoldine ... for I am convinced that Adèle had suffered a great deal from being the one he loved less. She felt in the way. She didn't even have her own name: her first name was her mother's and Hugo's name overshadowed her.'

as a kind gesture, the local bookseller presents her with a copy of Hugo's multi-volumed *Les Misérables*, thus revealing that he knows who she is. The camera pans slowly up the frontispiece to the author's name, in bold lettering at the top, and pauses there, before cutting to Adèle's horrified and angry reaction. Never seen in the film, heard only through his consistently loving, concerned letters (and these mostly read in Adèle's voice), Hugo is nonetheless represented as an oppressive presence. The extent of his celebrity is emphasised in contrast to the anonymity and increasing fragility of his daughter: the local doctor refers to him as 'the most famous man in the world'; when Adèle mendaciously announces her marriage by letter, the scene shifts briefly to Guernsey where a crowd of admirers and journalists wait outside the great man's house hoping for his appearance; the film's epilogue contrasts the two million mourners at Hugo's state funeral in 1885 with his daughter's scarcely noticed death in 1915. Despite her attempt to found a new identity, the repeated scenes of awaiting or collecting money orders at the bank demonstrate Adèle's dependence on her father, both for financial support and for his legal consent to her marriage. Throughout the film Adèle is shown writing her journal, more and more furiously as her hold on sanity weakens before Pinson's repeated rejections, as if to write herself into existence and erase her identity as the dependent daughter of a father adored and respected for his mastery of language. 'Je dénonce l'imposture de l'état-civil et l'escroquerie de l'identité',[5] writes Adèle, shot in semi close-up lying in bed and scribbling furiously whilst a voice-over provides the text, 'Je suis née de père inconnu, de père inconnu, de père inconnu, de père complètement inconnu...'[6]

Good fathers: *L'Argent de poche*

Les Deux Anglaises et le continent develops the theme of paternal absence, *L'Histoire d'Adèle H.* that of the father's oppressive

5 'I denounce the registry office records of identity as fraudulent'.
6 'I was born of an unknown father, of an unknown father, of an unknown father, of a completely unknown father...'

power. Some of Truffaut's films are also concerned to reimagine paternity in a positive way. In *L'Homme qui aimait les femmes*, Bertrand's fatherless childhood is briefly sketched in flashback, as the background to his adult avoidance of the company of men and obsessive desire for that of women. Yet the film contains one character who fulfils a benevolently paternal role. The elderly doctor who diagnoses Bertrand's case of mild venereal disease adopts an indulgent, 'men will be men' attitude to his patient's admission that he has had sexual relations with half a dozen women in the last ten to twelve days: 'What vigour! what youth!', and more significantly, as the proud author of a book on trout-fishing, first gives Bertrand the idea of publishing his own autobiographical novel. 'Rien n'est plus beau que de voir paraître un livre qu'on a écrit', he tells him, 'sauf peut-être de mettre au monde un enfant qu'on a porté neuf mois'.[7] The publication of the book will be the central achievement of Bertrand's life, and the doctor, though a very minor character, provides a fleeting image of a fatherly mentor who facilitates the younger man's self-fulfilment.

L'Argent de poche, made in 1976, is much more centrally concerned with the role of fathers. An occasionally sentimental, episodic film which scarcely has a plot to hold it together, it deals with the everyday life of a small town in provincial France and centres on the school, thus providing Truffaut with the opportunity to film with a cast composed largely of children, an idea he had nurtured since the filming of *Les 400 Coups* (Gillain 1988: 339). The film contains several 'good' fathers: almost all of the school-children whom we see in their home settings have loving two-parent families, most of whom gather weekly in that privileged site of Truffaldian happiness, the cinema. Twelve-year-old Patrick – one of the two most prominent characters – is motherless and responsible for the care of a father confined to a wheelchair, but the relationship between father and son is presented as cordial and mutually affectionate. Though Patrick's father is apparently unable to leave their flat, he is carefully linked in to the communal joy of the cinema: his window faces that of the projection room, so

7 'There's nothing more splendid than seeing your own work in print ... unless it's carrying a child for nine months and giving birth...'

that he can communicate with the projectionist and watch the technical process that produces the images on screen. The only child in the film to suffer neglect and abuse is Julien, whose bruises finally betray the ill-treatment he has stoically concealed and lead to the arrest of its perpetrators: two women, mother and grand-mother, the more sinister for remaining unseen until they are led out, handcuffed, to the police van, surrounded by angry neighbours. The grandmother's mane of wild white hair makes her a witchlike figure: these two, though counterbalanced by several loving maternal figures, belong amongst Truffaut's gallery of evil mothers.

The most central of the adult figures, the schoolteacher Jean-François Richet, becomes a father in the course of the film to his evident delight, a delight so intense that it distracts him from taking photographs of the birth, and which he shares with his class of children the following day in a funny, moving sequence of improvised questions from the cast of amateur child actors: 'Does it have hair?', 'How long is it?' 'How wide is it?' In a wholly affectionate portrayal of masculine theorisation opposed to feminine practicality, Truffaut films Richet's wife breastfeeding the baby (both of them perfectly happy), while Jean-François reads aloud from a manual on child-rearing, identifying all the problems the mother–child couple are clearly not having. 'The maternal relationship', he reads 'will influence the male child's future relationships with women'. 'Funny relationship you must have had with your mother!' replies his wife, tenderly. The exchange clearly alludes to the emotional problems of many Truffaldian heroes, whose unhappy experiences of childhood Richet later reveals he shares. However, in this semi-idyllic portrayal of what adult–child relationships might aspire to be, Richet has overcome his origins and chosen to be a teacher precisely in order to make childhood a happier time for his pupils. The sequence in which Richet makes a warmly emotional, and in the broadest sense political, speech to the assembled children (all boys, the school is just about to go mixed) about their rights and about the duties of adults, constitutes a reversed mirror image of the classroom scenes from *Les 400 Coups*: the stark, prison-like environment is replaced by a bright, noisy space, the harassed, contemptuous air of the schoolmaster by Richet's air of genuine liking for and interest in his pupils, the alienating, rule-based curriculum by a pedagogy that starts from the children's own interests and enthusiasms. Richet is an idealised, but (thanks partly to the film's improvisational techniques) agreeably underplayed and unpretentious representation of a father and a teacher.

Both sides of paternity: *L'Enfant sauvage*

The film which constitutes the most sustained and explicit portrayal of fatherhood is undoubtedly *L'Enfant sauvage*, made in 1970 six years before *L'Argent de poche*. Whereas the latter is concerned with communities and frequently fills the screen with crowds of children, *L'Enfant sauvage* is a much starker film, shot entirely in black and white, set at the very end of the eighteenth century mostly in the French countryside, largely played out between two characters. Based on a true story, *L'Enfant sauvage* begins with the capture of a 'wolf-boy', a child who has been living as an animal in the wild, and follows the process of his entry into human civilisation. At first the child is treated as a curiosity and a freak, displayed for profit and tormented by the other children in the Deaf and Dumb Institute where the authorities place him. He is rescued by Dr Itard, played by Truffaut, who takes him into his own home and slowly, painstakingly and despite many setbacks, succeeds in teaching the boy he names Victor to live in the human world, and above all to communicate through language.

The paternal nature of Itard's relationship with Victor is very marked in the film. When Victor is first brought to Paris he is measured and observed by two authoritative men of science, Itard and Professor Pinel, and whilst they agree that he was abandoned in the forest at the age of three or four but survived by adapting to his surroundings, the difference betwen their interpretations of the evidence is instructive. Their disagreement is emphasised visually by the framing of their dialogue in a window, a vertical bar splitting the pane and separating the two men as they observe the child outside in the garden. Whereas for Pinel the child is irredeemably sub-normal, a fact which also explains his parents' wish to dispose of him, for Itard the parents' desertion (possibly, he proposes, a result of the child's illegitimacy) caused the apparent sub-normality by isolating the child from human society in his formative years: for Itard the child has great human potential which has been blocked by parental neglect. Itard refuses to allow the child to be locked up in an asylum, adopting him to prevent this. Thus the script of *Les 400 Coups* is reversed: a child who was 'encombrant, dont il fallait se débarasser'[8] (Itard's words), instead of being handed over to an institution by his father, is saved by being taken into paternal care. The nine months of Victor's apprenticeship that transform him from a hirsute, naked little animal who runs on four legs, to a boy who, apart from his inability to speak, appears fully socialised, represent a second period of gestation: Itard all but gives birth to his son. This paternal birth though represents not the entry into life, but the entry into the domain of the Symbolic, or language, in psychoanalytic terms the domain *par excellence* of the father.

In Freudian theory, the child begins life in a state of imaginary unity with the mother, which must be left behind if 'normal' social and sexual development is to take place. The intervention of the father (or of a father figure), who imposes the Law against incest and thus forbids desire for the mother, does not destroy the child's identification with or longing for the mother, but represses these into the unconscious. For the male child, separation and repression are rewarded by identification with paternal power, with the right to be 'like Daddy'. For Lacan, this process coincides with the entry into language: the male child is compensated for his loss of the mother by entering language – or in Lacanian terminology the Symbolic Order – as a male subject, the 'he' who is the authoritative subject of patriarchal language. Whilst Truffaut was certainly not consciously employing such theories in his treatment of child development, they provide a useful lens for reading the films and are particularly enlightening in relation to *L'Enfant sauvage*.

A key sequence in Victor's acquisition of language concerns

8 'in the way, who had to be got rid of'.

Victor's liking for milk, the maternal associations of which are reinforced in the film by the visits Itard and Victor make to a neighbouring family, where the young mother always presents Victor with a bowl of milk to his evident pleasure. Itard makes use of Victor's desire for milk to encourage him to use language, withholding the milk until Victor attempts to articulate the word. Whereas the motherly friend, and Itard's housekeeper Madame Guérin, are happy to give the milk in response to any sign of desire, and the latter is delighted when Victor responds to receiving the milk with a sound that approximates the word, Itard insists on the importance of exchanging word for desired object. His journal, given in voice-over as we see Itard writing, records his analysis of the problem.

> Si le mot était sorti de la bouche de Victor avant la concession de la chose désirée c'en était fait. Le véritable usage de la parole était saisi par lui ... au lieu de quoi je n'avais obtenu qu'une expression insignifiante pour lui, inutile pour nous du plaisir qu'il avait ressenti.[9]

Here Itard attempts to produce in his adopted son the repression of immediate desire, specifically desire for milk/the maternal, and, through this, entry into the 'proper' Symbolic Order of language which operates as a system of controlled and rational exchange.

From his first appearance on the screen, Itard is the representative *par excellence* of a rational, ordered, scientific approach to life which is set in opposition to the uncontrolled, instinctive movements and emotions of the child. Itard is first seen dark-coated, standing erect at his writing-desk in a well-lit, symmetrically ordered room. His love and concern for the child are expressed through his actions and through occasional words, smiles and gestures, but Truffaut's understated acting style, together with the character's maintenance of scientific objectivity, mean that the surface of the film is curiously cold and unemotional. Using the journals of the historical Dr Itard, Truffaut intercuts scenes of Victor's successful

9 'If the word had come from Victor's month before he was given what he wanted, then the goal would have been achieved. He would have grasped the proper use of language ... instead of which I had only obtained an expression of the pleasure he felt, that was insignificant for him and useless to us.'

adaptation, his resistance and his escapes, with Itard's written commentaries on events, presented visually through images of him writing, aurally by Truffaut's flat, passionless voice-overs. Only at the most poignant moment of Victor's education, when Itard forces himself to inflict an unjust punishment on the boy so that Victor's outrage can prove his acquisition of a sense of justice, does he hold the boy close in an uncontrolled expression of tenderness. Frequently set in contrast to the gentler, more affectionate attitude of the female housekeeper, Itard's scientific detachment and emphasis on order and authority provoke an answering detachment in the spectator, and pose a question mark over the justice of his cause and the repressions it demands.

For although the narrative's structuring concern is the process of Victor's education, which concludes triumphantly as Victor returns voluntarily from his last escape, proving that – as Itard says – 'Tu n'es plus un sauvage. Tu es un homme. Un jeune homme extraordinaire, plein d'avenir',[10] the film is at pains to point out too what Victor has lost. Entry into the Symbolic Order, in other words, is shown to be essential to the acquisition of humanity but also costly. Several early scenes show Victor fleeing his captors to rush towards rivers or streams and plunge his head and arms into the water, or alone, swaying in the moonlight or soaked and ecstatic in gardens under the pouring rain, as if he had been torn from his proper element, or in Lacanian terms from the Imaginary domain of union with the mother. Each of Victor's flights, like that of Antoine in the closing sequence of *Les 400 Coups*, is towards water, and, as with Antoine, the water takes on connotations of a lost and desired maternal presence against the aridity of an over-regulated social order. The cups of water or milk with which Victor is rewarded for his efforts at language seem paltry by comparison. Victor's crises of tears and anger express his resistance to the painful process of replacing immediate desires and satisfactions with the laborious processes of language, social codes and manners: Madame Guérin reproaches Itard with spoiling all the child's pleasures by turning them into work.

10 'You are no longer a savage. You are a man. An extraordinary young man, with a future ahead of you.'

Victor's final escape takes him from the dark, austere house into a sunlit world of open fields, running streams and dense forests, the lyrical quality of the visual images reinforced by one of the loveliest and most poignant movements of the film's Vivaldi soundtrack. Victor, however, is no longer adapted to this environment: he falls from the tree he tries to climb, sleeps fitfully and uncomfortably in the open, gets caught at once when he tries to steal a chicken. His return marks both the triumph of Itard's project of socialisation, and Victor's irremediable loss of his place in the natural world.

The film's quality lies in its balancing of both sides of this equation. Desire for and revolt against paternal authority are here held in a paradoxical but persuasive tension. The Symbolic Order into which Victor is initiated is not merely repressive and deadening but also represents the positive achievements of civilisation. Thanks to Itard's patient commitment, Victor gains access to the joy of human communication, signified for example by the sequence in which Itard and the blindfolded Victor sit outside in the sun, each equipped with a drum and a set of bells, and Victor happily recognises and answers each of the sounds Itard makes by imitating them. Victor discovers play, when the neighbour's child pushes him around in a wheelbarrow, and creativity, when he invents a chalk-holder. He also learns the meaning of words and gestures of love, and invents a language of response, holding Itard and Madame Guérin's hands against his face to signify pleasure in their presence. At the same time, the film emphasises the loss attendant upon entry into a structured social order based on repression and obedience. The film closes as Victor ascends the stairs in the house to resume his ordered existence as Itard's pupil: an iris encircles Victor's face with darkness as he looks down towards Itard, to the accompaniment of a plaintive, melodic flute music. The image, which recalls the enigmatic final close-up of Antoine's face in *Les 400 Coups*, suggests not so much a celebration of the return to civilisation as a lament for the world Victor has lost, and a sense of uncertainty about his future.

Writing and repression: *Une Belle Fille comme moi*

The struggles between Itard and Victor centre above all on the written language. Victor never learns to speak, but Itard perseveres against all the odds to have his adopted son acquire the symbols of the written language which he himself prizes so highly, and this determined interposition of the word between Victor's desires and their satisfaction is, as we have seen, presented in part as oppressive. The written language can be seen as the domain *par excellence* of the Symbolic, for it is more rigorously codified, more subject to prescriptive rules than is the spoken language. To write means to internalise the rules of spelling and syntax and along with these a whole way of ordering the world. Whereas the spoken word is transient, the written word – particularly in its printed form – is durable, able to fix and preserve meaning, to confer upon it the stamp of authority. In Truffaut's films, the written word is in some instances the medium of patriarchal authority, the means by which those who resist the prevailing order are defined in its terms and thus (if the process works) safely assimilated.

Thus in *Les 400 Coups* Antoine is subjected to an educational diet of rote-learning and copying from the board, and his attempts at self-expression are consistently silenced or punished. His poem of complaint, written on the classroom wall, is erased and must be expiated by another, more orthodox form of writing – lines of verb declensions. Antoine's essay, a homage to one of his literary heroes, is punished as plagiarism, whilst his attempt to steal a typewriter (metaphorically, to appropriate language for himself) is punished by incarceration. At the police station the duty officer writes Antoine's 'statement' for him, limiting the boy's role to the addition of a signature. *Les 400 Coups* charts a struggle for narrative control over Antoine's life. In *Adèle H.*, Victor Hugo's massive paternal presence shadows his daughter's life and is symbolised by the great tomes of his novels, on which the name of the father looms large. To the authority of the father's language Adèle opposes the wild disorder of her own journal – handwritten not printed, disobeying the rules of grammar and syntax, subjective and without claim to universal truth. But the film which deals most explicitly – and most comically – with the repressive power of the written word, and with resistance to its authority, is *Une Belle Fille comme moi.*

Une Belle Fille comme moi (1972) was neither a commercial nor a critical success but Truffaut considered it 'possibly the most controlled and coherent of my films' (Gillain 1988: 295). It is the story of a struggle between two attitudes to life and to language, that of the respectable academic Stanislas Prévine who believes in the explanatory power of sociological theory, and hopes to advance his career by producing an authoritative thesis on 'Criminal Women', and that of the 'criminal woman' Camille Bliss, for whom the relationship between truth and language depends on the needs of the moment, and who hopes to use the interest of the sociologist to get out of prison.

The film opens in a bookshop where a female customer is unable to find the book she seeks, *Les Femmes criminelles* (*Criminal Women*) by Stanislas Prévine. The proprietor agrees that the book had been announced in the publisher's catalogue and is puzzled by its non-appearance: 'I really don't know what happened', he says, as the screen fades into flash-back. Thus the film narrative proper begins, the story of 'what happened' or of how Prévine's book failed to be published.

Stanislas, first seen in the film as he is escorted into the women's prison to interview Camille Bliss, is one of Truffaut's romantics, hopelessly gullible and immediately identified by his robustly self-interested interviewee as easy prey. Camille, who has 'the sexual energy and comic resilience of a Moll Flanders' (Houston and Kinder 1974: 2), provides him with a highly fictitious account of her life, during which she has engineered the deaths of two men and tried to kill two more; at the same time she seduces her interviewer into bringing her gifts and finally into proving her (dubious) innocence, so that she is released from jail. When her second attempt on her husband's life proves more successful, she manages to frame Stanislas for the murder and the film ends with Stanislas in jail, his thesis unpublished, and Camille rich and free. A summary of the plot would suggest that audience sympathy should be with Stanislas, but quite the reverse is true: despite his claims of an even-handed liking for both his characters (Gillain

1988: 296), Truffaut invites the spectator to enjoy the triumph of the amoral Camille.

Stanislas believes in the written word, both in the unconditional truth of the theory he has been taught – despite the cynical incredulity of his secretary he insists that Camille suffers from 'sublimated penis-envy' and seeks 'the love she was never given in childhood' – and in the capacity of his own thesis to capture the truth about Camille. Unaware both of Camille's blithe indifference to veracity, and of his own increasing bias as he falls for her, he earnestly records her words and transcribes them for his book, whilst the images on the screen reveal what really happened. Thus for example, as Camille records her calm and ladylike reaction to her husband's violence ('I behaved like the Queen of England') the screen shows her smashing several household objects over his head whilst screaming abuse. Stanislas's faith in the written word, and in the authority of father-figures such as Freud, his lawyer and the law itself, place him squarely on the side of patriarchal order, and indeed his dealings with Camille are less disinterested than he himself believes since both his conscious aim (his own self-promotion through the publication of Camille's story) and his unconscious aim (to make love to Camille) equate him with the film's other four men, each of whom seeks what Camille refers to as 'the same old thing', not only sex, but also the assertion of control over Camille's irrepressible autonomy.

If Stanislas is an only slightly caricatural version of a man of science (thus aligned within Truffaut's cast of characters alongside Dr Itard), Camille is a larger-than-life character filmed without pretensions to realism. The sociologist's use of language, like his neat bespectacled appearance, is sober and rational, framing experience within orthodox academic concepts, scarcely distinguishing between spoken and written registers, as his dictations to his secretary make clear. Camille's language is spontaneous, vulgar and vibrant, concerned not with the ordering and recording of truth but with self-assertion and self-promotion, as the discrepancy between the narrative on screen and Camille's voice-over version of the same events makes comically clear. The film's impact and humour depend on the opposition between these two characters and their modes of discourse. Stanislas is filmed in semi-realist vein, in the prison, in his secretary's flat, or searching for evidence, as he struggles to force Camille's story of sexual mayhem and casual murder into an acceptable thesis. Camille's story on the other hand tends to break into the modes of cartoon, slapstick comedy and musical, as if realism could not contain her. The flashback to her childhood, for example, sees her fly in slow-motion to the top of a haystack, propelled by a kick from her drunken father, and her husband Clovis barges through a door leaving a man-size hole reminiscent of *Tom and Jerry*. On their first meeting Camille responds to Stanislas's request to test the tape-recorder by grabbing the microphone and breaking into bawdy song; the camera tracks along the barred corridors of the prison as they are filled with Camille's loud, tuneless but life-affirming voice.

Although *Une Belle Fille* stands out as the most exuberant and comic of Truffaut's films, it contains marked echoes of the more serious *Les 400 Coups* and *L'Enfant sauvage*. Camille, with her unhappy childhood, passage through a youth detention centre, and indeed her eventual salvation through the telling of her story, has a distinct resemblance to Antoine, except that here the rebel is not in the weak position of the child but able to fight back and destroy the society that threatens her. Camille is also, as Truffaut himself puts it, a 'une grande sœur de *L'Enfant sauvage*'[11] (Gillain 1988: 294) in that she stands for total and instinctive self-gratification as opposed to repression and morality, and that her story is interpreted and recorded by a representative of the dominant, civilised order. Here however the educator is not a figure who invites the spectator's respect, but the pedantic and self-deluding Stanislas, so that the vitality of the pleasure principle triumphs over a civilised order presented as dull, cautious and pleasure-less (Stanislas faints when he finally finds himself in bed with Camille). Camille's philosophy of complete disregard for truth and total egoism is not being seriously presented for our approbation, but the film takes (and gives) great pleasure in allowing the amoral, verbally inventive 'savage' with her unlimited

11 'a big sister to the *Wild Child*'.

appetites to triumph over the imprisonment of both her body and her words: the non-appearance of Stanislas's book in fact emerges as a victory.

Writing and self-affirmation

However, Truffaut's films do not equate written language solely with the repressive power of the Father. We have seen that despite the emphasis on the repression that accompanies entry into the Symbolic, *L'Enfant sauvage* also celebrates the acquisition of language – specifically of written language – as enabling and creative. When Victor finally grasps the relationship between the arrangement of small wooden letters on the table, and the milk he wants to drink, he is elated both by the instrumental possibilities this presents and by his own achievement, so that he chooses to carry the letters with him to the neighbours' house and proudly set them out before the farmer's wife who rewards him with a bowl of milk. Jubilant music accompanies Victor's first copying of letters on the blackboard. Itard himself moves constantly between the education of Victor and the recording of that process in his journal, the 'real' journal that has survived the deaths of all those involved and permitted the recreation of events in Truffaut's film. Despite the losses entailed for Victor, Itard's in part successful attempt to transmit to him the capacity to express desire, to shape and communicate experience through symbolisation, are presented positively.

Indeed writing – as the story of *Adèle H*. suggests – can also be an important act of self-affirmation in Truffaut's films, though it is on the whole a way of asserting masculine identity either against the father's power or despite his absence. Adèle is the only one of Truffaut's heroines who writes; writing, for the most part, is bound up with the drama of masculine identity. In several films, the hero's publication of a book is as significant to the narrative as is his pursuit of happiness in relationships. The biographical connection is fairly transparent: Truffaut's career began with the transposition of his own unhappy story into a film that gained him fame and critical acclaim. Two of his films (*Jules et Jim* and *Les Deux Anglaises et le continent*) are based on the autobiographical novels of Henri-Pierre Roché, a man who also transformed the emotional pain of youthful experiences into works of art. Within several films, there is an intricate mirroring of the film narrative by a written narrative, as the heroes write and publish their own stories: not only Doctor Itard but also Antoine Doinel, Jim (*Jules et Jim*), Claude (*Les Deux Anglaises et le continent*) Bertrand (*L'Homme qui aimait les femmes*) each writes a book which could or explicitly does form the basis of the film. Pierre Lachenay (*La Peau douce*), Stanislas Prévine (*Une Belle Fille comme moi*) and Julien Davenne (*La Chambre verte*) are also writers, albeit in a less autobiographical vein.

The desire to tell one's own story and to be read is one of the emotions that drives Truffaut's narratives. As we have seen, *Les 400 Coups* is, amongst other things, the story of Antoine Doinel's attempts to impose his own version of his story against the competing narratives of those in authority. Failed and punished attempts at gaining narrative control of his own life punctuate the story: the poem written on the wall, the fictitious account of his mother's death, the plagiarised essay, the theft of the typewriter – until at last at the detention centre, for the first time, Antoine is invited to tell his story and is listened to, by the off-screen female psychologist. Shot in semi-close-up, focused solely on Antoine, this sequence is memorable for the range of emotions that flit across Jean-Pierre Léaud's face as he recounts Antoine's childhood: pain, mischief, incomprehension, longing, but above all the pleasure of telling.

In the later Doinel films, Antoine succeeds in recounting his story and publishes an autobiographical novel *Les Salades de l'Amour*, written in the course of *Domicile conjugal*. This does not exhaust his desire to write: the final Doinel film, *L'Amour en fuite*, makes the composition of Antoine's second novel central to the plot. As Antoine lives his affair with Sabine, he is also writing it as a novel. The film closes on a scene of triumphant narration, shot in close-ups of Antoine as storyteller (he begins in classic story-telling style 'One day...') interspersed with corresponding flashbacks. His compelling narration of the events that led him to love Sabine convince her that she loves him too, so that the happy ending rewards Antoine's powers as a storyteller, and the cycle concludes on a neat convergence of Antoine's two main routes to the establishment of identity: writing and love. The happy denouement is underlined by a final 'quotation' from *Les 400 Coups*: as Antoine and Sabine embrace, we cut to the young Antoine spinning ecstatically in the rotor. In the original film, the rotor was wholly on the side of pleasurable transgression, fusing sensuality, shared disobedience and a glimpse of creativity, whilst writing was a medium that excluded Antoine's voice. *L'Amour en fuite* would have us accept that Antoine has won the struggle to appropriate language for himself, without relinquishing the drive towards personal pleasure and freedom.

Similarly, in *L'Homme qui aimait les femmes*, Bertrand's writing of his autobiographical novel forms the basis of much of the narration, in the form of flashbacks, and 'gets the girl', since Bertrand's last lover is his editor who is first attracted to him through the manuscript. In this film there is no neat convergence of emotion and art: Bertrand's book constitutes his real achievement whereas emotionally he makes no progress. In a brief and curious flashback scene, Bertrand recalls his first visit to a prostitute as an adolescent, and the voice-over narration draws attention (without explanation) to the empty bookshelves in the prostitute's room. Bertrand's achievement is to create the missing book, to give to his multiple affairs and encounters a satisfactory and coherent form that will record relationships experienced as merely transient, and that will live on after him. As Geneviève (the editor) says in her concluding narration:

> Bertrand poursuivit le bonheur impossible dans la quantité, dans la multitude ... Mais de toutes ces femmes qui ont traversé sa vie il restera peut-être quelque chose, une trace, un témoignage, un objet rectangulaire, trois cents vingt pages brochés – on appelle ça un livre.[12]

12 'Bertrand pursued impossible happiness in quantity, in a multitude of women [...] But of all those women who passed through his life, perhaps there will remain a trace, a testimony, a rectangular object, three-hundred bound pages – what we call a book'.

The ability to write, and above all to be published, read and recognised, provide Truffaut's marginalised and fatherless heroes both with a sense of control over lives that can be reshaped in the telling, and with a pleasing sense that their names, thus their identities, really exist in the world. Once they have appropriated language for themselves, Truffaut's writers discover the pleasure of re-patterning the real, a pleasure explicitly celebrated in a brief scene from *L'Homme qui aimait les femmes*. Bertrand's book is in the process of being printed, and he watches the operator typing in an episode with a little girl in a red dress, an episode already shown visually on the screen and thus established as 'real'. Bertrand suddenly decides to change the dress colour to blue. Through a simple operation of the printing keys, reality becomes other – and the film echoes the process by showing a second version of the scene in which the dress is blue. The scene's sole function is to underscore the freedom of the author in relation to the real. Both *L'Homme qui aimait les femmes* and *Les Deux Anglaises* also devote scenes to the material presence of their heroes' books on public display in bookshop windows, for both the visibility of the writer's name and the availability of his words to potential readers constitute triumphant assertions of identity.

The book as privileged object: *Fahrenheit 451*

In *Adèle H.* and *Une Belle Fille*, the book is a monolithic object which stands for paternal repression and for the reifying power of the written language. The heroine of each film resists patriarchal authority, Adèle by flight, disobedience and her own unpublished writing, Camille by a total disregard for society's rules. Truffaut's male heroes, dispossessed heirs of a patriarchal tradition, are less inclined to open resistance, but may appropriate the book for what the films define as worthy ends. In these cases, the book ceases to be associated with authority and repression, and becomes a privileged object, representing the positive values of imagination, freedom and creativity.

In *Fahrenheit 451*, Truffaut carries this idealisation of the book to its extreme conclusion, identifying patriarchal power with the totalitarian state whose survival depends on the suppression of books, and thus making the book the token of courageous dissent and the defence of freedom. Based on Ray Bradbury's dystopian novel, *Fahrenheit* is set in a futuristic world reminiscent both of Huxley's *Brave New World* and of Orwell's *1984*, in which the population are drugged into docility by an unrelieved diet of propaganda and mindless entertainment, and possession of a book is a serious crime. The firemen whose function it is to find and ritually burn all books are an all-male team, uniformed and aggressive, wielding flame-throwers with irresistibly phallic connotations, commanded by a patriarchal figure whom the rebel hero must kill in order to find himself. The book-reading dissidents on the other hand are represented primarily by two female characters, who bring about the hero's conversion from defender of the dominant order to outlawed dissident, and the camp of the escaped 'book-people' opposes to the urban, military, phallic regime of the firemen a pastoral, gently anarchic counter-society in which each individual 'becomes' a book by memorising the text.

Both narrative and visual image focus obsessively on books, indeed one of the film's weaknesses is that we learn almost nothing of the origins or wider aims of this Brave New World beyond its book-burning policy. Books are hidden, sought, discovered, treated with a scandalous irreverence emphasised by lingering close-ups on the slow burning of covers and pages, died for, learnt by heart to preserve them against the barbarians: they come to represent in themselves all the human values which the film defends. The reverential treatment of the book as object, apparent in so many Truffaut films in the choice of printing works and bookshops as locations, and in repeated shots of the printing process, here reaches its most extreme point.

Writing in film: *La Nuit américaine*

Written language is characterised as both oppressive and liberating in Truffaut's films. Most often represented by the book, the written word may imprison its subject within the rigid codes of the Symbolic Order (*L'Enfant sauvage, Adèle H., Une Belle Fille*) or represent the freedom of imagination to transcend the limitations of the real (*L'Enfant sauvage, L'Homme qui aimait les femmes, Les Deux Anglaises*, the *Doinel* cycle). Given Lacan's identification of the Symbolic Order with patriarchy, it is interesting that Truffaut chooses to characterise both the book as dissidence against an oppressive social order (*Fahrenheit*), and resistance to the book as an instrument of that order (*Une Belle Fille*) as feminine. His heroes, sometimes helped by benevolent surrogate fathers, but more often fatherless and resistant to normative models of masculinity, find a way into language by writing their own stories, an achievement which the films present in positive terms. The celebration of writing is an important theme in Truffaut's cinema. And yet with the single exception of *Fahrenheit 451* – the only film in which patriarchal power is unequivocally aligned against the written word – this celebration is always accompanied by a note of disquiet. Antoine's writing brings him a very positive sense of achievement and identity, but in both *Domicile conjugal* and *L'Amour en fuite* it is apparent that in writing he assumes some of that power to define and control the lives of others against which he had himself fought in *Les 400 Coups*. Christine accuses Antoine of using his novel to 'settle scores' with his family. Colette points out the major discrepancies between her memory of their affair (authenticated by flashbacks to *Antoine et Colette*) and Antoine's fictionalised (and consistently self-glorifying) account of it in his novel. Given the irony that plays over the character of *L'Homme qui aimait les femmes*, a similar mistrust attaches to the authenticity of his account of relationships. Claude (*Les Deux Anglaises*) is seen to make literary use of Muriel's confidential letters, against her explicit request. Even when celebrated, the written language in Truffaut's world remains a medium tainted by its association with institutionalised control and the law of the Father.

There is, of course, another form of writing in Truffaut's work and one that is far less ambivalent. For Truffaut, both as critic and as New Wave director, the film-maker was an 'author' who 'wrote' on celluloid: in his films, cinema is a form of writing which avoids the traps of the Symbolic. The difference between written language and film language is established in a number of ways. For Truffaut the cinema is never allied with the State or with any other form of authority, but is always a place of escape and pleasure, so that film retains the imaginative power of written fiction without the overtones of paternal power. Truffaut (often to the annoyance of his more politicised contemporary Godard) understates the extent to which cinema too works through a codified 'language' and is an industry intricately imbricated with the State: in his films, the language of cinema carries no hint of repression. The individual enterprise of writing becomes the collective project of film-making, a project that involves both sexes and enriches the creativity of the 'author' with that of a host of collaborators.

There is not a film in Truffaut's repertoire, apart from the historical films set before cinema was invented, which does not incorporate some self-referential tribute to the pleasure of watching and/or making films. However, one film stands out in this respect: if *Fahrenheit* is Truffaut's eulogy to the book, *La Nuit américaine* is his panegyric to film. A film crew, led by the director Ferrand (played by Truffaut), gathers at the Studio Victorine in Nice to shoot a romantic drama entitled *Je vous présente Paméla* ('Meet Pamela'), succeeds in completing the film despite a series of difficulties, including the death of one of the leading men, and finally disbands to go their separate ways, bringing the framing film (*La Nuit américaine*) to a close. Banal as *Je vous présente Paméla* appears to be, it represents, for the purposes of the film, a worthwhile artistic project: its freedom from the constraints of pure commercialism or ideological orthodoxy is established early on by one of Truffaut's apparently gratuitous moments, when a visitor to the set asks the director why he never makes 'pornographic films or political films'. During the shooting, relationships between individual members of the cast are formed and dissolved, but the primary focus is on the joy of the shared, collaborative effort that goes to make a film, and on the controlling creativity of the director Ferrand. In one representative sequence, Ferrand concludes a voice-over monologue on the complexities of the director's role with the words 'le cinéma règne' ('cinema reigns'), which trigger the opening bars of an exuberantly triumphant musical score and a series of rapid cuts between shots showing aspects of the film-making process, concluding with a crane-mounted camera soaring into the sky to the music's crescendo. Film is unequivocally celebrated as a medium that both represents and transcends the real: films can be made out of 'anything', says Ferrand, for 'Les films sont plus harmonieux que la vie – il n'y a pas d'embouteillages dans les films, il n'y a pas de temps morts. Les films avancent ... comme des trains dans la nuit'.[13]

The question 'Where is the father?' finds its echo in *La Nuit américaine* through the character of Stacey, an actress engaged for a minor part in the film, whose unexpected pregnancy necessitates some adjustments to the scenario, and the paternity of whose child provokes some speculation. But here the question raises little anxiety, indeed the film completely loses sight of this small narrative thread and the identity of the child's father remains unknown. Meanwhile, the question in its wider sense receives multiple answers, for this is a film full of good fathers. Ferrand plays father to the family formed by the film crew, enabling and guiding individual creativity (whilst remaining firmly in control), and is supported by the discreetly benevolent producer who manages the financing of the film. Alexandre, the ageing star, plays the role of the father in *Paméla*, provides a benignly paternal presence on the set, and plans to adopt his young male lover. The husband of Julie, the female lead, is a doctor considerably older than herself, his fatherly role reinforced by the fact that he has helped her to overcome a nervous breakdown and to grow into the capable, adult woman she now appears to be. Towards the beginning of shooting Ferrand receives a package of books which he spills out on to the desk to be caught in close-up: each is on the subject of one of Truffaut's cinematic forefathers (Lubitsch, Buñuel, Bresson, Howard Hawks and several more), and Ferrand's recurring dream adds Orson Welles to the list. Though the film within a film, *Je vous présente Paméla*, tells a story of

13 'Films are more harmonious than life – there are no hold-ups in films, no lulls. Films move on like trains in the night.'

father/son conflict ending in patricide, this recalls the difficult relationships of other Truffaut films only in order to contrast them with the harmony that reigns here. And in this mythical world of happy families, good fathers and respectful sons and daughters, all made possible by the magical freedom of cinema, mothers too can be strong and benevolent, so that Julie can prevent the hysterical Alphonse from wrecking the film by sleeping with him in a spirit of affectionate professional solidarity, the pregnant Stacey in her turn plays mother to Julie in her hour of need, and the assistant director Joelle maintains a tough and competent professionalism that ensures the film's completion.

La Nuit américaine, then, is a film which combines a good deal of fascinating insight into the technical process of film-making with an enjoyably utopian, and sometimes comic, vision of creative harmony. In the process of film-making, or 'writing' in film, the negative power of the Father as the source of repression disappears, and the desire for benevolent, enabling father figures is realised. Film itself seems to stand for all that is most positive in Truffaut's world. The next chapter will explore the system of values, both aesthetic and ethical, of which this emphatic valorisation of cinema is a part.

References

Bazin, André (1975), *Le Cinéma de l'Occupation et de la Résistance* (preface by Truffaut), Paris, Union Générale d'Editions, Collection 10/18.

Houston, B. and Kinder, M. (1974), *Truffaut's gorgeous killers*, in Film Quarterly, 27: 2, pp. 2–10.

Gillain, Anne (1988), *Le Cinéma selon François Truffaut*, Paris, Flammarion.

7

The *définitif* and the *provisoire* (the absolute v. the provisional)

The lack of a socio-political dimension

Truffaut's films display mistrust of the institutions that impose social order: school (*Les 400 Coups*), army (*Baisers volés*), paternal authority (*Adèle H.*) and the written language, in as far as it may impose a limited model of reality and repress all that it excludes (*L'Enfant sauvage, Une Belle Fille comme moi, Les Deux Anglaises*). Truffaut's heroes on the whole occupy the margins of society (Antoine Doinel, Charlie Kohler, Adèle H.) and are not infrequently on the wrong side of the law (*Les 400 Coups, Tirez, Fahrenheit, La Mariée, La Sirène, Une Belle Fille*, briefly *Vivement dimanche!*). However, this direction of sympathy towards the delinquent and the unorthodox does not constitute a social or political critique, and we have seen (chapter 2) that the absence of clear socio-political themes in Truffaut's films has been judged by some critics to be a failing, particularly in the context of a national culture that values highly the political role of its intellectuals and artists. Truffaut's personal affinity for the Left led only episodically to political action, and the films rarely deal with politics either at the level of narrative or at the level of theme. Only *Fahrenheit 451* and *Le Dernier Métro* adopt a clear political position in their drama-tisation of struggles against repressive regimes, and in both cases political repression is represented primarily as a problem of artistic censorship, drawing the films back into a typically Truffauldian thematics of art and personal expression. Truffaut's films systematically ignore the political events and issues of the day, from the Algerian war (1954–62) through to the long awaited victory of the French Left at the 1980 and 1981 elections. Concerned rather to 'continue the tradition of cinema as fiction' (Gillain 1988: 14), the films deal primarily with questions of identity, love and friendship, the creative process itself, and death – staple themes of fiction from fairy tales to Hollywood.

The view that Truffaut's work is impoverished by its failure to engage with contemporary social questions[1] has been countered by those critics who defend the art of cinematic storytelling as in itself a serious and worthwhile social activity. Truffaut is widely acknowledged to be an exceptionally fine storyteller[2] and, as Anne Gillain argues, to tell stories well is no trivial achievement but rather a means to 'mobilise the collective imagination' (Gillain 1988: 14), in Truffaut's case through the whole sensual apparatus of cinema. Gillain's arguments, like those of Annette Insdorf and Carole Le Berre, suggest that beneath the films' apparently genial, apolitical and often romantic surface lie serious concerns that extend beyond the domain of the personal. These critics agree that whilst Truffaut's films remain silent about the political events and choices of their era, they nonetheless propose a set of aesthetic preferences and a system of values that are, if not political, at least relevant to the way we live in society.

The *définitif* and the *provisoire*

One way of approaching the films' system of values is through the underlying tension between what Truffaut tends to term 'le définitif' ('the definitive', 'the absolute') and 'le provisoire' ('the provisional', 'the impermanent'). The opposition between these

1 For example Roy Armes describes Truffaut's cinema as 'offer[ing] limited insights into the workings of contemporary society' (Armes 1985: 257); Terry Lovell finds it to be 'locked within a conservative romantic ideology' (Cook 1985: 136).

2 Armes, for example, balances his recognition of Truffaut's limitations with praise for work that 'ranks him as the finest story-teller to emerge from the New Wave' (Armes 1985: 257).

categories is articulated both in Truffaut's writing and in the films. In a piece written in 1978 in praise of a Sacha Guitry play, for example, he refers to Guitry's heroes 'aspir[ant] constamment à l'amour définitif avant de s'installer gaiement dans le provisoire'[3] (Truffaut 1987: 80). The 1968 film *Baisers volés* charts Antoine Doinel's desire for a grand and lasting passion with Fabienne Tabard, and his acceptance of her preferred alternative: a mutually tender but decidedly finite affair. The film's curious closing scene suggests that the yearning for an absolute is not, however, so easily overcome. Antoine has become engaged to the other, more accessible object of his affections, Christine, and the couple are seated on a park bench engaging in desultory conversation. Throughout the film, occasional brief sequences have shown a mysterious raincoated stranger following Christine: now the stranger reappears, approaches and, for the first time, speaks. 'Avant de vous rencontrer je n'avais jamais aimé personne. Je hais le provisoire. Moi je suis définitif.'[4] Dismissing Christine's relationship with Antoine as merely 'a provisional tie to a provisional person', he promises her a life of total fidelity in which 'nous ne nous quitterons jamais, même pas une heure',[5] then walks away leaving Christine to comment 'il est complètement fou, ce type-là' ('that guy is completely nuts'), to which Antoine assents a little hesitantly 'yes, yes, he must be...' Here the commitment to an absolute, uncompromising form of love is attached to an enigmatic, sinister and possibly crazy stranger – who nonetheless, both in his pursuit of women (*Baisers volés* shows Antoine as detective, often stalking his female quarry) and in his romantically idealising passion for a woman he scarcely knows, strongly reminds us of Antoine.

In *La Sirène du Mississippi* (1969) a typically shy Truffaut hero, Louis Mahé (Jean-Paul Belmondo), has recourse to the Lonely Hearts column of a newspaper to find himself a bride, and after some correspondence with Julie Roussel invites her to his home

3 'constantly seek[ing] a definitive love, before settling happily for the *provisoire*'.
4 'Before meeting you I never loved anyone. I hate impermanence [*le provisoire*] ... I am final and absolute [*définitif*].'
5 'we will never leave each other, not even for an hour'.

on the island of La Réunion where they will be married. The woman who arrives under Julie's name, however, and whom he marries, is in fact Marion Delgano (Catherine Deneuve), who has murdered Julie and stolen her identity. Even after discovering the truth Louis remains passionately in love with Marion, to whom he explains (in a scene romantically shot on a terraced roof under an evening sky) the difference between the letter-based relationship with Julie, and the passionate but brittle nature of their own couple. 'Dans nos lettres nous avons essayé d'établir quelque chose de solide, des choses définitives, puis tu es venue et tu m'as apporté le provisoire. Avant de te connaître j'ai cru que la vie était simple. Tu as tout embrouillé',[6] he explains. Here, *le provisoire* takes away the possibility of a once and for all happiness, but brings in its place a painful but also joyful sense of being alive. The scene is embedded in a narrative that shows Marion rejecting, fleeing, and trying to kill Louis as well as loving him: nothing definitive is established, though the final scene with its echoes of Renoir's *La Grande Illusion* shows the couple ploughing off through the snow together towards an uncertain but shared future. Both *Baisers volés* and *La Sirène* articulate a desire for the solidity of the absolute, but undercut this by placing the hero's central relationship (Antoine/Christine, Louis/Marion) on the side of the *provisoire*.

Truffaut's cinema plays out the tension between these two irreconcilable ways of being, sometimes expressing a yearning for the definitive, the permanent, the absolute, but articulating with some consistency a preference both aesthetic and moral for all that is impermanent, mobile, adaptable and provisional. Both Truffaut's conception of film as an artistic medium, and his preferred methods of making films, align film firmly with the *provisoire*.

6 'In our letters we tried to establish something lasting, definitive [*des choses définitives*] but then you came along and brought me the unexpected [*le provisoire*]. Before I knew you I thought life was simple. You've confused everything.'

Film-making methods and the *provisoire*: *La Nuit américaine*

Truffaut's films celebrate books and the process of writing, but also foreground the capacity of the written word to fix the open-ended, mobile stuff of experience in definitive form, reducing it to predetermined categories, as the earnest sociologist in *Une Belle Fille comme moi* would diminish Camille's anarchic vitality to the terms of a dry thesis. However, although the New Wave's *politique des auteurs* insisted on the analogy between writing and film-making, Truffaut's work expresses none of these reservations about the medium of film. On the contrary, Truffaut's films display unalloyed delight in the medium's capacity to shape the real into the form of stories whilst remaining true to the random and always incomplete nature of experience. In *La Nuit américaine*, a film about the production of a film, Truffaut shows that between the *auteur*'s original project and the completed film lies a complex, collective and largely unforeseeable process during which the different and sometimes competing creative inputs of actors, technicians, and artists must be harnessed together, the limitations imposed by budgets, temperaments, pregnancies and even deaths must be adapted to, and chance elements (objects, overheard snatches of speech) may be incorporated into the creative process.

Though the film's extremely favourable portrayal of the director Ferrand – played by Truffaut himself – could be judged narcissistic (Godard, who wrote to Truffaut to express his dislike of the film, asked 'How come the director's the only one who isn't screwing anyone?'), *La Nuit américaine* in many ways undermines the idea of the *auteur* as the artist who 'writes' their vision of the world on the screen. The emphasis falls rather on the collective nature of the production process, the determining effect of material constraints and the contribution of chance to the final product. In fact although *La Nuit américaine* is more concerned to celebrate than to describe realistically the process of film production, it does reproduce, through the fictional film crew, many of the real practices of the teams who made Truffaut's films under the auspices of his company Les Films du Carrosse. The film thus provides a useful point of entry into a consideration of the ways in which Truffaut's film-making practices favoured the principle of the *provisoire* over the *définitif*.

There is, first of all, a marked emphasis on the collaborative nature of the creative process, so that whilst Ferrand has the final word in all decisions, his creation is shaped and coloured by, for example, the props man's ingenuity, or the ability of the leading lady to persuade the jilted Alphonse to forget his pique and concentrate on the film. Ferrand does not realise a preconceived project so much as remain receptive to those around him and to the promptings of chance. An important effect of the emphasis on collaboration is the establishment of a short-term, provisional but close-knit community composed of all those who contribute to the film, from the producer to the lighting technicians. As they eat together, take group photos, find strategies to deal with the group's more awkward members (the infantile leading man, Alphonse, or the often inebriated female second lead), the team members come to resemble a family – though a family held together not by blood or a lifetime's commitment, but by a shared passion for cinema and an immediate project. The chosen and provisional nature of the family means that it need not subscribe to orthodox family morality: the film draws no moral distinction between hetero and homosexuality (the mystery lover of the likeable Alexandre turns out to be a young man) nor between single or married motherhood (the unknown paternity of Stacey's child is scarcely an issue). The distance between the film crew and the conventional family is marked by the outburst of the ironically named Madame Lajoie, wife of the production manager and the film's representative of an off-screen conservative moral majority. Frequently on the set in order to chaperone her husband, her constant knitting a sign of her aggressive respectability (evoking *les tricoteuses* or the women who knitted before the guillotine), Madame Lajoie observes the comradely promiscuity of the crew until she can bear it no longer and screams out her loathing for 'this *cinema* world where everybody sleeps with everybody else'. Madame Lajoie, however, is a comic figure whose views invite derision, and the film has shown the various sexual couplings that take place in a positive light, as part of an overlapping network of professional and/or friendly relationships. At the end of the film the group disbands, individuals go their separate ways towards new projects, enriched by the shared experience of creating a story.

La Nuit américaine romanticises but nonetheless reflects the collaborative production methods of the Films du Carrosse, outlined in chapter 2. Though each film was made by a differently composed crew, several members of the 'family' reappear in the credits of several films, indeed in some cases (notably Suzanne Schiffman) in almost all of them, thus making a consistent contribution to what we think of as Truffaut's filmic vision. Regular collaborators also transferred from one side of the camera to the other, so that technicians and administrators took on alternative identities within the fictional world constructed by the film. This team-based method of production, in which individuals change or acquire functions according to the needs of the film, differed markedly from the more formal methods of the studio-based *tradition de qualité*, against which the New Wave had defined itself. But it was in his treatment of the scenario that Truffaut most clearly reversed *tradition de qualité* practices.

As a critic, he had objected to the subordination of *mise en scène*, acting styles and editing to the demands of a pre-written script, in most cases an adaptation of a well-known literary work. Truffaut rarely employed professional script-writers, preferring to start from a (little-known) literary work, or simply an idea of his own, then to produce a working scenario for each film through a process of co-writing, collaborating with one of a small group of friends/colleagues (mainly Jean Gruault, Claude de Givray, Suzanne Schiffman or Jean-Louis Richard) and choosing his partner, in his own words, 'according to the needs of the scenario' (Le Berre 1993: 21).[7] Working either by correspondence or face to face, Truffaut and partner developed the initial project through a series of drafts, discussions and revisions, until filming began. The

---

7 With the exception of *La Sirène du Mississippi* which Truffaut adapted alone from the William Irish novel *Waltz into Darkness*.

scenario then remained open to adaptation and addition, not only at the visual level but also at that of plot and dialogue: in *La Nuit américaine* Ferrand and his assistant are shown writing the dialogue for the next day's shooting in the evening, after a hard day on location, and incorporating into the script words delivered spontaneously, under pressure of emotion, by their overwrought star. Julie's exclamation of 'What a nerve!' when she receives her own words presented as fictional dialogue signify a degree of self-reflexive irony on Truffaut's part, since he was much criticised by friends and ex-lovers for his tendency to use even the most intimate moments of his own life as material for scenarios.

In Films du Carrosse productions, then, the relationship between script and filming expressed Truffaut's inclination for the 'scénario toujours ouvert, toujours modifiable'[8] (Le Berre 1993: 9). Once the shooting itself was completed, the film remained in provisional form, since editing could still modify, inflect and even completely alter meaning. Truffaut's working method was one of overlapping projects, so that by the time one film finally reached its definitive form and went out to distributors, he (and the Carrosse team) were, in most cases, thoroughly involved in a new production. The final scenes of *La Nuit américaine* are scarcely concerned with the quality or the reception of *Je vous présente Paméla*, the production of which has formed the film's plot, but concentrate instead on the destinations of the departing members of the 'family', and on the pleasure of the now completed process of film-making: 'We hope you enjoy this film' says Bernard, the props man, interviewed for television as the team depart from the studio, 'as much as we enjoyed making it'. *La Nuit américaine* is not a film about film as product – indeed *Je vous présente Paméla* has the appearance of an unremarkable melodrama – but about film as process.

For what Truffaut celebrates, in this panegyric to his own life's work, is the transformational process whereby film can absorb the most disparate elements of everyday life, the most awkward and unexpected events, and weave them into a fiction that engages the

8 'open, endlessly modifiable scenario'.

emotions and the imagination. In an early scene, Ferrand happens to notice a vase in the hotel where the crew are staying: he immediately hands it over to the props man, seeing its possibilities as a small element in the developing narrative of *Je vous présente Paméla*. The vase suddenly becomes a doubly fictionalised object, part of the hotel décor in the film's frame narrative, and a significant detail in the décor of *Paméla*. The creative process appropriates random elements of the real, from objects to words, and also adapts to accommodate the unforeseeable. The discovery that one actress, Stacey, is pregnant – a condition uncalled for by the plot – at first seems to pose an insuperable problem, but this is finally overcome through careful editing of the scenes where she appears in a bathing suit. The film's leading man, Alexandre, dies in a car crash before shooting is finished, but by modifying the final part of the plot and carefully filming a double in long shot for essential scenes, the film is saved. Godard, attacking what he saw as Truffaut's bland romanticisation of the film industry, accused the film of ignoring the whole financial underpinning of film production (Truffaut 1988: 423), but whilst it is true that *La Nuit américaine* ignores the question of cinema's function within a capitalist economy, it does not conceal the determining role of finance in film-making. The character of the producer functions to recall the effect of budget on the director's artistic decisions, and the film's financial backers determine the final shape of the plot by the budget limitations they impose. The director's creativity is shown not to transcend material constraints but to depend on the capacity to adapt to and incorporate these.

La Nuit américaine expresses Truffaut's immense delight in the process of fictionalising reality into film, and in the power of the medium to reverse the flow of time and to refuse the definitive nature of the past. A film that systematically reminds us of how the filmic illusion is achieved – showing, for example, how a single scene is the result of multiple takes, or how the balcony window we see on screen may be no more than a piece of scaffolding supporting a frame – might serve to demystify and jolt the spectator into critical awareness: in Truffaut's hands, it serves rather to communicate the agreeable fact that, in the words of

Ferrand/Truffaut, 'les films sont plus harmonieux que la vie – il n'y a pas d'embouteillages dans les films, il n'y a pas de temps morts. Les films sont comme des trains ... comme des trains dans la nuit.'⁹ The verbal image connects with a recurring visual image in Truffaut's work: the poster advertising night travel on the French railways (seen in *La Mariée*, *L'Argent de poche*), in which a young woman dressed in a nightgown prepares to join her partner in a *couchette*, whilst outside the train window the stars sparkle in the night sky. The night train, mythologised by numerous films, is a richly evocative location, combining the intensity of confined spaces, the erotic charge of darkness, speed and the proximity of strangers, the merging of dream and reality as the traveller awakes from sleep to find him or herself in a new place. The fictional night train, if not the real one, carries the traveller/spectator smoothly along in a state of concentrated pleasure, removed from the complexities and repetitions of the static, everyday world, open to adventures and the excitement of new destinations. Film too provides these pleasures, moving freely in space and time, merging dream and the texture of the real.

Truffaut's films are not without self-irony, and when Antoine Doinel actually boards a night train in *L'Amour en fuite* and finds himself in a sleeping compartment in the company of the much-desired Colette, the resulting débâcle (they argue, he pulls the communication chord and makes his escape) might be read as an ironic comment on the gap between fictionalised ideal and awkward reality. But in *La Nuit américaine* the emphasis is solely on the magical power of film to transform the real. The stunt man sends a car hurtling over the cliff edge – but a flick of the switch reverses the film and brings it back to the road, recalling the reverse-motion shot that returns one of the *Mistons* from pretend-death to life; Alexander dies, but the film brings him back to life on screen, where his body, his voice, his unique personal style live on in an eternal present. If the life of the film crew is chaotic, beset by obstacles, conflicts, and tragedies, the film they create

9 'films are more harmonious than life – there are no hold-ups with a film, no lulls. Films move on like trains in the night.'

transmutes the muddle of the everyday into images that refer to the real, but are also richly patterned and allusive, evidence of human agency rather than mere chance. Film-making bestows the power to contest the inexorability of time, chance and even mortality. Though completion of the film inevitably consigns the final cut to the realm of the definitive, the emphasis within the film text is wholly on what Truffaut referred to as the medium's 'extraordinary power to really create life' (Desjardins 1993: 43), or in other words to assert the power of imagination over the fixity of the real.

Narratives, narration and the *provisoire*

The classic narrative is characterised by transparency, or the careful concealment of the fictional process, and by a coherent storyline ending in closure, that is by an ending that resolves dilemmas and answers the questions raised. In this sense the classic narrative supports a 'definitive' vision of the world as coherent, comprehensible, functioning according to rules and values that the spectators (in the case of film) may be expected to understand and share. In some senses Truffaut's films seem to conform to this pattern, which may help to explain the success of many of them within a mainstream market. Even though Truffaut's films generally privilege the exploration of emotion over the dynamics of narrative, they function effectively as stories, concerned to engage the spectator and to carry her or him along on the tide of curiosity and identification to the denouement. Even in the very early films Truffaut displays considerable skill as a storyteller, for example by economically providing the essential elements of characterisation, context and plot (minimal as this may be) in a few brief opening sequences.

Antoine et Colette, twenty-nine minutes long and thus demanding the narrative economy of a short story, provides a good example of this, establishing Antoine's personality and situation as well as opening the plot in four short sequences. First, Antoine waking up in his solitary bed-sitter, throwing open the shutters to look down on the morning bustle of the city, a shot then reversed to neatly capture Antoine's Rastignac-like[10] sense of freedom and of pitting himself against the metropolis. Second, a rapidly cut sequence showing Antoine travelling to work, clocking in and working in different sections of the record factory, shots which function iteratively or as single instances of what are regularly repeated actions. Third, a conversation with Antoine's close friend René leading into a brief flashback to *Les 400 Coups*, serving to establish the context of male friendship and to situate the action in relation to the well-known earlier film. And fourth, the concert hall, key location of the film's action, where an accelerating series of cuts shifts between Antoine, the aware but unresponsive object of his gaze who will turn out to be Colette, and the orchestra – the intensity of Antoine's desire marked by the soundtrack as the music rises to a crescendo. The scene is set for the story of unrequited love.

Closure, too, is generally observed: of the twenty-three films Truffaut made (excluding *Une Visite* and *Une Histoire d'eau*), eight end with the deaths of a central protagonist, six with the formation of a couple (or in the case of *Le Dernier Métro*, a triangle), four end with the completion of a project central to the plot (*La Nuit américaine*, *La Mariée* for example) and a further five with the completion of a significant stage in the lives of the protagonist/s. This would seem to place Truffaut's narratives more on the side of the closed and definitive text than on that of the provisional and open-ended.

However in a number of other senses the films contest the classic model. Transparency and the coherence of narrative structure demand that the spectator's suspension of disbelief should be total, but Truffaut's films both weave the spell of narrative illusion and deliberately draw attention to the processes that permit this. In the manner of Truffaut's narration there are elements that

---

10 Eugène de Rastignac is the young hero of Balzac's novel *Le Père Goriot* (*Old Goriot* 1835). An ambitious young student who discovers, in the course of the novel, the harsh rules that govern social success. Rastignac ends the novel looking down on the city spread out before him and expressing his determination to conquer it: 'A nous deux, maintenant!' ('Now it's between you and me!').

distance the spectator and quietly subvert the authority of the narrative, reminding us both that the world is more vast and various than a coherent narrative line allows, and that there is nothing truly inexorable about the particular direction the narrative is taking. Truffaut is not an experimental film-maker in the manner of a Godard, but he nonetheless employs a number of subtle distancing devices that work against the spectator's surrender to the power of the narrative. That 'peur de l'arrêt et de l'immobilité'[11] (Le Berre 1993: 168) that characterises the whole work is apparent in the insistence on the provisional and constructed nature of all stories.

Although each of the films is organised as a story, so that it is possible to provide a plot summary, most Truffaut films include apparently gratuitous scenes or sequences which can be forced – sometimes only thanks to some critical ingenuity – into the signifying system of the film as a whole, but which at a first viewing of the film seem simply to disturb the film's trajectory. Sometimes these are comic, as with the passer-by from whom Gérard of *Les Mistons* requests a light for his cigarette and who replies with disproportionate and unexpected emphasis 'No, sir! I never give a light – never! never!', or the police inspector in the last film *Vivement dimanche!* who manifests a strange and unexplained preoccupation with the relative ages of himself and his suspect, interrupting the film's 'functional' dialogue to pursue this. Sometimes these scenes establish, against the predominant movement of the narrative, a connection with apparently irrelevant but typically Truffaldian themes, as in the opening sequence of *Tirez sur le pianiste* where a *film noir* chase suddenly metamorphoses into an intimate male chat about relationships, or in *L'Amour en fuite* where a rather frothy plot about intersecting couples suddenly has Colette (now a lawyer) confronted with the moral dilemma of whether to defend a father accused of beating his child to death – a sub-plot that vanishes almost as quickly as it appeared. These deviations from the narrative line generally add enjoyment – either in the form of laughter or by posing a small enigma – and

11 'fear of endings and immobility'.

briefly remind us that the plot we are following is the result of an artistic choice; other narrative trajectories, other denouements were equally possible.

The same partial undermining of the fictional illusion is apparent at the level of narrative techniques or 'film language'. Truffaut's was relatively slow to start filming in colour, making the first six films (counting the short features) in black and white and changing to colour only with *Fahrenheit* in 1966. Black and white, to which he returned with *L'Enfant sauvage* in 1970 and *Vivement dimanche!* in 1982, is a more stylised and less realistic medium, since we normally view the world in colour, but one which in some ways Truffaut preferred. In his way of using colour film, he preserves some of the expressive qualities of the earlier medium, by (as it were) painting the image in colours that are implausible in realist terms but which both please the eye and carry metaphorical significance. *Fahrenheit* is thus a film dominated by the colours black, red and gold, the colours of the law-enforcers' uniforms and of the fire they use to fight the subversive force of the imagination, but which also turns against them; *L'Argent de poche* has the primary colours of childhood and, on the whole, happiness; *La Femme d'à côté* is almost entirely shot in shades of blue and yellow, with rare and significant flashes of blood red. The stylised use of colour paradoxically draws us into the film's emotions and at the same time reminds us of the fictional nature of the narrative. When the medium renounces transparency and becomes visible, the spectator's pleasure is double, arising both from the story itself and from sharing in the human capacity to shape and pattern the real, to transcend the apparently definitive nature of reality.

Truffaut's films also employ framing devices which foreground the act of storytelling and, like the use of colour, both intensify the film's emotional power and simultaneously maintain the spectator's awareness of her or his role in the fictional process. Six films (*Les Mistons, Jules et Jim, Antoine et Colette, Les Deux Anglaises, Adèle H., Le Dernier Métro*) employ the device of the extra-diegetic narrator, an unidentified voice-over supplementing and commenting on the narrative action, and a further three (*L'Enfant sauvage, L'Homme*

qui aimait les femmes, *La Femme d'à côté*) have intra-diegetic
narrators, or fictional characters who narrate part or all of the
story, in the case of *La Femme* directly to camera. In each of these
cases, the spectator is reminded of the process of narration and of
their own role as narratee, addressed, informed, and persuaded by
a storyteller.

Visual framing operates in a similar way, for innumerable
scenes in Truffaut's films are shot through windows or mirrors,
doubling and drawing attention to the framing operated by the
screen itself and thus foregrounding the constructed nature of the
image. Sometimes this framing reminds us that the camera is
adopting a subjective point of view, a technique much employed
but generally concealed rather than highlighted in classic narrative
cinema. Thus in *Adèle H.* we frequently observe Lieutenant Pinson,
the object of Adèle's love, through the windows of houses as she
spies on him, but when this device is repeated in Adèle's absence
and the camera peers through windows and half-open doors on its
own account, the effect is to draw attention to the process of filmic
narration. That is, where Truffaut's films employ the classic
technique of adopting a character's subjective viewpoint, they often
use this to disturb the illusion of overall narrative omniscience, as
in the scene in *Vivement* where the camera lingers inexplicably
with a passer-by in the street outside the Vercel's house, and
observes the couple arguing through a window. This highlighting
of the narrative process is still more marked when the subjective
viewpoint is detached from any fictional subject, as in *La Femme
d'à côté* when Bernard's violent explosion of anger against Mathilde
is filmed from inside the house, framed within the french windows,
despite the absence of any character observing from this vantage
point. Such devices do not break the fictional illusion, but they do
work to maintain a degree of distance on the spectator's part.
Truffaut's narrative structures and techniques maintain the tension
between emotional engagement and a more cerebral detachment,
between the story as definitive and the story as constructed,
provisional and arbitrary.

The *définitif* and the *provisoire* as theme

At a thematic level, Truffaut's films are consistently concerned with the tension between a yearning for the absolute and a finally more realistic and productive acceptance of the imperfect and the provisional. As an American critic, Vincent Canby, nicely puts it, Truffaut's films are in part about: 'a war between those who demand and desperately need to believe in the permanence of all things, and those who have had some fleeting glimpse of their impermanence, but who move blithely on, living on outside chances' (Canby 1975: 13). Love is the domain in which this war is most frequently waged, for Truffaut's absolutist characters tend to seek total happiness, complete fidelity and permanence in the couple, only to find that 'la solution couple ne marche pas' ('the couple solution just doesn't work'). If there are so many triangular relationships in Truffaut's films, this is because the introduction of a third party disturbs the symmetry of heterosexual pairing and raises questions about the viability of the couple as a basis for happiness.

The absolutists demand that love fill their lives and justify their existence. Some, like the sinister stranger in *Baisers volés*, choose absolute fidelity and devotion to a single partner and refuse to swerve from this, even in the face of rejection or death (Julie Kohler, Muriel in *Les Deux Anglaises*, Adèle H., Julien Davenne in *La Chambre verte*). Catherine (*Jules et Jim*) cannot bear to be abandoned by either of her lovers; Mathilde (*La Femme d'à côté*) struggles to escape from her desperate need for Bernard, but fails. Others (only male characters come into this category) devote their lives to the search for intense erotic and emotional fulfilment, but do so in an endless series of partners (Bertrand, 'the man who loved women', Maître Clément in *Vivement dimanche!*, to some extent Antoine Doinel, though Doinel straddles the categories of the *définitif* and the *provisoire*). The narratives direct sympathy towards these characters, but also connect their inability to change or compromise with death, either their own (Catherine, Mathilde, Maître Clément and in a sense Bertrand all commit suicide – Muriel and Adèle sink into illness or madness) or that of others (most of Truffaut's murderers belong amongst the absolutists, for example Catherine, Franca in *La Peau douce*, Julie Kohler, Mathilde, Maître Clément).

On the other side of Canby's 'war' are the compromisers, those who have learnt through experience that the demand for the absolute leads to death and suffering, that human happiness belongs in the realm of the relative, the provisional, and the impermanent. These are the characters who are capable of generosity because they can see beyond their own needs and desires: if Truffaut's films contain an ethical imperative, then it is expressed most clearly through this group of protagonists. Jules, the gentle friend and husband in *Jules et Jim*, Fabienne Tabard with her declaration that 'les gens sont formidables' ('people are wonderful'), Christine in the last two Doinel films, Anne of *Les Deux Anglaises*, both Julie and Joelle in *La Nuit américaine*, Jean-François Richet, the school teacher in *L'Argent de poche*, Geneviève in *L'Homme qui...*, the three central protagonists of *Le Dernier Métro* and Barbara in *Vivement dimanche!* – the list is not exhaustive, but demonstrates that the films are peopled by these adaptable and open-hearted individuals as much as or more than by the proponents of the *définitif*. All of them are presented positively and sympathetically. With the exception of Anne, all of them end the films alive.

Les Deux Anglaises, with its central opposition between the two sisters, demonstrates Truffaut's ways of depicting filmically these contrasting attitudes to life. Muriel, whose love for Claude is unique, intense and uncompromising ('Je veux Claude tout entier ou pas du tout. Si c'est non que ce soit comme la mort'),[12] is most often framed on the screen alone and still, engaged in writing letters (that she may never send) or her journal, or in thought. Her solitude and self-involvement are intensified by the use of mirrors, the camera focusing on her reflection, and by the use of a slow zoom in to extreme close-up that culminates in a shot of Muriel's (often half-concealed) eyes. Even in scenes of dialogue, the use of shot/counter-shot tends to frame Muriel's face in

12 'I want Claude absolutely or not at all. If I can't have him, I want my life to become a living death.'

isolation, and twice conversations with Claude are filmed not face to face, but with Muriel facing away from Claude and towards the camera, concerned more with her own thoughts than with communication. Muriel talks to herself, either in voice-over (the filmic version of the internal monologue) or aloud, in one scene speaking to the absent Claude as she walks down a London street. Conversely Anne is most often filmed with others and in motion, tracked by the camera as she walks, most strikingly in the long travelling shot that accompanies her walking along the river bank at the beginning of her happy rural retreat with Claude. Anne's dialogues tend to be shot not in shot/counter-shot but with both faces framed and visible, emphasising Anne's role as a woman whose attention is directed outside, towards the world she observes and represents in her art, and towards multiple others. Muriel tends to be filmed in interior shots, with low-key lighting, Anne in daylight intensified by additional lighting, thus in brighter and more varied colours.

Each sister chooses to lose her virginity with Claude. Anne's defloration is touched with humour, since she undresses in the riverside hut they are sharing to reveal red flannel undergarments which the narrator describes as 'quite impossible and rather military'; the scene is shot as a dialogue between the lovers and the image fades discreetly during the act itself, returning to show Anne's calm but not displeased expression and her verdict that 'c'est comme si tu jouais tout seul. Ce n'est pas encore nous'.[13] Muriel's defloration at the end of the film is shot with the camera entirely on Muriel's face, and the difficulty she has in emerging from her solipsistic world is signified by the painful struggle the couple share until her hymen breaks, and by the dramatic shot of red blood on the sheet. The film's sympathies are directed towards both sisters, towards Muriel's passionate and painful intensity of desire, as towards Anne's generosity, creativity and ability to combine sexual love and camaraderie. But the manner in which each sister is filmed emphasises that Anne's philosophy is the more liveable, the more humane, the more flexible and productive of happiness.

13 'it's as if you were playing by yourself. It's not us yet.'

La Chambre verte and the temptation of the *définitif*

The film that deals most explicitly with the temptation of the absolute is *La Chambre verte*, in which Truffaut takes the leading role as the reclusive, solitary Julien Davenne, a man so obsessed with fidelity to the dead that he can offer little to the living. Made five years after *La Nuit américaine*, *La Chambre* (based on a Henry James story) presents Truffaut in a role totally opposed to that of the film-director Ferrand: where Ferrand was creative and adaptable, Davenne is morbid and inflexible. The film balances sympathy for Davenne with recognition of the ethical inadequacy of his position. By shifting the action of James's story to the 1920s, Truffaut establishes a context that partially justifies Davenne's inability to leave the past behind: he is a survivor of the war in which France lost almost one and a half million soldiers. First evoked through the newsreel footage of the opening scene, the war is constantly recalled, both verbally and through the collection of gruesome slides of mutilated bodies in the trenches which Davenne inappropriately shows to his young mute protégé, Georges. Davenne's specific obsession with his dead wife Julie, to whom he has constructed a shrine in the green room of the title, is thus set against a wider concern with the tragic and untimely death of the young. The child Georges, who recalls both the 'wild child' (he too is a mute orphan, cared for and educated by a single surrogate father figure and his housekeeper) and the young Antoine (Georges too is imprisoned as the result of theft), is evidence of Davenne's capacity for kindness, and provides the film's almost unique moment of playfulness when Davenne daubs the child's nose with soap as Georges watches him shave. The fact that the narrative is structured as a love story also directs sympathy towards Davenne: Cécilia (Nathalie Baye) represents life against Davenne's death, colour and movement against his dark sepia tones and immobility, so that her growing attachment to him suggests the possibility of his redemption. The narrative concludes with Davenne's renovation of a tiny chapel, in the cemetery that is appropriately one of the film's key locations, where a candle burns to commemorate each of the dead he has known: since Cécilia helps with the project, and will light the final candle for Davenne himself, her love for him becomes visually associated with the mass of golden flames that replace the screen's hitherto mainly dark and shadowy images.

To this extent then, the film validates Davenne's position, but other elements in the film militate more conclusively against a sympathetic reading. Though the child serves to demonstrate that Davenne is not wholly without human sympathy, he also serves to confirm Cécilia's accusation that Davenne's love for the dead works against the living. Several scenes illustrate the child's devotion to Davenne, but when Georges inadvertently breaks one of the precious slide collection of dead soldiers, Davenne harshly sends him to bed without supper, which leads to his escape from the house, theft and subsequent imprisonment. Similarly, Davenne is first seen in the film comforting a friend on the death of his wife, but his friendship evaporates as soon as the widower transgresses Davenne's law of total fidelity by marrying again. Davenne can really love only the dead who, safely confined to the closed boundaries of completed lives, cannot challenge his view of them – his profession, as a writer of obituaries for a newspaper whose ageing readership is being steadily depleted by death, provides a metaphor for his philosophy so apt as to be almost (unintentionally?) comic.

Davenne's sense of his own integrity rests on the belief that to remember the dead is an expression of love and fidelity, and an act of resistance against the scandal of mortality, but the film suggests otherwise. The Julie he has created for himself out of photographs, casts of her hand, memories that solidify in the telling is now his creature, stripped of the demanding autonomy and changeability of a live other: as Davenne says to his widowed friend early in the film 'You can't lose them once they're dead, they belong to you.' The point is made most clearly in the scene of the dummy, where Davenne goes to collect the effigy of Julie he has had made by a local craftsman. Skilfully made, closely resembling the photographs of Julie, the figure is nonetheless horrible with its staring eyes and total immobility: the visual image signifies unmistakably that love for the dead is an extreme form of that possessive love that immobilises and reifies its object.

Davenne has its reluctant maker destroy it at once, a scene filmed from outside the windows of the workshop so that the hammer descending on the inert figure resembles a murder. Davenne's pleasurable anticipation of seeing the dummy, followed by the image of violent mutilation and destruction, suggests the proximity between the extremes of the emotional spectrum, between obsessive love and angry hatred, the desire to possess and the desire to kill. Truffaut's absolutists frequently kill the object of their love or, despairing, kill themselves.

Davenne's obsession with Julie and with the other dead is a form of death wish. Like Truffaut's other 'absolutists', he cannot deal with the awkward, changing and imperfect reality of relationships but must fix the loved one in immutable and definitive form, or die himself. As the chapel of remembrance nears completion he becomes increasingly anxious to 'complete the pattern' of candles: weakened by a period of self neglect motivated by the belief that Cécilia has betrayed him, he finally staggers to the chapel, is reconciled with Cécilia and dies. The final candle – his own – can thus be lit, and the narrative ends. The film's conclusion is confused in its sympathies: on the one hand Cécilia's love and the pathos of Davenne's death direct us towards identification with the hero; on the other hand, the desire that Cécilia should replace him as guardian of the chapel and keep all these candles burning until her own death is so patently absurd, and the obsession with fidelity to the dead so discredited by much of what has gone before, that the ending is far from satisfactory. It is not surprising that *La Chambre verte* was one of Truffaut's major box-office failures, despite its clear articulation of both the attraction and the danger of a yearning for the absolute and the definitive.

Le Dernier Métro: the Occupation, the *définitif* and the *provisoire*

One of the films that has been most reproached with a failure to address socio-political issues is *Le Dernier métro*, set under the German Occupation and thus unavoidably referring to a contentious period in French history. This story of a Jewish-owned theatre company surviving anti-Semitic policies, material shortages and censorship to greet the Liberation intact avoids the really difficult questions about resistance and collaboration. Truffaut, ever the cinephile, makes use of what have become standard filmic signifiers of the period to produce a pleasurably allusive surface: a soundtrack that includes the songs of Lucienne Delyle, sleekly sinister Gestapo cars in dark rainy streets, anonymous watchers in dark raincoats, Catherine Deneuve in her elegant 1940s suits and furs. Whilst the brutal reality of arrest, torture and the Holocaust are alluded to, the plot centres on relationships and on the survival of the theatre: one critic complained that the 'massive nature of the holocaust [is] reduced to the private level of a domestic tragedy' (Affron and Rubinstein 1985: 189). Critics objected too to the rather facile moral polarisation whereby the audience is positioned with the 'good' theatre troupe, emblematic of a French population broadly characterised as pro-Resistance, whilst 'the 'arch-villain', the collaborating journalist Daxiat, is just 'too convenient a diabolic device to concentrate all the poisons of an era into one thoroughly discredited personality' (Affron and Rubinstein 1985: 190). Such criticisms contain a good deal of truth particularly at a period when the French were beginning to come to terms, in the cinema as elsewhere, with the complex and painful reality of the Occupation.[14]

However *Le Dernier Métro* does not merely make use of the Occupation years as a picturesque background for a love story. We have defined the relationship between the *provisoire* and the *définitif* as a structuring opposition that constitutes a consistent value system in Truffaut's work, and *Dernier Métro* can usefully be read in the light of this opposition. One way of expressing the difference between the pro-fascist Daxiat and the theatre company, for example, is in terms of a conflict between Daxiat's insistence on definitive, essentialised identities, and the fluid, protean identities of the actors, which also extend to all those associated

---

14 Given the significant amount of collaboration with the occupying Nazi forces that occurred, the French found it difficult to explore the Occupation period in film as in other media. In 1971 Marcel Ophuls's challenging documentary *Le Chagrin et la pitié* to some extent opened the way to a re-examination of the period and was followed by several other films made in the 1970s and set in the war years, the best known probably being Louis Malle's *Lacombe Lucien* (1974).

with the theatre. Daxiat, representing the anti-Semitism of the Nazis and their French allies, insists that to be of Jewish blood means to be intrinsically corrupt, treacherous and decadent, so that the presence in the French theatre of any Jewish actor or director, regardless of individual characteristics, will corrode the entire medium. He also finds the new production of the *Théâtre Montmartre* to be 'effeminate', since for Daxiat the homosexuality of its director, Jean-Loup Cottins, signifies a contaminating and irreversible femininity. In contrast to this essentialist view, the film underlines the multiple, shifting and *provisional* identities of the members of the theatre troupe, for whom role-playing is not only a profession but also part of the fabric of everyday life.

As in *La Nuit américaine*, the frame narrative is structured around the production of a fictional work – here a play rather than a film. Thus we see several characters doubly fictionalised, as they act out scenes from the play on screen, and the temporary adoption of different identities is something that occurs throughout the film. But the role-playing does not end when the actors leave the stage: the film is less concerned to establish the personalities of the central protagonists than it is to display the fragility of the line that divides acting from 'being'. Marion is the only one who knows that her husband has not left the country, but is concealed in the cellar: she must play the part of the loyal but abandoned wife, acting out a false departure from the theatre each night before sneaking back to visit Lucas. Out of a mixture of loyalty and pride, she also maintains the role of the cool, detached employer against the increasing pressure of her desire for Bernard. Bernard himself is first seen in what Arlette terms 'le rôle de l'homme de la rue' ('the role of the man cruising the streets'), when he employs a rather predictable script in an attempt to chat her up, the theatrical nature of his performance highlighted visually by the fact that the 'street' is very apparently a studio set. As a member of the Resistance, he must also dissemble and conceal, so that when he leaves the theatre for the Maquis and explains to Marion that 'Where I'm going, I won't need make-up', she replies 'but you may need a disguise'. Lucas plays with the notion of being and looking Jewish, trying on a false hooked nose in an attempt to understand what Daxiat and his kind mean by 'Jewishness': 'J'essaie de me sentir juif' ('I'm trying to feel Jewish'). Being Jewish will not do, to satisfy an audience – particularly, here, an anti-Semitic audience – Jewishness must be performed.

The theme of identity as performance – hence as provisional and changeable rather than fixed and determined – is supported by the film's overall emphasis on the interpenetration of reality and fiction. As elsewhere in Truffaut, the spectator is occasionally gently detached from enjoyment of the fictional illusion by a reminder of its presence: 'Why did you say that to me?' asks Nadine in her role as the maid in the play she is rehearsing with Bernard. 'Because it's in the script!' he replies, suddenly shifting from the play to the level of the frame narrative, and reminding us too that we are willing accomplices in the fictional process, that Nadine and Bernard are also played by actors temporarily adopting roles. The final scene of the film operates the same technique on a larger scale, presenting the on-stage action (the secondary narrative) as primary narrative before suddenly revealing that what we thought was the continuation of the love story between Bernard and Marion is in fact simply a new play that they, as actors, are performing on stage. Such transitions emphasise the fragile line between performance and identity, and in that sense counter Daxiat's fascist desire to fix the individual within irrevocable categories of race, gender or sexuality, as well as questioning the model of coherent and consistent individual identity on which the classic narrative frequently depends.

The film does not explore the ideology of Nazism nor that of the French extreme-Right movements represented here by Daxiat. What it does make apparent is that Daxiat's order is exclusive and hierarchical, defining certain categories of human being as by nature inferior and expendable. Against this, the theatre represents a community that is inclusive and egalitarian, composed of disparate individuals held together by a shared project and by the ties of affection and solidarity that develop as they work towards its realisation. Like the film crew of *La Nuit américaine*, the team here is composed of men and women, straights and gays, established actors and backstage staff (such as the caretaker, Raymond, and the dresser, Germaine), Gentiles and Jews (the concealed Lucas but also Rosette, a young Jewish girl whose theatrical ambitions are encouraged by Marion and Arlette). Like most of Truffaut's characters who defend the principle of the *provisoire*, they are also good at adapting whatever material is to hand in the pursuit of their goals. These goals are closely linked: to produce the play successfully and thus ensure that one French cultural institution survives the war and provides pleasure for the deprived population; to resist the totalitarian order represented primarily by Daxiat's attempt to take over the theatre and by the anti-Semitic policies he supports. Adaptation plays a part in the achievement of each of these: Lucas discovers that from a certain position in the cellar he can hear every word of the rehearsals, and thus establishes a system whereby through Marion he can recover artistic control of the play without revealing his presence; Raymond improvises to provide props and lighting at a time of shortages and regular Allied bombardments, finally generating the necessary electricity by wiring up a bicycle to the lights and peddling furiously throughout the performance. Some instances of adaptation have more directly subversive aims: Bernard leaves the theatre with a record player under his arm, and a subsequent radio broadcast announces that a German Admiral has been killed by a home-made bomb adapted from a record player. On a lighter note, Marion buys a black-market ham (presumably to feed the hidden Lucas, despite his supposed 'Jewishness') and Raymond conceals it in a conveniently shaped cello case.

The love plot itself opposes the 'absolutist' ideal of total fidelity and exclusive monogamy observed elsewhere in Truffaut's world. If such an ideal is alluded to in the film it is only within the secondary narrative of *La Disparue*, of which we gain only disjointed glimpses suggesting a plot that centres on a doomed and tragic love affair. Within the film's story, the triangular nature of the love plot leads not to tragic consequences but to a happy conclusion. If Truffaut's playful deception leads the spectators to believe briefly that Lucas is dead and that guilt over his death has also destroyed the Bernard/Marion couple, when the camera draws back to reveal this scene as a secondary fiction it is replaced by the triumphant image of Marion flanked by her two men, one hand in Bernard's and the other in Lucas's, bowing to thunderous applause that celebrates both the Liberation of France and the happy resolution of all the film's narrative strands. Marion, it seems, loves *both* men. The conservative moral climate of the Occupation is little evoked in the film but is surely a relevant context. An important aspect of the collaborationist French government's ideology was summed up by Marshall Pétain's replacement of the Republican *Liberté, Egalité, Fraternité* by the nationalist and reactionary *Travail, Famille, Patrie* (Work, Family, Nation), and Pétain's 'National Revolution' like Nazi social policy insisted on women's maternal and domestic role and on a traditional view of marriage. The film thus ends with a rousing rejection of absolute, exclusive love that is also, in the Liberation context, a refusal of Vichyite sexual ideology. To this one could add that the theatre 'family' also represents an alternative and unorthodox response to Pétain's conservative view of the family defined by blood relationships and ruled by the father.

Le Dernier Métro can justifiably be accused of avoiding and simplifying many of the difficult political and ethical issues raised by the Occupation. Bernard's Resistance activities, for example, simply support the consistent identification of the theatre with the honourable struggle against Daxiat's values: the film makes no attempt to deal with the awkward fact that Resistance attacks on the occupying forces often led to the execution of innocent hostages. Anti-Semitism is evoked without explicit reference to the horror of the Holocaust, and the two Jewish characters end the film alive and well. The complex issue of French collaboration with the Nazis is neatly divided into, on the one hand, ideological complicity (concentrated and punished in the person of Daxiat who ends the film exiled and on the run) and, on the other, pragmatic acceptance of the situation (Marion accepts that she cannot employ Jewish actors, the ambitious Nadine is willing to charm Daxiat if this will advance her career, but these compromises are dissolved in the overall alignment of the theatre with 'good' values).

However, *Le Dernier Métro* is not merely an exercise in

cinematic exploitation of the period's mythologised charm. The film deals with Truffaut's habitual themes within the context of occupied Paris, mapping the value system that informs all of his films onto the struggle between a totalitarian order and the desire for a just, humane and liberal society. Totalitarianism is unequivocally aligned with the *définitif*, with an essentialised and changeless definition of nation, gender, and personal identity; in opposition to this stands the theatre as symbol of the right to dream, to redefine the self and relationships, to choose provisional forms of community rather than those based on blood or on an authorised social contract. Such a defence against the dark forces of fascism may seem flimsy, but the film makes little pretence at realism, opting instead for visual theatricality, moral polarisation and an unashamedly utopian ending.

Conclusion

Truffaut's films provide little explicit commentary on the social or political questions of their times. They are not committed films, nor especially critical or subversive. They do address important questions that are at once personal and social, and do so with intelligence, humour and imagination: the construction of gendered identity, the nature of patriarchal authority, the expressive and repressive power of language, the possible ways of sharing individual lives and forming communities, the nature of desire. Despite the collective rather than individual nature of the process of film-making – itself a theme of the films – the consistent vision and structure of values that the New Wave ascribed to *auteur* cinema are discernible here. We have described these in terms of the tension between recognition of the emotional pull of the absolute, the *définitif*, and the ethical and aesthetic preference for all that is provisional, transitory, and impermanent, the *provisoire*.

This opposition is present from the earliest films: in *Les 400 Coups* Antoine survives both an educational and penal system dedicated to fixing him into his place, and a temptation towards absolute love for his mother, by taking refuge in the pleasures of friendship, truancy and fiction. In *Jules et Jim* too, there is a struggle between the temptation of the fixed and permanent, and desire for an open-ended, fluid definition of love and relationships. Jules and Jim seek in Catherine the absolute of the 'eternal feminine' glimpsed in an antique statue; Catherine feels compelled to possess them both, and finally kills herself and Jim rather than accept the fact that she has lost him. But the film's happiest and, filmically, most innovative moments are all on the side of the *provisoire*: whilst the trio of Jules, Jim and Catherine remain together, desire circulating between them and never finally satisfied, the film is dazzlingly filled with images of movement and freedom. The three free-wheel on bicycles down a wide curving hill, the camera framing and re-framing them separately and in different combinations; at Catherine's behest they go searching in the countryside near the sea for 'traces of lost civilisation' and the camera searches with them, discovering disparate objects – a piece of china, a postcard, a broken cup, an empty packet of English cigarettes – which, to the accompaniment of a joyful soundtrack, take on the value of small treasures; the three race across a bridge, laughing and panting, even gender now a fluid category since Catherine is dressed as a boy and has become 'Thomas'. The song that Jeanne Moreau, as Catherine, sings in the later part of the film, recaptures nostalgically the mood of this period, and the characteristic pattern of Truffaut's love stories, with its refrain

> On s'est connu, on s'est reconnu
> On s'est perdu de vue, on s'est perdu de vue
> On s'est retrouvé, on s'est réchauffé
> Puis on s'est séparé.
> Chacun pour soi est reparti
> Dans le tourbillon de la vie.[15]

Whereas *La Nuit américaine* and *Le Dernier Métro* conclude unequivocally on the side of the *provisoire*, *Jules et Jim* presents a more complex picture. In one sense (as in *Le Dernier Métro*) the

15 'We met each other, then we met up again / We lost touch, we lost sight of each other / We found each other again, kept each other warm / Then we said goodbye. / Each one went their separate way / In the whirlwind of life.'

définitif is presented as in alliance with a conservative social order: it is the outbreak of war between France and Germany, with its reassertion of the primacy of national identity, that puts an end to the trio's period of shared freedom in Paris. Jules and Jim are obliged to join opposing armies, to become not the equivocally named 'Jules's and 'Jim' (the French-sounding Jules is Austrian, the English-sounding Jim, French), but a German soldier and a French soldier. Catherine, in this new climate, surrenders to normative definitions of a woman's role and becomes Jules's wife and the mother of his daughter. The spontaneity and invention of the Parisian period is never refound. At the funeral of Jim and Catherine some greater authority decrees that their ashes may not be mingled ('It was not allowed' the narrator tells us), and that despite her declared wish the ashes of Catherine may not be scattered to the winds but must be doubly enclosed, in a container inside a locked compartment in the cemetery. The film contains a sense – to be developed in later films – of an opposition between an oppressive social order aligned with the values of the *définitif*, and an attempt to invent new types of relationship and styles of living on the principle of the *provisoire*.

However, the *définitif* cannot here be reduced to an external and hostile force. *Jules et Jim* pursues the desire to move freely with the 'whirlwind of life' beyond early youth into maturity, and deals with the contrary desires for a stable and dependable love, and for children. The attempt, chiefly that of Catherine, to 'reinvent love' (as Jim describes it) founders on the misery caused by jealousy (Jules's resigned pain as Catherine transfers her love first to Albert, then to Jim, then see-saws between them; Catherine's jealousy as Jim settles for a secure happiness with Gilberte). The sweeping, circular camera movements that signified elation in the earlier part of the film are replaced by the fixed camera that observes Catherine's car driving round and round in a frustrated circle beneath Jim's window, as he resists this call for his attention. The sterility of Catherine's attempt to fix both men in her life, one as lover, the other as faithful friend, is signified by the failure of the Jim/Catherine couple to produce a child. Torn between the desire to live in the provisional, and the desire to have an absolute love that will give her life meaning ('What about me, Jim? But what about *me*?' she cries, before her first attempt to kill him), Catherine chooses death. As Jules leaves the cemetery and the film ends, only the swelling of the soundtrack to a jubilant reprise of Catherine's song, *Le Tourbillon de la vie*, reasserts the possible victory of the *provisoire*.

Truffaut's last film ends on quite a different note, though it too might be said to bring together both sides of the *définitif/provisoire* polarity. *Vivement dimanche!* was shot in 1982, and came out in 1983 little more than a year before its director's death. The film mingles *film noir* thriller with romantic comedy, and ties up both strands in a neat, tongue-in-cheek denouement, as the heroine, Barbara, pregnant and happy, marries the man she has saved from false conviction for murder, the ceremony performed by a priest whom they had previously taken for a gangster, the happy couple photographed by Barbara's ex-husband who has also played a part in both strands of the plot. A choir of children provide the soundtrack. A church wedding, pregnancy, perfect closure with all the plot's questions resolved – this would seem to be an ending both of the film and of Truffaut's career that privileges the virtues of the *définitif*. Suddenly, though, the photographer drops the lens from his camera. The film camera loses all interest in the wedding, church and central characters and concludes the film, as the credits roll by, with a lengthy sequence focused on the children's feet and the playful kicking around of the lens from one child to another. Ludic, exuberant, drawing attention to the world excluded by the narrative itself, and preventing any further fixing of the couple's happiness in the immobile images of the still camera, the final scene of Truffaut's entire cinematic production registers one final victory for the *provisoire*.

References

Affron, M. J., and E. Rubinstein (eds) (1985), *The Last Metro*, New Brunswick, Rutgers University Press.

Armes, Roy (1985), *French Cinema*, London, Secker & Warburg.

Canby, Vincent (1975), Truffaut's clear-eyed quest, *New York Times*, September 14, p. 13.

Cook, Pam (1985), *The Cinema Book*, London, BFI.

Desjardins, Aline (1973), *Aline Desjardins s'entretient avec François Truffaut*, Ottawa, Collection Les Beaux-Arts.

Gillain, Anne (ed.) (1988), *Le Cinéma selon François Truffaut*, Paris, Flammarion.

Insdorf, Annette (1989), *François Truffaut*, New York, Touchstone.

Le Berre, Carole (1993), *François Truffaut*, Paris, Editions de l'Etoile/Cahiers du cinéma.

Truffaut, François (1987), *Le Plaisir des yeux*, Paris, Flammarion/Cahiers du cinéma.

Truffaut, François (1988), *Correspondance*, Paris, Hatier.

Filmography

Une Visite, 1955 (*A Visit*)

7 min. 40 sec., b/w
Producer: Robert Lachenay
Assistant Director: Robert Lachenay
Script: François Truffaut
Camera: Jacques Rivette
Editing: Alain Resnais
Principal actors: Francis Cognany, Florence Doniol-Valcroze, Laura
 Mauri, Jean-José Richer. Filmed in the Paris apartment of Jacques
 Doniol-Valcroze.

Les Mistons, 1957 (UK/USA: *The Mischief Makers*)

23 min., b/w
Production Company: Les Films du Carrosse
Producer: Robert Lachenay
Assistant Directors: Claude de Givray, Alain Jeannel
Script: François Truffaut
Camera: Jean Malige
Editing: Cécile Decugis
Music: Maurice Le Roux
Principal actors: Gérard Blain (Gérard), Bernadette Lafont (Bernadette).
 Adapted from a short story taken from *Les Virginales* by Maurice
 Pons. Filmed in and around Nîmes.

Une Histoire d'eau, **1958** (UK: *A Story of Water*)

18 mins., b/w
Production Company: Les Films de la Pléïade
Producer: Pierre Braunberger
Production Manager: Roger Fleytoux
Script: Jean-Luc Godard
Camera: Michel Latouche
Editing: Jean-Luc Godard
Sound: Jacques Maumont
Actors: Jean-Claude Brialy (The Man), Caroline Dim (The Girl).
   Project begun by François Truffaut and completed by Jean-Luc
   Godard. Filmed on the outskirts of Paris during floods.

Les 400 Coups, **1959** (UK/USA: *Les 400 Coups*)

93 min., b/w
Production Company: Les Films du Carrosse, SEDIF
Executive Producer: Georges Charlot
Assistant Directors: Philippe de Broca with Alain Jeannel, Francis
   Cognany, Robert Bober
Script: François Truffaut and Marcel Moussy
Camera: Henri Decae with Jean Rabier
Editing: Marie-Joseph Yoyotte with Cécile Decugis, Michèle de Possel
Continuity: Jacqueline Parey
Sound: Jean-Claude Marchetti with Jean Labussière
Art Direction: Bernard Evein
Music: Jean Constantin
Principal actors: Jean-Pierre Léaud (Antoine Doinel), Claire Maurier
   (Mother), Albert Rémy (Stepfather), Patrick Auffay (René), Guy
   Decomble (Teacher) Jeanne Moreau (Woman in street). Original
   screenplay by François Truffaut and Marcel Moussy. Filmed in
   Paris and Normandy. The film is dedicated to André Bazin.

Tirez sur le pianiste, **1960** (UK: *Shoot The Pianist*; USA: *Shoot the Piano Player*)

85 minutes., b/w
Production Company: Les Films de la Pléïade
Producer: Pierre Braunberger
Production Managers: Serge Komor, Roger Fleytoux
Assistant Directors: Francis Cognany and Robert Bober

Script: François Truffaut and Marcel Moussy
Camera: Raoul Coutard
Editing: Claudine Bouché, Cécile Decugis
Continuity: Suzanne Schiffman
Sound: Jacques Gallois
Music: Georges Delerue
Songs: *Dialogue d'amoureux* Félix Leclerc, sung by Félix Leclerc and Lucienne Vernay, *Vanille et framboise*, Boby Lapointe
Art Direction: Jacques Mély
Principal actors: Charles Aznavour (Charlie Kohler/Edouard Saroyan), Marie Dubois (Léna), Nicole Berger (Thérèsa), Michèle Mercier (Clarisse), Albert Rémy (Chico), Serge Davri (Plyne), Richard Kanayan (Fido). Based on the novel *Down There* by David Goodis. Filmed in Paris and near Grenoble.

Jules et Jim, 1961 (UK/USA: *Jules and Jim*)

100 min., b/w
Production Company: Les Films du Carrosse, SEDIF
Executive Producer: Marcel Berbert
Assistant Directors: Georges Pellegrin and Robert Bober
Script: François Truffaut and Jean Gruault
Camera: Raoul Coutard
Editing: Claudine Bouché
Continuity: Suzanne Schiffman
Music: Georges Delerue
Song: *Le Tourbillon*, Boris Bassiak (Serge Rezvani)
Art Direction/Costumes: Fred Capel
Principal actors: Jeanne Moreau (Catherine), Oskar Werner (Jules), Henri Serre (Jim), Boris Bassiak (Albert), Vanna Urbino (Gilberte), Sabine Haudepin (Sabine). Based on the novel *Jules et Jim* by Henri-Pierre Roché. Filmed in Paris, on the south coast of France and in Alsace.

Antoine et Colette, 1962

29 min., b/w
Production Company: Ulysse Productions
Executive Producer: Philippe Dussart
Production Manager: Pierre Roustang
Assistant Directors: Georges Pellegrin
Script: François Truffaut

Camera: Raoul Coutard
Editing: Claudine Bouché
Continuity: Suzanne Schiffman
Music: Georges Delerue
Song: *L'Amour à vingt ans* lyrics by Yvon Samuel, sung by Xavier Despras
Photographer: Henri-Cartier Bresson
Artistic advisor: Jean de Baroncelli
Principal actors: Jean-Pierre Léaud (Antoine Doinel), Marie-France Pisier (Colette), Patrick Auffay (René). Filmed in Paris. Original screenplay by François Truffaut. This was Truffaut's contribution to the compliation film *L'Amour à vingt ans* (*Love at Twenty*).

La Peau douce, 1964 (UK: Silken Skin; USA: The Soft Skin)

115 min., b/w
Production Company: Les Films du Carrosse, SEDIF
Executive Producer: Marcel Berbert
Production Manager: Georges Charlot
Assistant Director: Jeran-François Adam
Script: François Truffaut and Jean -Louis Richard
Camera: Raoul Coutard
Editing: Claudine Bouché
Continuity: Suzanne Schiffman
Music: Georges Delerue
Principal actors: Françoise Dorléac (Nicole), Jean Desailly (Pierre Lachenay), Nelly Benedetti (Franca Lachenay), Sabine Haudepin (Sabine Lachenay). Original screenplay by François Truffaut and Jean-Louis Richard. Filmed in Paris, Normandy and Lisbon.

Fahrenheit 451, 1966 (UK/USA: Fahrenheit 451)

113 min., col.
Production Company: An Enterprise Vineyard Production
Producer: Lewis M. Allen
Associate Producer: Micky Delamar
Assistant Director: Bryan Coates
Script: François Truffaut, Jean-Louis Richard, David Rudkin, Helen Scott
Camera: Nicholas Roeg
Editing: Thom Noble
Continuity: Kay Manders

Music: Bernard Herrmann
Sound: Bob McPhee
Art Direction/Costumes: Syd Cain and Tony Walton
Principal actors: Oskar Werner (Montag), Julie Christie (Linda and
Clarisse), Cyril Cusack (The Captain), Anton Diffring (Fabian).
From the novel *Fahrenheit 451* by Ray Bradbury. Filmed in the
suburbs of London and at Pinewood Studios.

La Mariée etait en noir, 1967 (UK/USA: *The Bride Wore Black*)

107 min., col.
Production Company: Les Films du Carrosse, Les Artistes associés
(Paris), Dino de Laurentiis Cinematografica (Rome)
Executive Producer: Marcel Berbert
Production Manager: Georges Charlot
Assistant Director: Jean Chayrou and Roland Thénot
Script: François Truffaut and Jean-Louis Richard
Camera: Raoul Coutard
Editing: Claudine Bouché with Yann Dedet
Continuity: Suzanne Schiffman
Sound: René Levert
Music: Bernard Herrmann
Art Direction: Pierre Guffroy
Principal actors: Jeanne Moreau (Julie Kohler), Claude Rich (Bliss),
Jean-Claude Brialy (Corey), Michel Bouquet (Coral), Michael
Lonsdale (Morane), Charles Denner (Fergus), Daniel Boulanger
(Delvaux). Based on the novel *The Bride Wore Black* by William
Irish. Filmed in Cannes and Paris.

Baisers volés, 1968 (UK/USA: *Stolen Kisses*)

90 min., col.
Production Company: Les Films du Carrosse, Les Artistes associés
Executive Producer: Marcel Berbert
Production Manager: Roland Thénot
Assistant Director: Jean-José Richer
Script: François Truffaut with Claude de Givray and Bernard Revon
Camera: Denys Clerval
Editing: Agnès Guillemot
Continuity: Suzanne Schiffman
Sound: René Levert
Music: Antoine Duhamel

Song: *Que reste-t-il de nos amours?* Charles Trenet

Art Direction: Claude Pignot

Principal actors: Jean-Pierre Léaud (Antoine Doinel), Claude Jade (Christine), Delphine Seyrig (Mme Tabard), Michel Lonsdale (M. Tabard), Harry Max (M. Henri). Original screenplay by François Truffaut with Claude de Givray and Bernard Revon. Filmed in Paris. The film is dedicated to Henri Langlois's Cinémathèque française.

La Sirène du Mississippi, 1969 (USA: *Mississippi Mermaid*)

120 min., col.

Production Company: Les Films du Carrosse, Les Productions Artistes associés and Produzioni Associate Delphos (Rome)

Executive Producer: Marcel Berbert

Production Managers: Claude Miller and Roland Thénot

Assistant Director: Jean-José Richer

Script: François Truffaut

Camera: Denys Clerval

Editing: Agnès Guillemot with Yann Dedet

Continuity: Suzanne Schiffman

Sound: René Levert

Music: Antoine Duhamel

Art Direction: Claude Pignot with Jean-Pierre Kohut-Svelko

Principal actors: Jean-Paul Belmondo (Louis Mahé), Catherine Deneuve (Marion/Julie Roussel), Marcel Berbert (Jardine), Michel Bouquet (Comolli). Based on the novel *Waltz into Darkness* by William Irish. Filmed on the island of La Réunion, Antibes, Aix-en-Provence and near Grenoble. The film is dedicated to Jean Renoir.

L'Enfant sauvage, 1970 (UK/USA: *The Wild Child*)

83 min., b/w

Production Company: Les Films du Carrosse, Les Productions Artistes associés

Executive Producer: Marcel Berbert

Production Managers: Claude Miller, Roland Thénot

Assistant Director: Suzanne Schiffman

Script: François Truffaut and Jean Gruault

Camera: Nestor Almendros with Philippe Theaudière

Editing: Agnès Guillemot with Yann Dedet

Continuity: Christine Pellé
Sound: René Levert
Music: Vivaldi
Art Direction: Jean Mandaroux
Costumes: Gitt Magrini
Principal actors: François Truffaut (Dr Itard), Jean-Pierre Cargol (Victor), Françoise Seigner (Mme Guérin), Jean Dasté (Dr Pinel). Based on the report on Victor from the Aveyron by Jean Itard (1806). The film is dedicated to Jean-Pierre Léaud. Filmed in the Auvergne and in Paris.

Domicile conjugal, 1970 (UK/USA: *Bed and Board*)

100 min., col.
Production Company: Les Films du Carrosse, Valoria Films (Paris), Fida Cinematografica (Rome)
Executive Producer: Marcel Berbert
Production Managers: Claude Miller, Roland Thénot
Assistant Directors: Suzanne Schiffman, Jean-François Stévenin
Script: François Truffaut, Claude de Givray and Bernard Revon
Camera: Nestor Almendros
Editing: Agnès Guillemot, Yann Dedet, Martine Kalfon
Continuity: Christine Pellé
Sound: René Levert
Music: Antoine Duhamel
Art Direction: Jean Mandaroux
Make-up: Nicole Félix
Principal actors: Jean-Pierre Léaud (Antoine Doinel), Claude Jade (Christine), Hiroko Berghauer (Kyoko). Original screenplay by François Truffaut, Claude de Givray and Bernard Revon. Filmed in Paris.

Les Deux Anglaises et le Continent, 1971 (UK: *Anne and Muriel*)

132 min., col.
Production Company: Les Films du Carrosse, Cinétel
Executive Producer: Marcel Berbert
Production Managers: Claude Miller, Roland Thénot
Assistant Director: Suzanne Schiffman
Script: François Truffaut and Jean Gruault
Camera: Nestor Almendros
Editing: Yann Dedet, Martine Barraqué

Continuity: Christine Pellé
Sound: René Levert
Music: Georges Delerue
Art Direction: Michel de Broin
Costumes: Gitt Magrini
Principal actors: Jean-Pierre Léaud (Claude Roc), Kika Markham (Anne Brown), Stacey Tendeter (Muriel Brown), Sylvia Marriott (Mrs Brown), Marie Mansart (Claire Roc), Philippe Léotard (Diurka). Based on the novel *Les Deux Anglaises et le continent* by Henri-Pierre Roché. Filmed in Paris, the Cotentin Peninsula and the regions of Vivarais and the Jura.

Une Belle fille comme moi, 1972 (UK: *A Gorgeous Bird Like Me*; USA: *Such a Gorgeous Kid Like Me*)

100 min., col.
Production Company: Les Films du Carrosse, Columbia Films
Executive Producer: Marcel Berbert
Production Managers: Claude Miller, Roland Thénot
Assistant Director: Suzanne Schiffman
Script: François Truffaut and Jean-Loup Dabadie
Camera: Pierre-William Glenn, Walter Bal
Editing: Yann Dedet, Martine Barraqué
Continuity: Christine Pellé
Sound: René Levert
Music: Georges Delerue
Songs: *Sam's song*, Jean-Loup Dabadie, sung by Guy Marchand, *Une belle fille comme moi*, Jacques Datin, lyrics by Jean-Loup Dabadie, *J'attendrai*
Art Direction: Jean-Pierre Kohut-Svelko and Jean-François Stévenin
Costumes: Monique Dury
Make-up: Thi Loan N'Guyen
Special effects: Jean-Claude Dolbert
Principal actors: Bernadette Lafont (Camille Bliss), André Dussolier (Stanislas Prévine), Philippe Léotard (Clovis Bliss), Guy Marchand (Sam Golden), Claude Brasseur (Maître Murène), Charles Denner (Arthur). Based on the novel *Such a Gorgeous Kid Like Me* by Henry Farrel. Filmed in and around Béziers.

La Nuit americaine, 1973 (UK: *Day for Night*)

115 min., col.

Production Company: Les Films du Carrosse, PECF (Paris), PIC (Rome)

Executive Producer: Marcel Berbert

Production Managers: Claude Miller, Roland Thénot, Alex Maineri

Assistant Directors: Suzanne Schiffman, Jean-François Stévenin

Script: François Truffaut, Jean-Louis Richard and Suzanne Schiffman

Camera: Pierre-William Glenn, Walter Bal

Editing: Yann Dedet, Martine Barraqué

Continuity: Christine Pellé

Sound: René Levert, Harrik Maury

Music: Georges Delerue

Art Direction: Damien Lanfranchi

Principal actors: François Truffaut (Ferrand), Nathalie Baye (Joëlle), Jean-Pierre Léaud (Alphonse), Jacqueline Bisset (Julie Baker), David Markham (Dr Nelson), Nike Arrighi (Odile), Valentina Cortese (Séverine), Dani (Liliane). Original screenplay by François Truffaut, Jean-Louis Richard and Suzanne Schiffman. The film is dedicated to Lilian and Dorothy Gish. Filmed in La Victorine Studios, Nice.

L'Histoire d'Adèle H., 1975 (UK/USA: *The Story of Adèle H.*)

95 min., col.

Production Company: Les Films du Carrosse, Les Productions Artistes associés

Executive Producer: Marcel Berbert

Production Managers: Claude Miller, Roland Thénot, Patrick Millet

Assistant Directors: Suzanne Schiffman, Carl Hathwell

Script: François Truffaut, Jean Gruault with Frances Guille

Camera: Nestor Almendros

Editing: Yann Dedet, Martine Barraqué

Continuity: Christine Pellé

Sound: Jean-Pierre Ruh, Michel Laurent

Music: Maurice Jaubert

Art Direction: Jean-Pierre Kohut-Svelko

Make-up: Thi Loan N'Guyen

Costumes: Jacqueline Guyot

Principal actors: Isabelle Adjani (Adèle Hugo), Bruce Robinson (Lieutenant Pinson), Sylvia Marriott (Mrs Saunders), Joseph

Blatchley (Bookshop owner). Based on *The Diary of Adèle H.* edited by Frances Guille, Lettres Modernes, Paris. Filmed in Guernsey and Senegal.

L'Argent de Poche, 1976 (UK/USA: *Small Change*)

105 min., col.
Production Company: Les Films du Carrosse, Les Productions Artistes associés
Executive Producer: Marcel Berbert
Production Managers: Roland Thénot, Daniel Messere
Assistant Directors: Suzanne Schiffman, Alain Maline
Script: François Truffaut and Suzanne Schiffman
Camera: Pierre-William Glenn with Jean-François Gondre, Florent Bazin, Jean-Claude Vicquery
Editing: Yann Dedet, Martine Barraqué
Continuity: Christine Pellé with Laura Truffaut
Sound: Michel Laurent, Michel Brethey
Music: Maurice Jaubert
Art Direction: Jean-Pierre Kohut-Svelko
Make-up: Thi Loan N'Guyen
Costumes: Monique Dury
Principal actors: Jean-François Stévenin (Jean-François Richet), Virginie Thévenet (Lydie Richet), Nicole Félix (mother of Grégory), Francis Devlaeminck (M. Riffle), Tania Torrens (Mme Riffle), Ewa Truffaut (Patricia), Laura Truffaut (Madeleine Doinel). Original screenplay by François Truffaut and Suzanne Schiffman. Filmed in and around Thiers.

L'Homme qui aimait les femmes, 1977 (UK/USA: *The Man Who Loved Women*)

118 min., col.
Production Company: Les Films du Carrosse, Les Productions Artistes associés
Executive Producer: Marcel Berbert
Production Managers: Roland Thénot with Philippe Lièvre, Lydie Mahias
Assistant Directors: Suzanne Schiffman, Alain Maline
Script: François Truffaut, Michel Fermaud, Suzanne Schiffman
Camera: Nestor Almendros with Anne Trigaux, Florent Bazin
Editing: Martine Barraqué

Continuity: Christine Pellé
Sound: Michel Laurent, Jean Fontaine
Music: Maurice Jaubert
Art Direction: Jean-Pierre Kohut-Svelko, Pierre Compertz, Jean-Louis Povéda
Make-up: Thi Loan N'Guyen
Costumes: Monique Dury, Nicole Banal
Principal actors: Charles Denner (Bertrand Morane), Brigitte Fossey (Geneviève Bigey), Nelly Borgeaud (Delphine Grezel) Nathalie Baye (Martine Desdoits), Leslie Caron (Véra). Original screenplay by François Truffaut, Michel Fermaud, Suzanne Schiffman. Filmed in and around Montpellier.

La Chambre verte, 1978 (UK/USA: *The Green Room*)

94 min., col.
Production Company: Les Films du Carrosse, Les Productions Artistes associés
Executive Producer: Marcel Berbert
Production Managers: Roland Thénot, Geneviève Lefebvre
Assistant Directors: Suzanne Schiffman, Emmanuel Clot
Script: François Truffaut and Jean Gruault
Camera: Nestor Almendros with Anne Trigaux, Florent Bazin
Editing: Martine Barraqué
Continuity: Chritine Pellé
Sound: Michel Laurent, Jean-Louis Ugnetto
Music: Maurice Jaubert
Art Direction: Jean-Pierre Kohut-Svelko, Pierre Compertz, Jean-Louis Povéda
Make-up: Thi Loan N'Guyen
Costumes: Monique Dury, Christian Gasc
Principal actors: François Truffaut (Julien Davenne), Nathalie Baye (Cécilia Mandel), Jean Dasté (Bernard Humbert), Jane Lobre (Mme Rambaud). Based on themes in novels by Henry James. Filmed in Honfleur and Caen.

L'Amour en fuite, 1979 (UK/USA: *Love on the Run*)

94 min., col.
Production Company: Les Films du Carrosse
Executive Producer: Marcel Berbert
Production Manager: Roland Thénot

Assistant Directors: Suzanne Schiffman, Emmanuel Clot, Nathalie Seaver

Script: François Truffaut, Suzanne Schiffman, Jean Aurel, Marie-France Pisier

Camera: Nestor Almendros with Florent Bazin, Emilia-Pakull-Latorre

Editing: Martine Barraqué

Continuity: Christine Pellé

Sound: Michel Laurent

Music: Georges Delerue

Song: *L'Amour en fuite*, Alain Souchon

Art Direction: Jean-Pierre Kohut-Svelko, Pierre Compertz, Jean-Louis Povéda

Make-up: Thi Loan N'Guyen

Costumes: Monique Dury

Principal actors: Jean-Pierre Léaud (Antoine Doinel), Claude Jade (Christine), Marie-France Pisier (Colette), Dani (Liliane), Dorothée (Sabine), Daniel Mesguich (Xavier Barnérias), Julien Bertheau (M. Lucien). Original screenplay by François Truffaut, Suzanne Schiffman, Marie-France Pisier. Filmed in Paris.

Le Dernier Métro, 1980 (UK/USA: *The Last Metro*)

128 min., col.

Production Company: Les Films du Carrosse, SEDIF, TFI, Société française de producteurs

Executive Producer: Jean-José Richer

Production Managers: Roland Thénot, Jean-Louis Godroy

Assistant Directors: Suzanne Schiffman, Emmanuel Clot

Script: François Truffaut, Suzanne Schiffman, Jean-Claude Grumberg

Camera: Nestor Almendros with Florent Bazin, Emilia-Pakull-Latorre, Tessa Racine

Editing: Martine Barraqué, Marie-Aimée Debril, Jean François Giré

Continuity: Christine Pellé

Sound: Michel Laurent, Michel Mellier, Daniel Couteau

Music: Georges Delerue

Songs: *Bei mir bist du schön* music by Sholom Secunda, lyrics by Cahn-Chaplin, Jacob Jacobs and Jacques Larue; *Prière à Zumba*, A. Lara and J. Larue; *Mon Amant de St. Jean*, E. Carrara and L. Agel, sung by Lucienne Delyle; *Sombreros et Mantilles*, J. Vaissade-Chanty, sung by Rina Ketty; Cantique: *Pitié mon Dieu*, A. Kunc

Art Direction: Jean-Pierre Kohut-Svelko, Pierre Compertz, Jean-Louis

Povéda, Roland Jacob

Make-up: Didier Lavergne, Thi Loan N'Guyen, Françoise Ben Sousson

Costumes: Lisèle Roos

Principal actors: Catherine Deneuve (Marion Steiner), Heinz Bennent (Lucas Steiner), Gérard Depardieu (Bernard Granger), Jean Poiret (Jean-Loup Cottins), Jean-Louis Richard (Daxiat), Sabine Haudepin (Nadine). Original screenplay by François Truffaut, Suzanne Schiffman, Jean-Claude Grumberg. Filmed in Paris.

La Femme d'à côté, 1981 (UK/USA: *The Woman Next Door*)

106 min., col.

Production Company: Les Films du Carrosse, TF1

Executive Producer: Armand Barbault

Production Managers: Roland Thénot with Jacques Vidal, Françoise Héberlé

Assistant Directors: Suzanne Schiffman, Alain Tasma, Gilles Loutfi

Script: François Truffaut, Suzanne Schiffman, Jean Aurel

Camera: William Lubtchansky with Caroline Champetier, Barcha Bauer

Editing: Martine Barraqué, Marie-Aimée Debril, Catherine Dryzmalkowski

Continuity: Christien Pellé

Sound: Michel Laurent, Michel Mellier, Jacques Maumont, Daniel Couteau

Music: Georges Delerue

Art Direction: Jean-Pierre Kohut-Svelko, Pierre Compertz, Jacques Peisach

Make-up: Thi Loan N'Guyen

Costumes: Michèle Cerf, Malika Brohin

Principal actors: Gérard Depardieu (Bernard Coudray), Fanny Ardant (Mathilde Bauchard), Henri Garcin (Philippe Bauchard), Michèle Baumgartner (Arlette Coudray), Véronique Silver (Odile Jouve), Roger van Hool (Roland Duguet). Original screenplay by François Truffaut, Suzanne Schiffman, Jean Aurel. Filmed in Grenoble.

Vivement dimanche!, 1982 (UK: *Finally Sunday*; USA: *Confidentially Yours*)

111 min., b/w

Production Company: Les Films du Carrosse, Films A2, Soprofilms

Executive Producer: Armand Barbault

Production Managers: Roland Thénot, Jacques Vidal

Assistant Directors: Suzanne Schiffman, Rosine Robiolle, Pascal Deux

Script: François Truffaut, Suzanne Schiffman, Jean Aurel

Camera: Nestor Almendros with Florent Bazin, Tessa Racine

Editing: Martine Barraqué, Marie-Aimée Debril, Colette Achouche

Continuity: Christine Pellé

Sound: Pierre Gamet, Jacques Maumont, Bernard Chaumeil, Daniel Couteau

Music: Georges Delerue

Art Direction: Hilton McConnico

Principal actors: Jean-Louis Trintignant (Julien Vercel), Caroline Sihol (Marie-Christine Vercel), Fanny Ardant (Barbara Becker), Philippe Laudenbach (M. Clément), Philippe Morier-Genoud (Superintendent Santinelli), Jean-Louis Richard (Louison). Based on the novel *The Long Saturday Night* by Charles Williams. Filmed in and around Hyères.

Select bibliography

See also the References sections at the end of each chapter.

Books by Truffaut

Hitchcock/Truffaut, édition définitive, Paris, Ramsay, 1983. First published in 1966, this major study of Hitchcock, which Truffaut wrote in collaboration with Helen Scott, is based on a series of recorded interviews with Hitchcock (Helen Scott acted as interpreter). The book reveals almost as much about its author as it does about its subject. (Trans. Helen G. Scott. *Hitchcock*, New York, Simon & Schuster, 1967.).

Les Films de ma vie, Paris, Flammarion, 2nd edn, 1987. First published in 1975, a collection of articles and reviews, some of which had not been published previously, edited by Truffaut himself. The book is organised, on a loosely chronological basis, under the headings 'The Big Secret' (the silent period), 'The Talkies', 'Some Outsiders' and 'My New Wave Buddies' and opens with a 20 pp. essay exploring the difficult relationship between artists and critics. (Trans. Leonard Mayhew. *The Films in My Life*, New York, Simon & Schuster, 1978.).

Le Plaisir des yeux Paris, Cahiers du cinéma, 1987. A second collection of Truffaut's writings on cinema including 'Une certaine tendance du cinéma français'. A valuable source of information with insights into Truffaut's ideas on film-makers and film-making.

Correspondance 1945–84, Paris, Hatier, 1988; also Paris, Livre de poche, 1993, Jacob, G. and de Givray, C. (eds). Five hundred letters spanning the years between early holiday camps in Normandy and his death. Personal and professional, witty and dark, these letters capture most sides of his complex character and shed a revealing (though perhaps not as revealing as they might have been) and invaluable light onto his work and life. (Trans. Gilbert Adair. *Correspondence 1945–84*, London, Faber & Faber, 1989.).

Books on Truffaut

Allen, D. *Finally Truffaut*, 2nd edn, London, Secker & Warburg, 1985. Revised and enlarged version of the original 1974 monograph which examines the films in chronological order. The approach is a wide-ranging one and, since the author knew Truffaut personally, there are illuminating asides on the relationship between the director's life and his films.

Baecque, A. de & Toubiana, S. *François Truffaut*, Paris, Gallimard, Collection NRF Biographies, 1996. Substantial and detailed biography written with the cooperation of Truffaut's family and friends by two *Cahiers du cinéma* critics and containing material from Truffaut's personal archives. Sympathetic to the man and his work but avoids hagiography.

Cahoreau, Gilles *François Truffaut 1932–84*, Paris, Julliard, 1989. The first biography, detailed but erring on the side of the politely discreet.

Collet, J. *Le Cinéma de François Truffaut*, Paris, Lherminier, 1977. 'Not really a book, more of a mosaic, a collection of notes dealing with an absent text' is the way Collet chooses to describe his own study of Truffaut. While bearing witness to the strengths and weaknesses of the 'film-by-film' approach, it provides discussion of the films up to *L'Homme qui aimait les femmes*, and offers useful and often perceptive readings of the films. There is a closing chapter dealing, in part, with the central theme of writing.

Gillain, Anne *Le Cinéma selon François Truffaut*, Paris, Flammarion, 1988. A compilation of interviews with Truffaut, undertaken by a variety of journalists and scholars and edited by Gillain. The book presents discussion of each film taken in chronological order. Although an *auteur*'s statements concerning his or her works invite caution, the book is a rich mine of information touching on a wide variety of thematic, technical and human interest aspects of the films.

Gillain, Anne *François Truffaut, le secret perdu*, Paris, Hatier, 1991. An illuminating critical study of Truffaut's films employing a psychoanalytical perspective based on the writings of D. W. Winnicott. Discusses the films in pairs under thematic headings (e.g. *Les 400 Coups* and *La Femme d'à côté* under 'Family Secrets'). Argues that Truffaut's fictions achieved popularity because they give pleasurable form to fundamental and shared emotional drives. Gillain's argument on *Les 400 Coups* can be found in English as 'The script of delinquency: François Truffaut's *Les 400 Coups*' in Susan Hayward and Ginette Vincendeau: *French Film Texts and Contexts*, London and New York, Routledge, 1990, pp. 174–87.

Insdorf, Annette *François Truffaut*, Cambridge, Cambridge University Press, 1994. This is the third revision and update of a perceptive and comprehensive reading of Truffaut's work It comprises a detailed and cogent evaluation of the influence upon it of the films of Hitchcock and Renoir.

Le Berre, C. *François Truffaut*, Paris, Editions de l'Etoile/Cahiers du cinéma, 1993. A carefully argued study that stresses the presence of raw and violent emotion beneath the films' pleasant surface. Interesting on Truffaut's working methods and their relevance to the films' meanings.

Monaco, J. *The New Wave*, New York and Oxford, Oxford University Press, 2nd edn, 1976. The first and only major review of the Nouvelle Vague with four substantial chapters on Truffaut covering the Doinel Cycle, the question of genre and 'intimate politics'. First published in 1973, the book contains readings of films, up to and including *La Nuit américaine*, which remain fresh, valid and illuminating.

Petrie, G. *The Cinema of François Truffaut*, London, A. Zwemmer, 1970. One of the first major studies in English covering the films made before 1970, the book takes a scholarly and thematic approach ('A Cinema of discovery', 'Hidden Languages') and culminates with a discussion of 'styles' in *La Sirène du Mississippi*. Petrie's own direct and unfussy style generates analyses of the films which are rich in insights and unsparing in illustration.

Index